From Flappers to Flivvers...

We Helped Make the '20s Roar!

Charged with the pep of
changing times, it was an era
of real heroes and reckless
daredevils...and with so many
"swanky" guys and gals kicking
up their heels, the less-than-
bold had plenty to watch! Our
thanks to all *who were there*.
Without the stories they've
shared with us today, this
book would not be possible.

FOLLOWING THE LEAD of the decade's many endurance fads, these die-hard dancers struggle to keep moving at a dance marathon in Washington, D.C. in 1924. All across the country, exhausted shufflers snoozed on partners' shoulders, often competing for first-prize awards of $1,000. Spectators flocked to contests just to witness the antics of cranky couples—after 6 or 7 days, they kept one another awake with smelling salts, ice or even pinches, punches and kicks.

Editor: Bettina Miller
Contributing Editor: Clancy Strock
Assistant Editors: Deb Mulvey, Mike Beno, Kristine Krueger, John Schroeder, Michael Martin, Henry de Fiebre
Art Director: Gail Engeldahl
Art Associate: Julie Wagner
Photo Coordination: Trudi Bellin
Editorial Assistants: Blanche Comiskey, Joe Kertzman
Production Assistants: Ellen Lloyd, Judy Pope
Publisher: Roy J. Reiman

© 1995 Reiman Publications, L.P.
5400 S. 60th St., Greendale WI 53129

Reminisce Books
International Standard Book Number: 0-89821-149-2
Library of Congress Catalog Number: 95-69124
All rights reserved. Printed in U.S.A.

Photos on the cover and this page: UPI/Bettmann

For additional copies of this book or information on other books, write: Reminisce Books, P.O. Box 990, Greendale WI 53129. **Credit card orders call toll-free 1-800/558-1013.**

Contents

7 Prologue

The 1920s waved *Toot, Toot, Tootsie, Good-bye!* to the recently faded Victorian era and said a big hello to modern times of the Jazz Age. It was a decade of *Puttin' on the Ritz* that ended with a crash.

9 Chapter One ⇝ When Flappers Were in Fashion

In this unabashed time of "Oh, you kid" and "23 skidoo", hair and skirts got shorter, and knees (both ladies' and "the bees") were news. Turned-up nose, rolled-down hose...*Yes, Sir, That's My Baby!*

29 Chapter Two ⇝ Radio Was the Rage

This was a modern-day miracle—sound from a *box* bringing music, comedy and sports right into our homes! Now get the chores done, be quiet and don't bother Dad—it's time for *Amos 'n' Andy*.

49 Chapter Three ⇝ What a Trip That Was!

"Pardon our dust!" As the flivver joined the flapper, everyone got mobile and trips to the country, or even cross-country, became more and more popular. *California, Here I Come!*

69 Chapter Four ⇝ Cherished Photos

The affordable Brownie box camera came along just in time for folks everywhere to record zany antics of the era. These delightful reader photos of family and friends will be enjoyed for decades.

89 Chapter Five ⇝ "The Silents" and Other Fun

The song declared *Ain't We Got Fun* and boy, did we! From singing 'round the parlor piano to a day at the circus or picnic in the park...from dance crazes to talking movies that amazed us—the '20s offered plenty!

109 Chapter Six ⇝ How We Got Around

Folks still used horses, trolleys and trains in the '20s, but the auto was honking its way into our hearts, while the flying feats of our beloved "Lone Eagle" had *everyone* moving as they danced the Lindy.

133 Chapter Seven ⇝ Lasting Memories of Life in the '20s

Most admit that even in this time noted for acts of reckless abandon, daily life was business as usual...filled with work, school and church. But looking back, everyone agrees there's never been another time like it!

BUSTLING WITH LIFE, this New York City street scene captures a
slice of our most razzle-dazzle decade to date. Coming in the
aftermath of the Great War and before the Great Crash, those
prosperous years between were ripe for frolic.

Prologue

By Clancy Strock, Contributing Editor, Reminisce Magazine

THE DECADE of the 1920s is perhaps the most remarkable 10 years in the history of the United States. That's quite a statement, but you're likely to agree with it after you've finished reading the hundreds of personal recollections of those years gathered in this book.

This energetic decade was like the threshold of a giant door. On one side was a world that had changed very little in a century or two...while on the other side came an age of eye-popping change, innovation and progress.

In between those two very different worlds came the '20s. I was born in 1924, which put my baby feet astride both those worlds.

The decade started off with a surge of optimism. Our "doughboys" had come home after fighting "the war to end all wars" to marry the girls they left behind, start families and find work. (My father, who'd never been far from his hometown, had been whisked to France to serve. His outfit got so close to the fighting they could hear the roar of cannon fire! Luckily, the armistice was signed and he returned in 1920 to marry my mother.)

Off to a Roaring Start

From beginning to end, the remarkable decade called the "Roaring '20s" brought change. In January of 1920, "the noble experiment" called Prohibition went into effect, and in that same year, women were empowered to vote in a national election for the first time.

Commercial radio broadcasting also made its debut, and station KDKA in Pittsburgh made history by broadcasting the election returns. The winner was a low-key man from Ohio named Warren G. Harding, who did most of his campaigning by simply sitting on his front porch and letting voters interested in his views come to *him*. (Why can't we find another like this one?)

The League of Nations held its first meeting in Geneva, Switzerland, although the United States declined to take part. The League was an optimistic idea designed to promote world peace and tranquility, and hopes were high all around the world for its success.

And although few realized it at the time, prospects for mystery lovers greatly improved: Agatha Christie published her first whodunit in 1920.

So the decade began with omens of good things ahead...but ended with a sickening thud on Black Thursday, October 24, 1929, when the stock market went into a meltdown that ended October 29 with the country's entire financial system in ruin.

In between those bookends, you'll find 10 years packed with events that changed our lives forever. The headlines told of heroes and scoundrels who are still an important part of our American folklore.

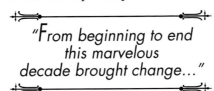

"From beginning to end this marvelous decade brought change..."

We hatched good ideas (tetanus shots and penicillin)...and bad ideas (installment-plan buying and speakeasies).

Of the bad ideas, none could top Prohibition. Certainly the most unexpected result was that it actually led to an *increase* in the consumption of booze and general lawlessness.

For the first time, crime became an organized activity. Al Capone bragged that he "owned" every sheriff in the state of Illinois...and the nice lady next door went to dances carrying a teddy bear—its hollow tummy filled with white lightning or homemade bathtub gin.

I grew up on a small farm in northern Illinois, and there was a reputed bootlegger living down the road from us who made his illicit product from the bounty of his orchard. I still recall how on hot summer nights, we'd sit on the front porch and count the cars that made brief stops at his home.

The Ku Klux Klan made its unfortunate comeback with a vengeance, claiming 2 million members. (Our own family was shocked to discover KKK robes hidden in an attic trunk that belonged to a recently deceased and much-respected relative. Who knew?)

From the White House came the Harding administration's lurid Teapot Dome scandal, involving the cover-up of kickbacks taken for granting oil leases on federal land. This media event was every bit the match for Watergate a half century later.

On a brighter note, *Reader's Digest, Time* and *The New Yorker* were launched. Tabloid newspapers, however, became popular focusing on—what else?—sex, violence and celebrities.

Gramma and Grampa, as well as a good many other level-headed people, were scandalized by those young women called "flappers". Their skirts were so short that you could see their knees. They refused to wear corsets, donned bathing suits that revealed an awful lot of bare leg, and went to speakeasies where they drank bootleg liquor and danced the Charleston to that *dreadful* jazz music. What was the world coming to? How much moral decay could the country withstand?

But all of this was more than outweighed on the "good" side of the ledger.

On the Bright Side

For example, when President Harding died while in office, he was succeeded by Calvin Coolidge—a man of few words but strong actions. He threw the leftover scoundrels out of the White House, cut taxes and reduced the national debt by $3 billion...then retired without running for a second term. What a guy!

We had more heroes than we could count during the 1920s. The biggest was Charles Lindbergh, and one by-product of his fame was that air travel increased by 400 percent within a year after his nonstop flight to Paris. Old and young idolized the dashing "Lone Eagle", and I named my pony "Lindy".

We also had sports heroes aplenty, like Babe Ruth, who swatted an incredible 54 home runs in 1920 and continued to break records throughout the decade. Other heroes of mythical stature were Jack Dempsey, Red Grange, channel-swimmer Gertrude Ederle, golfer Bobby Jones, tennis stars Bill Tilden and Helen Wills, and a thundering horse named "Man O'War".

Meanwhile, the silver screen was illuminated by Clara Bow, Mary Pickford and Douglas Fairbanks, Harold Lloyd, Buster Keaton, Charlie Chaplin, Tom Mix, Hoot Gibson and America's favorite dog, "Rin-Tin-Tin".

I dimly remember the first "talkie" I ever saw. It was *Rio Rita*, and our family took a half day's drive all the way to Chicago to enjoy it.

Oh yes, and let's not forget the mightiest mouse of them all, Mickey, who made his screen debut in an animated short feature.

Authentic "American" music also made its appearance, thanks to George Gershwin, Duke Ellington and Louis Armstrong. They ushered in what we now recall as "The Jazz Age".

On the radio we listened to the A&P Gypsies and the Cliquot Club Eskimos for entertainment, and Graham McNamee, H.V. Kaltenborn and Floyd Gibbons for the news. National radio was established by NBC and CBS, giving us a "radio family" coast to coast.

Ground-Breaking Events

Wyoming broke new ground by electing—could you believe it?—the first woman governor.

Wheaties and Rice Krispies first showed up on grocery shelves, along with Mounds and Milky Ways.

Main Street merchants began worrying about national chain stores as A&P opened an average of three new stores a day across the land, and J.C. Penney grew by 100 stores a year.

Electric refrigerators, electric shavers, antifreeze for the car radiator, hybrid corn, and hand-held cameras loaded with Kodak film all were hints of more good things to come in our lives.

The first motel opened in 1926. And a newfangled amusement called the crossword puzzle turned up in a newspaper in 1924. It was a fine birthday present for me (though as a newborn I didn't know it), because I've since become a crossword puzzle addict.

Science began making important breakthroughs, too. Vaccines for tetanus and whooping cough promised a defense against two common killers, and Alexander Fleming discovered penicillin.

CROSSWORD KID? One of the many contributions of the '20s was the crossword puzzle. Clancy Strock is an avid puzzler... perhaps 1926 photo at left shows a young Clancy enjoying his favorite pastime in its infancy.

But there was still a lot in our lives that could stand improvement. There were no real school buses, which meant that endless generations of grampas-to-be could bore their grandchildren with tales of walking 4 miles to school through "howling blizzards and waist-deep snow...and uphill both ways!"

Few people under 60 can appreciate one of the landmark events of that decade. The 5-1/2-day work week was born! Ford even pioneered a 5-day week, but better yet, International Harvester made a paid 2-week vacation standard for its workers. Suddenly, at least part of the work force was going to have leisure time (although it was to be

"The 5-day work week was a landmark event..."

quite a while before all companies adopted these ideas).

I vividly recall the joy in our family when I went to work for a company that had a 5-day work week. It precisely doubled the amount of family time we could enjoy together.

But there were also ominous rumblings off in the distance. Across the world, a man named Mussolini marched on Rome and formed a Fascist government. Another man, named Hitler, was jailed after his Munich "Beer Hall Putsch" failed, and used his time in the slammer to write *Mein Kampf.* The German economy crashed.

Here at home, cool heads issued unheeded warnings about the land boom in Florida (as folks bought nonexistent property sight unseen) and rampant speculation in the soaring stock market.

Just about half of the U.S. still lived on farms, and 40% of all wage-earners made less than $2,000 a year.

Farmers were in a desperate recession, and coal miners were still making as little as $2 a day, which turned their attention to John L. Lewis and his drive for a militant labor union.

In 1928, Herbert Hoover ran for president and was opposed by a cocky New Yorker named Al Smith. Smith's Bronx accent grated upon middle-American ears, and his Catholic faith became a major issue.

I still remember listening to my dad and a neighbor, leaning against the barnyard fence, talking about the election. "If Al Smith is elected, America will be run by the Pope," the neighbor warned. I had no idea what a "pope" was, but it sounded scary.

So, the 1920s was a decade of good news and bad news, good guys and bad guys, good times and bad times, but mostly optimism...and plenty of it.

In the pages that follow, you'll read about it all, as told firsthand by the people who still remember that remarkable decade.

We thank each and every one of them for their stories and cherished photos, because their memories need to be preserved for all of us to enjoy...and to learn from. ➡

Chapter One

When Flappers Were In Fashion

When Flappers Were in Fashion

HEMLINES were on the rise as daring new styles and the boyish "bob" took hold across the country. It was time to wave good-bye, forever, to the prim pompadours and confining corsets of the Victorian Era. Leading the march against age-old convention were those feisty flapper gals...kicking up their heels and strumming ukuleles as they played their way through the Jazz Age.

"MY MOTHER, Mary Freischle, had exquisite taste and always dressed in the latest fashion," recalls Bea Taus of Fremont, California. "She was an immigrant and had come to America with all of her belongings in a small wicker suitcase. After growing up on a poor farm in Poland, she was awed by the finery she saw when she settled in the big city of Chicago."

Call it the Flapper Era or the Jazz Age or the Roaring Twenties, in the heart of America where I grew up, the *roar* of the times was rather muted. Most of the flappers we saw were in the movies of the day, as portrayed by Clara Bow ("The Hottest Jazz Baby in Films"), Joan Crawford, Mary Pickford, Vilma Banky and others.

We heard about gangsters but didn't personally know any. There were rumors of people who made bathtub gin and there were a few alleged bootleggers in the area. There were whispers about certain local ladies who had been seen smoking cigarettes. One tavern had a "family entrance" for the convenience of women who didn't want to be seen walking in the front door.

On the whole, life was rather serene.

Yet there's no denying that the Twenties was one of those decades when rebellion was afoot. It was a time to break away from tradition and move on to new things. Not that people were demonstrating in the streets or storming city hall. A lot of the rebellion was symbolic rather than earthshaking.

Traditionalists in for a Shock

Perhaps it went hand in hand with women finally having a chance to vote in national elections. Freed from second-class citizenship, they also decided to shuck some other things. Long hair, for example.

It's hard for us today to appreciate how deeply traditionalists were shocked when women decided to "bob" their hair. Outraged fathers stalked out of the house. Grandparents were scandalized. Husbands were speechless. Ministers thundered that it foretold a total breakdown in national morality.

My mother certainly was not a chain-smoking, champagne-sipping flapper. Nevertheless, in her 1920 wedding photo, she's clearly wearing bobbed hair. I can only imagine how upset her conservative father must have been.

Worse still, women began showing their legs as hemlines soared up, up, up...nearly to the knee. Before the Twenties, a brief flash of ankle as a lady alit from a carriage was about as much excitement as onlooking men could handle. But now...!

Women showed up on tennis courts unencumbered by long dresses. Bathing suits were actually brief enough for swimming. What was the world coming to?

Families Were Scandalized

In our family, Aunt Florence was the family scandal. She went away to some college in Iowa and came home a Thoroughly Modern Millie...bobbed hair, short skirts, language salted with slang, rolled stockings and unbuckled overshoes—a ruined woman in the eyes of the family.

In the meantime, jazz had come up the Mississippi River and spread across the country. It was perfect music for a decade intent upon breaking with the past...lively, loud and unconventional. You just weren't a flapper if you didn't know how to do the Charleston, spangled dress glittering, a "headache band" on your forehead and long, long beads flashing around your hemline.

What a spree it was! Cigarette sales doubled as women began smoking in public. And sipping bootleg hooch from teacups or out of their own flasks. And driving cars. Some even went off to law school or trained to be doctors ...could you believe it?

The stories on the following pages are from people who were there when women decided it was time to kick aside the traces of Victorian Age conventions once and for all. Yes, indeed, this new age was "the cat's meow".

—*Clancy Strock*

Flappers Ushered in Lively New Era

By Carolyn Mays
Homosassa Springs, Florida

WHEN THE flapper era blew open the closed doors of the Victorian period, my sister Kelly was just the right age. I wished I could be one of those rebellious flappers, too, but I was a little too young and too shy to try.

There was nothing timid about Kelly, though. She started rolling down her long cotton stockings into thick rolls and displaying her bare knees at a time when ankles had barely been seen uncovered. And when winter came, she fearlessly shortened the legs of her long underwear until she grew brave enough to discard them entirely.

The Charleston, Black Bottom and new fast dances filled dance halls across the country with contests. Kelly was part of a wave of teenagers who ignored the disapproval of their parents and danced to the lyrics, "Roll 'em, girls, roll 'em! Roll 'em down and show your pretty knees!", which played over and over on our Victrola.

Grandfather had always been the family barber and gave Kelly's dark curly hair the latest cut called a "mon-

SISTER ACT. Kelly (on right) was the rebellious flapper, says Carolyn Mays. Sister Mildred is on left.

key bob". Grampy prided himself on keeping up with the times, but even he had misgivings about these new styles.

However, Grampy soon became the regular barber for all of her friends, who would rush to him with pictures

or drawings of the latest hairstyle fad.

Flappers like Kelly overwhelmed horrified parents and neighbors with their bobbed hair, dancing feet, short dresses, made-up faces and necks adorned with dog collars or long swinging beads.

Over time, their skirts grew shorter and shorter as belts became lower and wider. Slender fingers flaunted cigarettes in long holders, and cotton stockings were replaced by silk ones with ornamental clocks running up the sides.

On Sundays, church took a backseat to movies and rides in convertibles. Shrieks of delight and unfamiliar songs accompanied by ukuleles filled the air.

On weekdays, long sleek cars overflowing with hooky-playing teenagers streaked through country towns, leaving bewildered bystanders scratching their heads.

It was a carefree, fun-loving, trendsetting era. Traditions, decorum and false modesty were tossed by the wayside. Yet there was an openness and gaiety in the flappers' daring behavior that filled others with envy. When Kelly left the Victorian age behind, she opened new doors for the women of the future. ⇥

BEES KNEES. Short skirts and bobs were in, and Helen Tillapaugh of Fort Wayne, Indiana wore them with grace.

Young Flapper Had Fun—with Dad's Blessing

MY mother was among the first in our town who dared to bob her hair, and my father was a modern man who encouraged me to have fun.

Daddy put few limits on my activities, but he had one condition. "You can do anything you want," he'd say. "But always keep it clean." Thanks to his wise advice, bathtub gin never fit into my schemes.

In every other way, though, I was a real flapper! I wore my skirts above my knees, which were rouged, and I can still roll my hose without garters. (There's an art to that.) As the years passed, our dresses got shorter and shorter—almost to the point of indecency.

My hair was cut in the latest style with bangs pointed in the center, making the face look heart-shaped.

Our favorite reading material was

Whiz Bang magazine, which we often memorized, and the phrase "Oh, you kid!" followed almost any expression we uttered. One of our favorite sayings was, "Send up the ice cream and onions…man up here wants out." (The fact that it made no sense made little matter to us!)

I drove a Model T sports roadster to school, then our goats chewed the top off. But that was no big deal —by then, "strip-downs" were the style.

And don't tell me flappers didn't make good wives and mothers! Through all my harum-scarum adventures, I was always particular about my boyfriends. I married a wonderful man at 17, and we sent all four of our children to college.

—*Blanche Morris*
Clovis, New Mexico

Sister Cherished Her "Charleston Girl"

I CHERISH the memories of my flapper sister, who added so much to my childhood. Alice epitomized the Roaring '20s with her short dresses, rolled stockings, chewing gum and pot-shaped felt hats adorned with cutout posies.

She even drove an old Ford coupe with a rumble seat, and if there was a flat, *she* changed it.

Alice was named "Miss Portsmouth" in our New Hampshire hometown, and she won first prize for doing the Charleston. No wonder she was in great form—she was kicking up her heels all day, every day.

She won the prize wearing the dress of my dreams, a lavender lace with chiffon inserts all around the bottom to make it flare. The dress was stored in an old chest in the attic, and I was forever going up there to hold and admire it.

I kept asking Alice if I could have the dress when she didn't want it anymore, and I've never forgotten the deep disappointment I felt when it eventually disappeared.

The day came when Alice married and left on her honeymoon. Living on a farm, I would go down to the pasture to

MISS CHARMING...That's what my sister Alice was called, says Jennie Ouellette. Alice was dignified for high school graduation (left) and "flappered" at Dad's gas station (above).

deal with my loneliness. I had never known a day without her, and now my Charleston girl was gone. Life would never be the same without that fun-loving character.
—*Jennie Ouellette*
Sanford, Maine

When Sis Walked, She Shimmered

MY BIG SISTER was a flapper, and Mom and Dad spoiled her rotten. It seemed she had nothing to do but dress up and drive all over the county in Dad's car.

I loved to get into her closet and go

BIG SISTER Ethel (below) was a "spoiled" flapper, says Evelyn Martin (right), who was 5 in 1928. Evelyn sported bangs; Ethel "spit curls".

through her things. It was a treat just to feel the materials of her short-skirted frocks. Many had crystals and bugle beads and shiny fringe all over them. When Sis walked, she seemed to shimmer, and you could always see her dimpled knees between her rolled stockings and hemline.

Most of the dresses had ribbon headbands to match, and Sis' cloche hats were loaded with bunches of fruit (especially cherries) and every kind of flower and feather.

I especially liked getting into her cosmetics and the huge crystal jar of bath powder with a fluffy round puff. To keep her Billie Dove spit curls in place, she used some sort of green gel that stiffened them like concrete.

Our grandmother was constantly horror-struck by the new fads and fancies, and I know Nannie had a real fit when she found out Sis had a silver flask in her beaded purse.

My sister really enjoyed the '20s, though, for she had the courage of her convictions—and she's just as forward-thinking today!
—*Evelyn Martin*
Lakeland, Florida

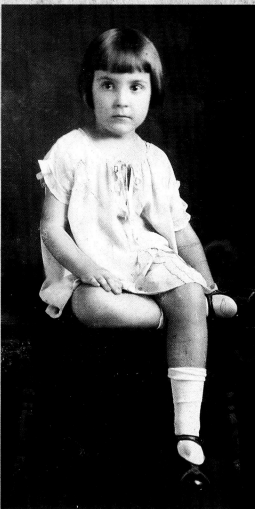

BEFORE AND AFTER. Her mother's hair hung down in ringlets (inset) before she went "modern" and bobbed it, says Lois Sudborough. That's Mama later, not only with bobbed hair, but driving a car. How modern can you get!

SMILE AND WAVE. Marcelled hair and a *long* string of pearls were the look of the '20s, says Mrs. F.V. Lane of Walla Walla, Washington, who sat for this portrait in 1925. Back then, women spent most of Saturday in the beauty shop, getting ready to look like this for a night on the town—going to dinner or a vaudeville show, or just strolling and window-shopping.

Flapper or Proper Matron? Mother Couldn't Decide

AS A young married woman with small children, Mama was torn between being a sensible matron and keeping up with the flapper style.

Wanting to please her conservative mother-in-law, she sometimes wore a whalebone corset, heavy lisle stockings and dresses that fell well below the knees.

Other times, Mama wanted to be young and daring like her teenage sisters (I vividly recall Mama, Harriet and Alice in the kitchen practicing the Charleston). Then she wore a one-piece undergarment called a teddy or chemise, silk stockings with garters, and a fashionable dress with a long waist and short skirt.

Dad liked the modern look and encouraged Mama to wear the flapper styles and keep her hair bobbed. (Mama explained the hairstyle to her mother-in-law by saying that long hair was too hard to care for when she was confined to bed in childbirth.)

We had a great-aunt who lived nearby. She wore long skirts with old-fashioned long drawers underneath and was scandalized by Mama's silk stockings. She'd reach down and feel Mama's legs to make sure there were really stockings there! Apparently it would have been an even greater sin to go bare-legged.
—*Lois Sudborough, The Dalles, Oregon*

Little Girl Loved Flapper Mom's Look

I THOUGHT my flapper mother was absolutely "it" in her low-waisted pleated dress, red silk stockings, high heels and dangling red earrings.

Her friend wore a sundress with a "V" cut in the back. This was the "in" thing and considered quite daring—although the bottom of the "V" was no more than 5 inches below the neck!

The two of them also wore long intricately woven beads, and when they danced the Charleston, those beads flew as fast as their feet. I learned this dance at a tender age and was so proud to be able to dance it with Dad and his friends. I'm sure they were just humoring me, but I felt grown up.   —*Helen Dutcher Lynn Haven, Florida*

"My Gal Sal" Became Her Signature Tune

MY MOM was a flapper before she married, and for 10¢ admission, she liked going to the local dance hall with her flapper friends and dancing all night. This was "the place" to meet boys, and Mom never lacked for dance partners.

At one dance, Mom and her friend Frances entered a singing contest and performed *My Gal Sal*. They must have been pretty good, because they won first prize—which was a bottle of hooch!

My Gal Sal became Mom's signature song, and through the years, Mom was asked to sing it whenever there was a family gathering.

As her golden years approached, Mom often told me that she wanted *My Gal Sal* played at her funeral. Everyone in the family knew of her fondness for that song, and when the time came, each and every one asked me if I intended to carry out her wishes.

The funeral director was upset that I would even think of such a "desecration" to a solemn service, but I insisted. The organist played the song as though it were a hymn, and despite our pain, we all smiled to think Mom was looking down at us…happy with this tribute of "her song".
—*Bette Mann*
North Fort Myers, Florida

She Envied Older Girls' Flap-Flapping Galoshes

WHEN I WALKED to my country school, I had to keep all four buckles

OH, YOU GRANDKID! Betty Ewig of Port Washington, Wisconsin shared this photo of her daughter, Rachel Gahan, wearing a dress and headband from the flapper era. Betty's mother, Anita Allen, made the dress for herself in the early 1920s.

fastened on both overshoes or risk losing them in the sticky black Iowa mud. On city streets with paved sidewalks, however, the high school girls strode along with their unbuckled overshoes making a defiant *flap-flap-flap*. I was too young to disobey my mother, so my overshoes stayed buckled, but my heart was with the big girls.

By the late 1920s, someone invented a slide fastener called a zipper to replace the buckles. Shoe salesmen called the new galoshes "flappers". They came in chic shades of tan and light brown and made the same satisfying sound as unbuckled galoshes when worn unzipped.
—*Isabelle Winship, Warden, Washington*

The Height of Style

WE FLAPPERS wore heavy unbuckled overshoes, short dresses with lots of fringe and long strands of pearls knotted around our necks. Large fancy garters kept our stockings below the knees, and we wore "headache bands" around our bobbed hair. Bathing suits were made of itchy wool and covered a lot more than today's styles. For sports, we wore middy blouses and bloomers.

The boys favored striped blazers and large bearskin coats in winter, and straw hats were the style in summer.

Everyone had a ukulele, and it was considered "smart" to smoke and carry a flask. I still play my ukulele!
—*Gladys Castner, Clearwater, Florida*

Dances Kindled Romance

DURING THE Roaring '20s, I often walked a mile to an open-air dance pavilion called Victory Park in Slatington, Pennsylvania.

I went with four or five other girls. This was always more fun than going with a date because you got the chance to dance with more young men. They came in groups, too, so many a romance was kindled as we did the Charleston and fox-trot as a lively orchestra or Big Band played.

When the dances ended at midnight, the fun continued on the return walk. Everyone in town knew the young people were on their way home because of all the loud laughter. When the weather called for rain, we wore well-decorated yellow slickers…and in winter, we wore four-buckle galoshes with never a thought of using the buckles. —*Luella Althouse*
Allentown, Pennsylvania

PHOTO PHLAPPER. Mae Dodd Milford considered herself the ultimate flapper when she had this photo snapped at the studio where she worked, says her daughter, Elizabeth Winter of Long Beach, New Jersey. The photo was displayed in the studio's window.

Flappers Adapted Theme Song

THE flapper days changed my life, and I still recall a popular song of the time with lyrics that went: "I long to be in Tennessee, in my Dixie paradise, where sunshine fills the skies and songbirds harmonize. Lawdy, hear my plea, take me where I want to be. I long to be in Tennessee, in my Dixie paradise."

Well, we flappers sang that tune… only with new words: "I roll my own, I roll my own, just an inch below my knee, so the wicked boys can see the dimple in my knee. Lawdy, hear my plea, make a wicked vamp of me. I roll my own, I roll my own, just an inch below my knee."
—*Evalyn Carlson, Maywood, Illinois*

First Bobbers Might as Well Have Dropped a Bomb!

AT A SLUMBER PARTY one night, a group of us teenagers started talking about the new short hairstyle, when one of the more adventurous girls shouted, "Let's all cut our hair!"

At first it was just a joke, but as we pored over pictures of movie stars and celebrities who had embraced the "short cut", we decided it would be a great idea. Our hostess' mother even agreed to help us, and pretty soon, I no longer had long curls falling below my shoulders.

Nothing could have prepared me for the reaction I got when I went home and walked in the kitchen the next morning. If a bombshell had dropped at my father's feet, he could not have looked more stricken.

After staring at me for what seemed an eternity, he murmured, "Honey, what have you done?" Then he turned quickly and went out to the barn.

Mother stood tight-lipped for a full minute, then told me we'd go to a hairdresser the next day. "Your curls were your father's pride and joy," she informed. "And the Bible says a woman's hair is her crowning glory."

I couldn't speak over the lump in my throat. I'd never stopped to consider how my parents would feel! I went to my room and cried for hours.

The next day, a hairdresser improved my shaggy appearance. Mother's only comment was, "If I'd known you wanted short hair, we would have had it done right in the first place." That experience taught me a valuable lesson —never do anything important on impulse!

—*Viola Zumault*
Kansas City, Missouri

SHORT AND SWEET. Viola Zumault cut her long curly locks on impulse at a slumber party. She and her friends admired the new look adopted by celebrities—but her parents' reaction was quite different!

"Bold Hussies" Kept Bobs Under Wraps

GETTING A HAIRCUT today is no big deal, but in the '20s, it often became a major event.

One evening after supper in 1925, my father took me to Johnny Cable's barbershop in Lyndonville, Vermont to have my long locks cut. Grandmother had advised him that my heavy hair was "sapping my strength", thus causing my frequent colds and sore throats.

When we got inside, two men were reclined in barber chairs with their up-turned faces lathered and ready to be shaved. I thought that was what was going to happen to *me*, so I burst into tears and refused to get into the chair. My father finally gave up and took me home—without the bag of popcorn from Mr. Beauchesne's cart promised for good behavior.

Not long after that, bobbed hair for ladies came into fashion. My mother and her neighbor, Edna, admired the style and took it upon themselves to visit Mr. Cable's barbershop to have their long tresses cut.

They were quite happy with themselves...until their husbands came home at suppertime. The men took one look at their wives and threw a fit. (This was the first time I heard the expression "bold hussy".)

For a long time after that, my mother and Edna wore dust caps in the house and hats anytime they went outside.

—*Lois Brown*
Worthington, Massachusetts

First Chop Sparked A Chain Reaction

SEVERAL ladies in our town cut each other's hair after seeing movie star Clara Bow's bob. Since they weren't professionals, a few of the cuts looked *really* funny, so Mother went to the new beauty shop to have her hair cut.

When she came home, she rushed into the house and covered her hair with a scarf. We kids were shocked. Her long wavy hair was gone—snipped all the way up to her ears.

When Dad asked what the scarf was for, Mother reluctantly removed it. I thought Dad was going to faint. His usual smile faded as he quietly asked, "How could you do such a thing?"

He immediately left for the woodshed and cut enough wood to last for 3 days! When he finally came back in, his last words on the matter were, "I hope it grows back fast."

—*Ruth Jorgensen*
Eugene, Oregon

Teen's Bold Move Paved Way for Sisters

BEFORE it was fashionable, my mom was a feminist. When she was in her late teens, both she and her twin sister wanted bobs. Since this was frowned on as a "naughty girl's" style, however, their strict papa declared, "Absolutely not!"

Mom took matters into her own hands and headed for the woodshed, armed with a wavy piece of mirror and a pair of dull scissors. She whacked

UNDER COVER. Lois Brown's mother did her housework in a dust cap after having her long hair cut into a fashionable flapper bob—and incurring her husband's wrath!

DOUBLE HEADER. When her mother, Jeneva Miller (left), was denied permission to bob her hair, she went to the woodshed and did it herself, says Joyce Dennis. That encouraged her twin sister, Eva, to follow suit. Four other sisters figured if Jeneva and Eva could do it, so could they —and they did!

away at her long red hair until it was short enough to suit her, then went back to the house to face her parents.

Five sisters soon followed Mom's headstrong lead with their own stylish bobs. After all, if Jeneva had survived *her* act of defiance, they would, too!
—*Joyce Dennis, Lemoyne, Ohio*

She Dished Out Criticism— But Later Ate Those Words!

MY MOTHER was a beautiful woman with glossy coal-black hair. She was also a wonderful mother, wife, neighbor and friend.

For years, Uncle Bert and Aunt Fannie had been our next-door neighbors. We were very close to them, so it was something of a shock when Aunt Fannie insulted my mother after she bobbed her hair. Mother, she said, had violated all the rules of ladylike decorum. What was she thinking of…a prominent woman of the community bobbing her hair? What kind of an example was she setting?

Mother was deeply hurt by such harsh words from her friend, but she held her head high and continued to keep her hair short.

A year or so went by, when one afternoon there was a knock at our back door. There stood Aunt Fannie with bobbed hair! She had come to apologize.
—*Marie Vincent Salt Lake City, Utah*

***CALL HER BOBBIE.** That's what Doris Muschetto's dad did after Doris took a pair of dull school scissors to her long braids. Doris just cried and wore a hat all summer.*

She Cried SOS to Sis

WHEN THE GIRLS started bobbing their hair, I wanted mine cut, too. I had long braids down my back, which my dad must have liked, because he refused to give me the money to go to the barber. So I decided to cut my hair myself.

My hair was thick, and I only had a dull, stubby pair of school scissors, but I managed to cut it way above my ears.

When I saw what I had done, I started crying. My mother had died some years before, so I put on a hat and ran to my older sister's house.

As soon as I took my hat off, she quickly called a neighbor, who tried to straighten it out…but it was *so* short! I wore that hat all summer until my hair grew a little longer.

When my dad saw my new hairdo, he just smiled and started calling me "Bobbie".
—*Doris Muschetto Justice, Illinois*

Their Bobbed Hair Really Got Dad's Goat

WHEN MOTHER got her long black hair cut short in the early 1920s, my father was so angry he wouldn't even speak to her.

Despite having witnessed the consequences, not long after that, two of my sisters "faked" a note from Mother and took it to the barber, asking him to bob their hair. He did.

When they appeared at the dinner table with their bobbed hair and spit curls, my father took one look and declared, "If we're going to be eating with nanny goats tonight, we're not eating!"
—*Leanora Strecker Cincinnati, Ohio*

Befelled by Second Thoughts As Curls Began to Fall

MY TWO SISTERS bobbed each other's hair when I was 14. I wanted mine cut the same way, but my parents wouldn't give their consent.

One day I begged and begged until Mama finally told me to go out to the barn and ask Papa. When I did, he replied, "Go ask Mama." That was as close to permission as I was likely to get, so my sister put an apron around my shoulders and started snipping.

About halfway through, I decided I didn't want my long curls cut off, but it was too late! My parents refused to look at me afterward, but they eventually decided the shorter cut was cute.
—*Mrs. Harry McElhatten Mesa, Arizona*

DUTIFUL DAUGHTER. Marcelle Seidl was 19 in 1922 when her mother forbade her from joining the flapper craze by cutting her shoulder-length hair. Marcelle obeyed her mother, but you couldn't tell it by this photo. "I pinned up my hair in little 'pugs' and bought this wig to cover it," laughs Marcelle, of Milwaukee, Wisconsin. To accentuate the flapper look, she made the sequined dress she's wearing in this tinted portrait.

Madame's Miraculous Machine Worked "Magic"

MY GRANDMA KATE was a "young" grandmother who belonged to several women's clubs and always dressed in the latest fashion. She had pretty dark hair, but it was fine and thin no matter what she tried. How she envied her friends' luxurious locks!

Sometime around 1925, a friend told her about a "curling iron" she had just purchased. Grandma bought one and was ecstatic with this new look.

She began curling her hair every morning…but often let the iron get too hot in the gas burner. This made the hair burn and break off, and after several months, her hair got thinner and thinner. This worried her a little—but not enough to quit using the iron.

Then one day there was a huge advertisement in the paper with a picture of "Madame Schenke from Germany" and her miraculous "permanent-waving machine". Guess who was her first customer? The two of them even got their picture in the paper together!

In those days, women getting permanents had their hair wrapped around little metal rollers. The electric machine that did the "magic" was a huge monstrosity with larger tubes into which the rollers fit. The tubes and rollers were so heavy that customers put bath towels behind their necks to keep their heads from falling backward!

When Grandma was finished, she

LATEST FASHION WAVE. When the marcelled look caught on, Mrs. William Lambert of Brentwood, Tennessee wore it well.

was thrilled to see little bitty curls all over her head—and permanent ones, at that! Grandma was Madame Schenke's best advertisement, and from that day forth, she was never without a permanent wave. —*Maxine Van Tornhout*
St. Petersburg, Florida

Mom Didn't Raise a Flap Over Her New Nickname

WHEN our mother had her long hair bobbed, we were surprised to see it life in perfect waves. It had never been curly until she got the heavy hair cut off!

Later that summer, when we went on our annual camping trip, everyone

called her "Flapper Fanny" after a cartoon character who had an upturned nose and wore rolled-down hose with short dresses.

Mom didn't mind being called Flapper Fanny while we were camping, as long as everyone called her Lula back at home. —*R. Lucille Crawley*
Sunset Beach, California

Another Use for Early-Day Washboards?

ALTHOUGH I was just a young girl during the '20s, I was very good at "finger-waving", and lots of the older girls came to my house so I could wave their hair for them.

One day I fixed my cousin's girlfriend's hair. When he saw her that evening, he immediately asked, "Did you have to sleep on a rub board to get your hair to look like that?" —*Leona Lamon, Adamsville, Alabama*

Country Cousin Became An Accidental Flapper

MY COUSIN, who'd lived in the country, came to board with my family in the mid-1920s. She wore her long shining brown hair in a neat ball at the nape of her neck and rolled the front on rags or paper every night to wave it.

Irene found a job at the knitting mill and had some money to spend, so when she learned about the new curling irons, she bought one. This wasn't today's electric type with heat control, but a simple metal one with wooden handles which was heated over the burner of our oil cookstove. However, Irene found it worked better than rags and paper *ever* did.

One evening, Irene was distracted as she did her usual beauty routine. When she returned to the kitchen, she picked up the curling iron and rolled it around a strand of hair. The smell of burning hair was awful, and when she unwound the curler, the entire section of hair came off and left a stub about 3 inches long! Irene and Mom both cried as I stood watching, dumbfounded.

The next day, Irene went to one of those new beauty parlors and had the rest of her hair trimmed off and got a permanent wave. She looked beautiful, but so different. After that, she became a true flapper, wearing short skirts and using powder and rouge. —*Grace Myers, Sarasota, Florida*

She Had a Swell Solution

THERE WERE NO beauty parlors in our small Iowa farm town—and no permanents, bobby pins or setting gel. If you didn't have naturally curly hair, you either wore it straight or curled it with a curling iron.

My hairstyle had a "spit curl" in the middle of the forehead. To make it, I'd wet my fingers and rub them on a bar of soap, then work the soap into my hair. The sculpted curl would harden and last all day!

Sometimes we would boil flaxseed, then strain and cool it for use as a setting gel…but it flaked when we combed it out. —*Lauren Marshall, Osage City, Kansas*

BEAUTY TIP. When Lauren Marshall was a high school freshman in 1924 and styled her hair with a spit curl, she used a bit of *clean* ingenuity to keep that lock locked down.

J.C. Allen and Son

COUNTRY COUTURE. In rural America, the fashions of the Roaring '20s had little impact. Mothers still made clothes for their families from material that lasted and got their ideas from the mail-order catalogs.

Rural Families Unfazed By Latest Fashion Craze

THE FASHIONS of the Roaring '20s didn't have much impact on rural Louisiana. Mothers still made most of their families' clothes as well as the household linens during those years.

The material we used then wasn't colorfast and would shrink, too. The careful housewife soaked new fabric in cold water and a little salt or vinegar overnight, hung it out to dry, then ironed it. This would shrink the material and set the color so it didn't "run" during washing. *Then* the work of making a dress could begin!

Catalogs from Sears Roebuck and Montgomery Ward were our fashion guides. Mothers used a basic pattern, often on brown paper, to copy the styles. My grandmother had two or three patterns and could make several different dresses by using a sleeve design from one, a skirt from another and so on.

We took off school dresses as soon as we got home so they could be worn for several more days. Starch helped them look newer and stay clean longer—although it also made them so stiff that they creased when we sat down!

Girls wore boys' clothing, like long pants, only when working in the fields or picking berries. During winter, we stayed warm by wearing long ribbed stockings or one-piece union suits under our dresses.

Children got a new pair of high-tops once a year, just before school started. These had to last until Easter—then we went barefoot! —*Gypsy Boston Shreveport, Louisiana*

Rag Curls Looked Anything But Ragged

THROUGH most of high school in the '20s, I slept in rag curls every night. Remember those? Starting at our scalp, we'd wind a section of hair neatly around a long rag, then wind the rag up over the wound hair and tie the ends in a knot. It wasn't too comfortable sleeping on all those knots, but after untying and brushing the hair around our finger the next morning, we had nice long curls. —*Doris Schutt, Cleveland, Georgia*

Saving Her "Sin Money" Didn't Make Waves

WHEN WOMEN began defying their husbands by cutting their long tresses and getting short bobs and permanents, my mother saved her "sin money" for weeks to pay for a permanent.

After shedding all her heavy hair, she discovered it was naturally curly and she didn't *need* a permanent. In grateful thanks, she gave her sin money to the missionary fund. —*Marjorie Johnston Tucson, Arizona*

Fashions Were Stylish and Elegant

AT THE START of the 1920s, we wore our skirts long with a wide sash at the waist. We also wore wide silk headbands, and I had an uncle who would tease me by saying, "Do you have a headache?" whenever he saw me wearing one.

For evening wear, we added a very long strand of colored or pearl beads and a small beaded bag.

The first shorter dresses fell below the knee, and it was so exciting to put on a dress that didn't come down to your ankles. I'll always remember my senior prom dress—pink chiffon, with a soft full skirt featuring painted butterflies outlined with colored beads.

My date gave me a corsage of sweet peas. Did I Charleston that night!

—*Lillian Yale, Neffs, Pennsylvania*

ANKLES AWAY! When skirts finally came above the ankle, Lillian Yale (at far right and wearing headband above) thought this liberating style was the cat's meow.

WHEN FLAPPERS WERE IN FASHION 19

Powder Box Holds a Special Place in Her Heart

ALTHOUGH I had all the love and necessities growing up, I never had any "extras" besides a few hair ribbons.

There just wasn't money for jewelry or scarves, so I was thrilled when my boyfriend gave me a powder box he bought at a jewelry store in the early '20s.

SPECIAL GIFT. This beaded powder box was from her best beau over 70 years ago, says Etta Kennedy.

It could be carried dangled from your wrist by the cord, or the ring at the end of the cord would fit on a finger.

The black satin box is about 3 inches long and there's a mirror under the lid with a divided bottom portion to hold powder and rouge. The top is decorated with beads arranged in a flower design.

I felt extra special when I carried this fancy powder box to a movie or on an outing with my date…and in 1924, I married the giver of this lovely gift. We had eight children and 53 wonderful years together.

—Etta Kennedy, Wooster, Ohio

Sharing Accessories Was Twice the Fun

WOMEN often wore their hair draped over one ear, so my mother and her friend would split a pair of earrings and each wear one on the exposed ear.

Dressy shoes had patent leather on one side and velvet on the other, and dresses were sleeveless, trimmed with lace and ruffles, with short skirts that fell above the knee. The most popular undergarments were black and lacy.

—Mary Fisher
Brockton, Massachusetts

This Farm Wife Showed Style

MAMA MAY HAVE been a farm wife living on a dirt road far from the city, but she had style. She went to church wearing a big beaver hat trimmed with huge ostrich plumes, and she was the

first in the neighborhood to get her hair bobbed.

We kids might have had some home-made clothes, but we had our share of store-bought fashions from the National Bellas Hess catalog of New York City …and, of course, Sears Roebuck and Montgomery Ward in Chicago.
—*June Chatterton, Milan, Illinois*

Long Necklaces Were Made for Twirling

MY OLDER SISTER and our cousins wore low-waisted dresses with long, long necklaces.

I can still see them twirling the end of the necklace in one hand while resting the other hand on one hip as if they were "somebody". It looked silly to me, but they always laughed a lot, so I guess it was good clean fun!
—*Marjorie Andrasek Garden City, Kansas*

DOWNTOWN. Bradley's in Delavan, Wisconsin was *the* place to shop in the '20s…and it's still in business after 142 years! Ferne Vance of nearby Elkhorn remembers her dad driving her there by horse and buggy for her first store-bought coat. Ferne also remembers the pneumatic tubes that took the money to the bookkeeping loft. Bill McKoy, who now owns the store, supplied the photo (see men's display, page 25). How about those hats!

Mom Nearly Fainted At Flapper Photo

I REALLY WASN'T a flapper…but you wouldn't know it by this picture.

I used to drive our Model T from Decatur to Bloomington to attend teacher's college in Normal, Illinois. One day, some classmates and I had our pictures taken on a lark. The off-the-shoulder dress (a definite *no-no*), boa and spit curl really topped off the look.

I had the time of my life, but when my parents saw the picture, they said I had disgraced the entire family. I thought my mom would faint!—*Emma Wright, Pana, Illinois*

THE BRIDE UNVEILED. Virginia Wallerius of Haledon, New Jersey shared the gorgeous portrait at right of her mother, Clara, shown seated. When wedding dresses got shorter in the flapper era, they sometimes caused a stir. Florence Palmer's memory below tells of one such incident.

Bride's Skirt Put the "Hitch" In Getting Hitched

WHEN I SEE today's short, short dresses, I think of my 1927 wedding, which took place when skirts were short for the first time in history.

We went to our minister's house with just two relatives and a friend for a simple ceremony. The minister told me to sit on the piano bench while he asked us a few questions.

My dress was new, so I'd never even sat down in it. When I did, I was shocked to see that a good portion of the skirt seemed to vanish! I tried pulling on it and changing positions, but there just wasn't enough yardage.

I was so embarrassed that I can't even recall what questions the minister asked. Apparently my answers were the right ones, though, because my marriage was a *long* and happy one.

—*Florence Palmer, Marshall, Illinois*

DARING DIPPERS. Despite strong protests from her mother, Geraldine Marshall of Osage City, Kansas appeared in public wearing a "revealing" black suit with orange stripes. She's second from right in this 1926 shot.

SHEER BEAUTY. A doctor's wife in Decatur, Illinois, Elsa Tearnan looked elegant in chiffon as she posed for this 1925 photo. From the family album of Sara Pora of Windsor, Maine, this cherished picture of her Aunt Elsa includes typical home furnishings of the day.

Dad's Resoled Shoes Were Guaranteed for Miles

WHEN MONEY was short, my dad resoled our shoes using old tires. He'd cut an old tire in half, then two of us girls would hold onto it while he pulled hard with pliers to get the cord lining loose.

He'd cut a piece of the lining to fit the sole and nail the cord on with the help of a shoe iron. Those "new" soles lasted longer than the uppers!
—*Hilda Brandt, Waukesha, Wisconsin*

Dress Code Kept the "Roar" Out of Girls' Wardrobe

DESPITE THE FADS of the Roaring '20s, the vice-principal of our school directed a committee to enforce strict dress codes for the girls in my high school.

All fashion extremes were banned, including low-cut or very thin blouses, and loose-knit sweaters if worn without a dress waist. Anything in silk, satin, georgette or voile was taboo.

Modesty and simplicity were the

BLOOMER BRIGADE. Clad in the required uniform, this girls' gym class from Young America, Indiana took to the rural roads for a hike back in 1927.

watchwords. Fancy hairdressing, cosmetics and elaborate jewelry were banned. The highest heel we could wear was the Cuban—no French heels allowed!

The greatest demand for modest attire was in gym class. White long-sleeved middy blouses were cut straight up and down so that no feminine curves were exposed. A triangular black satin scarf at the neck, black cotton stockings, tennis shoes and black bloomers completed the uniform.

The bloomers were voluminous, with 2-inch overlapping pleats at the waistband. The legs were gathered in elastic at the bottom and fitted above the knee so that the extra fabric draped over and concealed the kneecap.

Enclosed in this bulk, it wasn't always easy doing calisthentics or participating in basketball, hockey, baseball and track!
—*Stella Rouse, Santa Barbara, California*

'Brain-Binders' and Anything Russian Were the 'Cat's Pajamas'

THE EXTREME BEHAVIOR of the Roaring '20s never applied to us. My friends and I didn't smoke cigarettes or sample moonshine from a hip flask, though we did bob our hair. We tied it with an inch-wide ribbon in the middle of the forehead, then made a big bow in back. My disapproving mother and aunts called these ribbons "brain-binders".

With World War I over, the Russian revolution created an interest in everything Russian as songs like *A Russian Lullaby* became popular. The more affluent began wearing step-in "Russian boots"...but I was just happy to graduate from rubbers to grown-up galoshes.

Galoshes were exceedingly ugly overshoes that had about six metal buckles, but we didn't close them. We spread them as wide as the tongue permitted, and the flaps slapping against each other made the most satisfying *swish* and *jingle* with every step!

In search of a more sophisticated look, we began fastening all but the top two buckles. The turned-down top made a cuff that fit neatly around the ankle, while the tongue, left upright, made an artistic butterfly in front.

The boyish figure was "in", so our abbreviated dresses hung straight from the shoulder. Waistlines dropped lower and lower until they were only inches above the hemline—which hovered around the knee.

That exposed quite a lot of silk hose, and those of us who weren't bold enough to roll our stockings down kept them neat with ornate round garters just below the knee.

When King Tut's tomb was discovered, we started wearing black patent leather sandals with wedge-shaped cutouts. Later, everything became Chinese red—coolie coats replaced bathrobes, and dragons appeared everywhere.
—*Katherine Funck Grayling, Michigan*

Bloomers Had Us "Snap Happy"

I LIVED during the Roaring '20s and love it when I can find someone today who likes reminiscing about what a wonderful time that was.

Yes, I was a flapper, complete with yellow slicker and bobbed hair—but really, our clothes weren't too different in the mid-'20s. The girls all wore middy blouses rolled up at the sides and pinned to look more in style.

We also wore sateen bloomers in blue, red, green or purple. They were fitted tightly below the knees with an elastic cuff.

Oftentimes on hot afternoons in our country school, one girl would snap an elastic cuff, then another girl would snap hers. Pretty soon, the *snap-snap-snapping* sounds were coming from every desk! I'm sure the teacher heard but was too embarrassed to say anything.
—*Genevieve Brandon Sterling, Illinois*

BREECH BOYS. When Cecil Spray was 12 (far left), he and his brothers all wore breeches. A year later and after much pleading, Cecil (above right) and brother Buddy finally graduated to the long trousers of big boys.

Short Pants Were Tops In Boys' Dress Clothes

YOUNG BOYS wore knee breeches for dress wear during the early 1920s. We called them our "Sunday clothes" because we wore overalls on weekdays.

Sometime in the mid-'20s, styles began to change and younger boys began wearing long trousers. By 1928 when I was 12, I was convinced all boys my age—and even younger—were wearing long pants, and I tried to convince my father to let me wear them. But he couldn't accept this and thought it was a sign that boys were trying to grow up too soon.

After several months and much asking, my father finally agreed that when my 10-year-old brother was a little older, he'd buy long pants for both of us. By 1929, he realized clothing styles were indeed changing and we both had long trousers to wear. —*Cecil Spray Austin, Texas*

Garters Led to His Darkest Moment

THE long black stockings worn with knickers or knee pants in the teens and '20s were a constant source of trouble for young boys.

To keep mine up, Mother fashioned a harness of elastic tapes that fit over my shoulders and extended down my

thighs. A special garter snap hooked to the top of the stockings, which were forever coming loose and sagging.

As I grew older, the harness was abandoned for an elastic leg band that rolled onto the stocking tops. The stockings still sagged, though, prompting the constant admonition: "Robert, pull your stockings up!"

Finally I was old enough to wear long

AW, MA! Raymond Larson hated to get dressed up, says his wife, Dorothy. Ray, now of White Cloud, Minnesota, preferred bib overalls and bare feet back in 1928. Mom didn't mind showing *her* knees, as was the fashion then.

1928

pants. Hooray—no more above-the-knee stockings! But I still had to keep up the short socks, as it was almost a sin to be seen with them down around the shoe tops. Garters solved that problem. Men had been wearing those for years.

One day, I'd just completed a recitation in front of my sixth-grade class. Our teacher walked over to where I had been standing, picked up a garter and held it high, asking, "Does this belong to anyone?"

The answer was obvious, but you can be sure I didn't claim it. That was one of my life's darkest moments.

—*Robert Brayton Oklahoma City, Oklahoma*

Buster Brown Moniker Lasted a Lifetime

AS A CHUBBY CHILD, I looked a lot like the "Buster Brown" character who advertised shoes and clothing with his little dog, "Tyge".

After a few years, everyone called me Buster. When I started school, my parents reminded me to tell the teacher my name was Carl, not Buster, but everyone continued to call me that. Soon the nickname was shortened to "Bus", and it stuck.

To this day, that's what everyone calls me. Younger children in our family sometimes ask me why I'm called "Bus", but when I explain, they just look

puzzled. They're too young to remember Buster Brown!

—*Carl Crumpton, Topeka, Kansas*

First Haircut Turned Him Into a Real Buster!

WE LIVED in the Brownsville section of Brooklyn in the '20s, and one day when I was very young, Mama announced she was taking me to the barbershop.

I followed her to this unknown territory with great trepidation. Like the Biblical hero Samson, my curly hair had never been cut!

As we entered the shop, Mama announced that I was to have a Buster Brown. The barber went to work, and I wasn't allowed to look in the mirror until the job was done.

When I finally saw my reflection in the mirror, I screamed. I had a part down the center of my head, bangs to the eyebrows, and the sides combed straight down, ending with a curl. All I needed was a little sailor suit to complete the picture!

I cried all the way home and refused to be seen in public for a week. I finally solved the problem when I cut off the hated bangs with a pair of scissors. Mama was heartbroken, but I think she understood. We took another trip to the

SMILE, BUSTER. George Biringer of Bella Vista, Arkansas says brother Buddy gladly sported the Buster Brown look in '22.

barbershop, but this time for a *real* boy's haircut.   —*Barnet Chernick Brooklyn, New York*

Teens' Big Date Was Nixed by Knickers

JUST BEFORE my 14th birthday, my parents decided I could attend a church dance with my cousin Junior as my escort.

Mother modified one of her flapper-style gowns for me, and on the big day, my cousin Ivernia came over with her marcel iron to crimp my hair and help me apply a touch of makeup.

I felt like a princess, ready for the ball—until Junior arrived. At first glance, this 6-foot budding Adonis looked like a dream boat in his father's white dinner jacket…but then I looked down and saw, oh no, *knickers!*

As the adults exclaimed what a nice-looking couple we made, my eyes met Junior's. I knew from his expression that he'd already made his arguments at home, and knickers had prevailed.

When Junior and I got to the dance, we peered in and listened to the band for a while but never got up the courage to go inside. (Not with those knickers!) Instead, we walked to a nearby theater and watched a film with a vaudeville show headlining "Three of the Seven Little Foys".

Later, we told our folks all about the band (we *had* heard it, after all) and said we'd had a wonderful time at the dance. How could we ever explain to adults about knicker-sensitive teenagers?

—*Sara Hewitt Riola Lakewood, New Jersey*

CLOTHES MADE THE MAN back in the '20s, just as they do today. And for shoppers in Delavan, Wisconsin, Bradley's was the store to get those clothes, as this impressive window display proves. Bill McKoy owns the store now and is only the third owner in the store's 142-year history! Stick around—those styles will probably be back.

Sister's Sketch Draws Memories

By Jim Hingley, Key Largo, Florida

MY OLDER SISTER, Dorothy Hingley Fall, was a talented fashion illustrator. Back in the '20s, photographs did not print well in advertisements, and when my sister was 24, she started drawing illustrations for Blum's Department Store in Philadelphia. I think she earned about $100 a week.

Sometimes Dot preferred to work at home, so I'd take the streetcar downtown and pick up the clothes she was supposed to draw.

One time when I was bringing home a mink coat on the subway, the women began staring at me with evident curiosity. I'm sure they couldn't imagine what a 15-year-old boy was doing hauling around a $350 mink!

"Modeled" for Sis

When I got home, Dot ordered me to put the coat on and stand over by the dining room window so she could see how it looked when the light fell on the fur. I posed there for 20 minutes—filled with terror that my buddies would walk by and see me in a woman's coat!

Looking back, my exciting "delivery boy" days are still so clear. I even remember the department store's phone number and "Miss Myers", who entrusted those fancy clothes to a teenage kid.

My sister had a natural talent and practiced it to the fullest. Today, I'm left with only a copy of one of Dot's drawings, but the following memory that she'd handwritten to go with it makes this sketch special:

I bought this dress when I was working in New York. It was a Chanel of tomato-red mesh, and the minute it came into the studio to be sketched for an ad, I fell in love with it.

My kid sister dropped in and lost her heart to the Chanel. She had a bid to the Penn State prom, and to her, it was the perfect prom dress...overlooking the fact that 17-year-olds did not wear backless dresses in 1929!

She completely ignored the dainty white dress I'd put aside for her and insisted on the Chanel. She finally wore me down and I agreed to lend it to her, along with the dyed-to-match slippers with rhinestone heels. I'm not sure if the dress had anything to do with it, but my kid sister later married her prom date.

SMILING SIBS. "This picture is a favorite because it shows how much my sister Ruth and I cared for each other...and still do!" says Ralph Bray of Grand Forks, North Dakota. "Her fox stole and my knickers were the fashion of the day, as was my letter sweater (below)."

ILLUSTRIOUS SKETCH. In his memory above, Jim Hingley explains why this drawing penned by his sister Dot is so special.

Mom Dressed Her Family in Style

MY PARENTS were married in Safford, Arizona in 1923, just as the Roaring '20s were beginning to growl.

Mother was already known for her stylish flair, so she loved the hats, feathers, jewelry and ribbon headbands that came into fashion. On her wedding day, she even wore a fashionable Spanish-style hair comb.

In 1927, the family moved to Silver City, New Mexico, where the big event every summer Saturday was a dance at the open-air pavilion. Mom went decked out in the latest fashions, and Dad would tease her about "getting all gussied up". She'd retaliate by accusing him of getting "all spiffied up" for the young ladies.

In keeping with the times, Mother also loved to dress up her two little girls in the fashions of the day, hair ribbons and all. —*Nate Skousen Jr. Rio Rancho, New Mexico*

SPIFFY SHOTS. Nate Skousen's parents' 1923 wedding photo (above) set the pace for the family's many fashionable photos.

Coeds Used Caution Breaking Through to Roaring '20s

By Blanche Weaver, White Bear Lake, Minnesota

COILED COED Blanche Weaver had only *contemplated* the controversial "bob" at the time this freshman photo was taken.

MOST of my classmates at South Dakota State College had never strayed far from home in 1921, but we slowly learned times were changing.

We read that at other schools, girls called "flappers" were wearing unbuckled overshoes and smoking cigarettes, while boys called "lounge lizards" wore raccoon coats and slicked their hair back in a style known as patent leather hair.

We didn't leap onto this bandwagon rashly, and the first breakthrough was hair. Most girls wore theirs drawn back into a knot. I wore mine close to my head with little coils rolled over my ears. When a few coeds began bobbing their hair (mostly the "fast" girls who sneaked into the dorm through the fire escape after hours), controversy reigned. *To bob or not to bob?*

My roommate, Mildred, found the new style unladylike. "What would your mother and father say?" she'd exclaim. As a sophomore, she had my respect, but every time I wound my hair into coils, I longed for a bob. Even the president of the YWCA had one! But Mildred still thought it was crude.

A girl named Nina down on the second floor of our dorm was known for giving initial haircuts, so Mildred kept me away from her. I had to account for every *minute* away from our room.

One night when Mildred had a dinner date, I went to Nina's room. Since our doors had no locks and Nina knew

---

"Mildred stormed up to the door..."

---

about Mildred, she hooked a chair under the doorknob.

She'd lopped off half my hair when Mildred, who had come home early, stormed up to the door. She pounded, yelled and rattled the doorknob while Nina frantically finished cutting. When I returned to my room, Mildred snorted, but I looked into the mirror and saw a new person.

"You'd better write your father," she ordered. To keep the peace, I did. (He must have been very surprised, because it was the *only* letter I wrote him from college.) When I went home for the first time with my new look, I was relieved that both parents approved.

For the rest of my college years, bobbed hair was the rule, not the exception, and Mildred eventually gave in. During my senior year, a few overshoes went unbuckled, but I knew of no coeds who sneaked cigarettes.

And if the boys didn't go in for raccoon coats, at least they wore fewer suits or ties. We had broken through to the Roaring '20s. ⊷

He Still Recalls Poem Written "To the Flapper"

THE ROARING '20s are still vivid in my mind, and when I was in school back in 1928, we had to memorize a poem called *The Barefoot Boy.* Around this time, our local paper published an anonymous poem titled *To the Flapper*, which I also memorized:

> *Blessings on thee, little dame,*
> *Bareback girl with knees the same.*
> *With thy rolled-down silken hose*
> *And thy shoes with open toes.*
> *With thy tiny turned-up nose*
> *And thy short, transparent clothes.*
> *With thy red lips, reddened more,*
> *Smeared with lipstick from the store.*
> *With thy makeup on thy face*
> *And thy bobbed hair's jaunty grace.*
> *From my heart, I give thee joy,*
> *Glad that I was born a boy!*

—*Mike Tkachuk, Lublin, Wisconsin*

COLLEGIATES HAD CLEAN FUN. Natalie Baker of Canandaigua, New York says her grandparents (center) chaperoned Phi Gamma Delta's "Junior Week House Party" in '22. Her father is standing second from the left and her mother is at far left in the middle row.

Chapter Two

Radio Was
The Rage

Radio Was the Rage

The big excitement these days is something they're calling "the information superhighway". Supposedly it will change our lives. If you're old enough to recall the 1920s, you're entitled to chuckle and say, "Ha! A lot they know!"

Hitching up computers that talk to each other is a nice trick, but it's no great shakes compared to the decade of the '20s when *voices came out of the air and right into our homes!* Even from far-off mythical places such as Pittsburgh, New Orleans, Cincinnati and Omaha, for goodness sake!

You could be living on an isolated ranch in Montana and listen to a live broadcast of an orchestra in New York City. With a twist of some dials, you had a seat behind first base at a major league baseball game.

You could hear national election returns as they were being tabulated. You could laugh along with famous entertainers who until then had only been names in the newspaper.

It Was Revolutionary

Don't tell those of us who are offspring of the '20s about communications revolutions. We were there for the *really big one.*

At our northern-Illinois farmhouse, the radio was a long black metal box with an amazing array of dials and switches on the front and a big "tulip horn" speaker perched on top. It was powered by a collection of batteries in the basement. Only Dad was allowed to operate it.

Daytime reception was iffy, but Dad usually managed to catch the farm market reports from the Chicago Board of Trade, broadcast by, I believe, WLS ("The Prairie Farmer Station") in Chicago. For the first time, he was able to get up-to-the-minute market reports, something of critical interest to a farmer.

The very best reception was on below-zero, clear winter nights. Nowadays, Dad would be called a "channel-surfer" since he wasn't as much interested in the programs as he was in swooping across the dial to discover far-off radio stations. He had his little logbook handy, and each new station he picked up was a prized trophy to be jotted down.

"Last night I tuned in WLW in Cincinnati," he'd boast to a friend he met in the hardware store the next day.

"That's nothing," the friend would one-up him. "I caught a station in Denver!"

Discovered New Horizons

Here we were, living in a plain little farmhouse, a family that seldom ventured beyond the borders of our county—and now our horizons stretched as far as radio waves would carry. For the first time, we knew how baby birds felt when they discovered how to fly away from the nest.

It's often said that radio in those days was "theater of the mind" because the listener's imagination was free to roam where it would. When Mary said to Jimmy, "That's the most beautiful house I've ever seen," every listener saw *their* idea of a beautiful house. Everyone was happy.

Today we have "talk radio" and Top 40 radio and country radio. And it's everywhere—in the car, the bathroom, the bedrooms, the tractor and the barn. It's with us on the beach and while we jog and while we travel on the bus or plane.

But I miss the days when the whole family gathered around the radio, filled with wonder, staring at the set and sharing the magic that suddenly transformed and enriched our lives. To learn firsthand what it meant, read the stories that follow, written by people who were there when radio was in its infancy.

—*Clancy Strock*

WARING'S
BANJO
ORCHESTRA
TYRONE, PA.

Chicken-Coop Radio Entertained Entire Town

By Virginia Richardson Sutter
Owen, Wisconsin

MY BROTHER, Lawrence, was always engrossed in some kind of fascinating project. Being 7 years younger, I was his willing helper. Whenever I asked what he was doing, his answer was the same: "Watch and you'll find out."

In the summer of 1921, I found out about radio.

Lawrence dreamed of receiving messages by wireless. He was forever asking Dad to buy just one more piece of equipment in hopes of making it work.

We'd sit for hours, headphones clamped over our ears, while Lawrence

---

"People lined up outside to listen for themselves..."

---

twisted and adjusted the dials. We never heard anything but static.

Never, that is, until one Sunday afternoon when we heard voices! One sounded familiar, and it didn't take long to realize we'd somehow intercepted a telephone conversation—the local ladies' man arranging a date!

Became a Summer Project

In 1921, Lawrence's friend Fletcher came to spend the summer with us in Owen, Wisconsin. He said he'd built a radio that really worked and couldn't wait to show Lawrence how to do it. This was before commercial radios were available, so this was a pioneering effort in our little town.

The boys decided to build the radio

COOPED UP. The chicken coop behind Virginia became the local radio station.

in a former chicken coop in our backyard. After an order had been sent off for the parts, there was a flurry of activity as the coop was scrubbed clean and painted.

When the radio parts arrived, the boys mounted each component on a separate 6-inch square of Bakelite. Each had its own switch or dial, and once assembled, it made an impressive sight. I gladly ran errands so the two boys could work uninterrupted.

A group of townsmen armed with posthole diggers and logger's tools raised two 50-foot poles for the aerial. That event drew quite a crowd. We all held our breath until the first pole shuddered into place in our backyard, then moved to another yard down the block to watch the second pole go up. A wire was strung between them.

The boys were finally ready. There were many anxious moments as they tried to synchronize all those dials, listening for some indication that all the effort hadn't been in vain.

There were three sets of earphones and three stools in that little coop. I sat beside the boys listening, and I'll never forget the elation I felt when the first faint strains of music came through the earphones!

Radio Drew a Crowd

We were listening to Madame Schumann-Heink singing *The Rosary*. In the coming days, the stations we heard most frequently were KDKA Pittsburgh and WGY Schenectady.

It didn't take long for word to get around. Soon people were lining up outside the tiny coop to hear for themselves.

Some people came from sur-

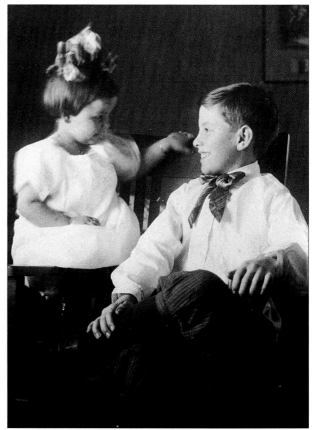

RADIO KIDS. Virginia Richardson and her brother, Lawrence, had their picture taken in a studio in the '20s. The photo was supplied by Virginia's daughter, Cynthia Ebert of Ripon, Wisconsin.

rounding towns. One night the owner of the local lumber mill even waited in line for a turn! The local druggist often called during baseball games to ask for the latest scores.

When winter came, the set was reassembled indoors. Tuning was a ticklish process; in fact, we probably did as much tuning as listening. But sometimes it paid off, letting us listen to a station as far away as Havana, Cuba.

In the coming years, I came to realize that radio was going to be more than just a pleasant summer diversion. On August 2, 1923, we heard about the sudden death of President Warren G. Harding in San Francisco. Somehow, it had greater impact than seeing it in the paper the next day.

How little we realized during that summer of the radio all the wondrous advances in communication the coming decades would bring. Having lived through it, I'll never take them for granted.

To Teen, Historic Broadcast Was Just Another Experiment

By Russ Rennaker, Kokomo, Indiana

I HUNKERED DOWN in my chair, pulled up my bib overalls and clamped my Brandes headset over my ears. This was going to be something special. The date was November 2, 1920, and I was 13 years old.

I was an amateur radio operator with my small set and call letters 9CRC.

For weeks, I'd been listening to a Dr. Conrad in Wilkinsburg, Pennsylvania, as he played records over his amateur radio station, 8XK. But tonight was going to be something different.

Dr. Conrad had written to me, asking that I be sure to listen in on this particular night and let him know how the reception was. I was an official "listening post" in Indiana for his experiments in radio broadcasting.

All I knew about Dr. Conrad was that he was an enthusiastic radio amateur who played records. What I didn't know was that he was assistant chief engineer of Westinghouse. A Westinghouse executive who listened to Dr. Conrad's popular broadcasts thought a real demand for radio receivers could be built if programming were available. He talked the company into building a radio station.

On the evening the station was to begin broadcasting, Dr. Conrad wouldn't be there; instead, he would be 5 miles away at 8XK, standing by in case the new station's equipment failed.

The static crackled in my earphones, and then I heard a voice. But it wasn't the familiar voice of Dr. Conrad.

"This is L.H. Rosenberg, speaking to you from the radio facilities atop the Westinghouse Building in East Pittsburgh, Pennsylvania. This is the first broadcast over the newly licensed KDKA. We are going to bring you the returns of the Harding-Cox presidential election. Stand by..."

I yawned and pressed the earphones tighter. I reached for the pad I used to write my comments to Dr. Conrad. To me, it was just another experiment. I had no idea I was witnessing a historic event—the beginning of professional broadcasting. ⇥

"Opry" Offered 4 Hours of Pure Entertainment

WE HAD no electricity in the Ozark Mountains, but a few neighbors owned battery-powered radios. On Saturday nights, if the reception was good, we'd sit as quiet as falling snowflakes and listen to the *Grand Ole Opry*— or, as one clown in the group used to call it, the "Grand Ole Uproar".

From 8 o'clock until midnight, we kids were in our own little Heaven. After a hard week's work in the fields, we could snuggle down, half-asleep, for 4 hours of entertainment and total relaxation.

At the end of the program, the announcer always drawled, "Well, it's time for the tall pines to pine, the papaws to pause, the bumblebees to bumble all around, while the grasshopper hops, the eavesdropper drops and gently the ol' cow slips away. This is George D. Hay, the solemn ol' judge, saying so long, ever'body."

Sixty years later, the memory still makes my skin tingle and brings tears to my eyes. Those hours of simple entertainment and pleasure are indelibly etched in my memory.
—*Eldon Patton, Guymon, Oklahoma*

Radio Broke Down Walls Of Solitude for Farm Boy

By Kenney Hicklin, Kansas City, Missouri

MY INTRODUCTION to radio came on August 2, 1923, while visiting my cousins. The eldest was tinkering with a little gadget, but I wasn't much interested until he took off his earphones and announced, "President Harding is dead!"

I didn't put much stock in the news, coming as it did from a wireless contraption way out there in the country.

But the next day's newspaper confirmed it—the president had died suddenly in San Francisco. Far across the land, in a Vermont farmhouse, John Calvin Coolidge had taken the presidential oath of office by lamplight at 2 o'clock in the morning

It wasn't until the winter of 1926-27 that I got to listen to radio regularly. Early one evening when I arrived home

━━◆━━━━━━◆━━

"Inside our home was a new Crosley radio..."

━━◆━━━━━━◆━━

on horseback from school, I looked up into the starlit sky and saw something new—a wire stretched from the farmhouse gable to the smokehouse.

Inside our home at the end of a lead-in wire was a new Crosley radio, complete with a 6-volt storage battery, two "B" batteries, a "C" battery and a loudspeaker. My mother had paid $100 for it—a considerable sum in our circumstances. But today I salute her vision.

New World Opened

On those long winter nights, 5 muddy miles from the nearest village, that radio defied the forces of isolation to bring us the news and weather—and later, entertainment.

A whole new world opened up to us, as we listened to *Amos 'n' Andy*, St. Louis Cardinals baseball games and music…wonderful music where there had been none before.

I'd listen to far-off stations like KOA in Denver, KMOX in St. Louis and KFNF and KMA in Shenandoah, Iowa. One evening I was thrilled when a DJ in Kansas City announced the next number: "And now, *The Wreck of the Old Ninety-Seven* as requested by Kenney Hicklin, Route 1, Sampsel, Missouri."

The radio's storage battery had to be taken to town periodically for recharging, and if the roads were impassable, we were in for a lonely radio-free hiatus.

In 1928, we gave up on our Model T auto with its magneto electrical system and acquired a car equipped with a storage battery. We soon discovered the car battery was interchangeable with the radio battery. When the radio battery weakened, we'd switch them. The car recharged the radio battery while the radio used the car battery. It was like discovering perpetual motion.

Today television is king, and it is a marvel. But for me, it was radio that came along when I needed it most.

AMOS 'N' ANDY. Freeman Gosden ("Amos", left) and Charles Correll ("Andy") were stars of what many folks considered the best radio show on the air.

I'll never forget those winter nights more than 70 years ago, when radio waves came bounding over the dark hills at the speed of light to pierce a wall of solitude and bring the wonderful world to a young boy in rural Missouri.

Radio-Building Skills Came in Handy During War

AFTER MY FAMILY bought our first radio, a simple crystal set, a friend and I decided to build our own sets, following directions from a science magazine. We used several of the items recommended in the article, including graphite from a pencil for the "cat's whisker".

Years later, in a German POW camp, we used similar materials to build a secret radio set. We got the parts by bribing a guard with food from our Red Cross parcels. With our secret radio, we could pick up signals and programs from clandestine mobile units broadcast by the BBC. The camp's massive barbed-wire walls served as a giant antenna!
—*Frank Florence Jr.*
Butler, Kentucky

Dad's 'Dream Machine' Brought Boxing to Town

By Ralph Browne
Carlsbad, California

WHEN THE FIRST RADIO with a loudspeaker came to our small farming community on the Canadian prairie in 1926, it was a major public event. The few household radios in Arcola, Saskatchewan were equipped with earphones, allowing only one person to listen at a time.

My father was a telegrapher with the Canadian Pacific Railway, and an avid radio enthusiast. He spent hours reading everything he could find on advances in the technology.

One day he saw an advertisement in an American magazine extolling the virtues of a powerful 26-tube radio equipped with a loudspeaker so a family could listen together. He was hooked.

Dipped into Savings

For days thereafter, the only thing Dad could talk about was that radio. He and Mother had endless discussions about whether we could afford it. Finally, Mom surrendered. Dad took the money from our limited savings account and ordered his dream machine.

In the days that followed, Dad talked about the radio with everyone who came by the depot. There was so much interest that he agreed to unveil it at the community hall.

After what seemed an eternity, the radio and its accessories arrived. They were packed in a large wooden crate,

and it took three men to unload it from the express car.

It was decided that the radio would make its debut a couple of nights later, when the Jack Dempsey-Gene Tunney fight was to be broadcast.

On the big night, two of Dad's friends helped him set up the radio. Sitting on stage, it looked huge—much larger than a steamer trunk. The front of the gleaming mahogany cabinet had black Bakelite dials for tuning, volume control and other adjustments. On top was a towering horn-type speaker. It was an impressive sight indeed.

Dad unpacked the tubes with care and inserted them while his friends strung the outdoor aerial. Then it was time to see if the radio would bring in

"After some fine-tuning, WGN came in loud and clear..."

any of the stations carrying the fight. After a lot of "fine-tuning" amid bursts of static, WGN came in loud and clear from Chicago. Dad was the happiest man alive!

About 50 people showed up to hear the fight. Dad gave a short talk on developments in radio and predicted that within a few years, batteries would not be required—people could plug their radios right into light sockets!

Dad urged all to crowd in close so they would be sure to hear. He checked the connections and turned on the switch, explaining that it would take a few minutes for the tubes to warm up.

His Man Lost

At first, there was only static, but with a little fine-tuning, we soon heard the announcer on WGN calling the fight round by round. When Gene Tunney won, the crowd applauded. Dad was disappointed…he was a Dempsey fan.

After the fight, some people stayed to talk as Dad tuned in other stations. Some of the children, including me, dashed out into the warm summer night.

One of my friends bragged that he was Gene Tunney and could lick any kid in town. I responded by bopping him on the nose, and we wrestled each other to the ground. We were separated by people coming out of the hall.

When we all returned home, Dad served ice cream to celebrate. He gave me an extra scoop, calling me his "Jack Dempsey son". I've had a warm spot in my heart for radio and ice cream ever since.

THE UPSET. Boxing fans were thrilled to be able to hear the Jack Dempsey-Gene Tunney fight on the radio on September 23, 1926. But many were stunned when Tunney beat the champ. There was a rematch a year later, but Dempsey lost again.

RADIO HOME. It was in a tent in the backyard of this home in Defiance, Ohio, where William Thompson (below left) and his pal Richard Reineke first heard a radio broadcast from far-off Los Angeles, California.

It was a gala evening, even though only one person at a time could hear a portion of the broadcast from WJR Detroit. The expression on the face of the one wearing the receiver made it worth waiting our turn! —*Doris Schutt Cleveland, Georgia*

They Shared with Operator

SOME FAMILIES had radios with headphones, but our RCA didn't. In 1926 when we listened to the *Grand Ole Opry* on Saturdays, Father would ring up "central", the local operator, and suspend the receiver so she could hear the program until she closed the switchboard for the night. I think she appreciated that radio just as much as we did! —*Emma Jordan, Lantana, Florida*

"Silent Night" Let Amateurs Try for Distant Stations

RADIOS were a novelty at first. Home mechanics spent many hours building superheterodynes powered by a row of batteries. Every Monday was "Silent Night" in Chicago. Local stations ceased broadcasting to give amateurs a chance to pick up distant stations.

I built a crystal set and stored it under the bed, using the bedsprings as an antenna. I always looked forward to the Wayne King broadcast from 10 p.m. to midnight. It was a pleasure to lie in bed with the earphones on, listening to *Melody of Love* and other good music. —*George Biringer Bella Vista, Arkansas*

Sounds of Far-Off Station Tuned Him in to New Hobby

FOR MY 10th birthday in 1929, my father gave me a kit for a crystal set. I immediately assembled it and picked up WLW in Cincinnati from our home in northwestern Ohio.

A friend and I persuaded my parents to let us stay up all night in a tent in the backyard, tuning the "cat's whisker" to see if we could pick up more distant stations.

We played with the set for a while, but heard nothing except WLW and Detroit's WJR. We both fell asleep.

About 3 a.m., we woke up and tried again. Suddenly we heard: "You are listening to dance music coming from the Ambassador Hotel's beautiful Coconut Grove ballroom through radio station KFI, on 640 kilocycles, located in Los Angeles, California."

We were so excited we barged out of our tent, dashed into the house and woke my parents and younger brother!

From that exciting beginning, amateur radio became my hobby. I operated amateur station W6PMV for 34 years. —*William Thompson Irvine, California*

Newspaper Made Building Radio Set Crystal Clear

WHEN the *Detroit News* published daily installments on how to build a crystal set radio, my father started his homework each evening by reading the directions in the newspaper.

He wound wire 'round and 'round an oatmeal box, then on each succeeding night, he added parts as the instructions directed.

I'll never forget the first evening we heard voices and music as we passed around a borrowed set of headphones between our family and the neighbors.

RADIO CAR. What might have been the first car radio was built in 1926 by his dad, says R.B. Freeman of Gettysburg, Pennsylvania.

Wonders of Radio Kept Dad Out 'Til 3 a.m.

WHEN I was little, we lived in River Park, a suburb of South Bend, Indiana. My father worked at a drugstore in South Bend and closed up each night at 10 minutes before 11. The last streetcar to River Park left at 11, and if he didn't catch it, he had to walk 4 miles home.

Mom always waited up for him, but one night in 1923, he wasn't on the streetcar. When hours passed and he still hadn't shown up, she was in a panic!

About 3 a.m., a car drove up and Dad bounded into the house, full of excitement. He started telling Mom about the "fantastic box" he'd been listening to, with music coming over the air. Mom knew Dad didn't drink, so she assumed he must have lost his mind!

When Dad finally calmed down, he explained he'd been listening to a friend's radio, enjoying band music and other programs from as far away as St. Louis and New York City, and said we were going to get a radio of our own.

Ours was the first battery-operated radio in the neighborhood. What a thrill it was to put on the earphones and listen to music and talking!

Every night, neighbors and relatives dropped in to hear our "newfangled contraption", as Grandpa called it.
—Maxine Van Tornhout
St. Petersburg, Florida

Brothers' Ingenuity Let Both Listen at Once

MY BROTHER Sam and I built a crystal set and sold vegetables from our garden to raise money for a set of earphones. But only one of us could listen to the radio at a time.

We solved that by putting the earphones inside one of Mother's large-mouth pitchers, then putting our ears close to the mouth. That way we could both listen at the same time!
—Hugh Choat, Trussville, Alabama

First "Squawk Boxes" Interested Only Hobbyists

IN THE EARLY 1920s, radio was really an oddity. Only the hobbyist indulged, and when he invited you to come listen to his "squawk box", it was usually late at night, because the reception was better. Amid the static,

you could actually understand a few words. But it was still marvelous—after all, it was coming through the air.

By the late 1920s, this marvel was quite commonplace. We could actually hear the voice quality of Bing Crosby, Russ Columbo, Morton Downey, Paul Whiteman and other big names of the decade.
—Chet Noland
Federal Way, Washington

"Contraption" Didn't Keep Family up Too Late

IN 1925, my father received a letter from his brother, who was stationed at Fort Lewis, Washington. In that letter, my Uncle Roy described his new radio:

"Since we got our radio about 2 months ago, we've logged around 60 stations. I quit work at 4:30 and am home in 15 minutes, then we have supper at 5 p.m. While eating, we usually listen to Vincent Laparello's Concert Orchestra, playing in the Garden Room of the Hotel St. Francis in Frisco. They are on 5 nights a week at this hour.

"We also hear Creatore's Orchestra, which plays at the Million Dollar Theater in Los Angeles. Pittsburgh is the farthest eastern station we have heard.

"There's a world of entertainment to be had from a set, although the best of them are none too good under some conditions. At any rate, we don't let the darned contraption keep us up any later than 10 or 10:30." *—Mary Mahoney*
Omaha, Nebraska

LITTLE LISTENER. Rosemond Davis developed an early love of radio, as the photo at right taken in Milford, Illinois shows. She was just 11 months old when a newspaper photographer caught her with earphones on her head and a cookie in her hand. Above, Rosemond again tried on the earphones (this time without a cookie) after finding the old radio in an uncle's basement. "It doesn't work anymore, but considering its age, it's not in bad shape," she reports. Rosemond, who now lives in Dixon, California, says she is still a radio buff, preferring the pictures of her imagination rather than those on television.

How Could Voices Come From Nuts and Bolts?

By Marjorie Brubaker, Arcadia, California

I'LL NEVER FORGET the first time I saw and heard a radio. Everyone in our church in Cincinnati, Ohio had been invited to come see "something very special and new". Sitting before us was mechanical equipment unlike anything we'd ever seen before. The sanctuary buzzed with excited chatter.

Then a hush fell over the crowd. When the clock reached a certain hour, voices began coming out of that equipment. Even more amazing, the voices joked and spoke the names of some of the members of our little congregation. How could this be? *Voices* coming from nuts and bolts!

Then we learned the voices belonged to some men from the congregation who were at WLW, a local radio station. We were amazed. Voices were out there in the air, we were told, and it was possible to reach out and bring them into the room!

Radio fever filled the air. Everyone in our neighborhood, including my father, built a crystal set with a round Mother's Oats box tightly bound with burnished wire from top to bottom. Later, my father tried to build a tube radio, but his interest cooled when the $5 tube burned out!

Everyone seemed to be abuzz about this invention. It was the main topic of conversation on streetcars, as people discussed "how I built my crystal set" or "the programs I received last night".

Later, when the Depression began, my future husband always kept a crystal set in his college dorm room tuned to WLW. A wire the width of a hair connected the set to several other rooms.

Since no electricity was involved, anyone in the hookup could listen in anytime the station was on the air. ✄

EARLY RADIOS were crystal sets, or, like this Magnavox M4, great horned outfits. In the '20s, $25 was a lot of money. The old ad is from Alice Dow of Columbus, Ohio.

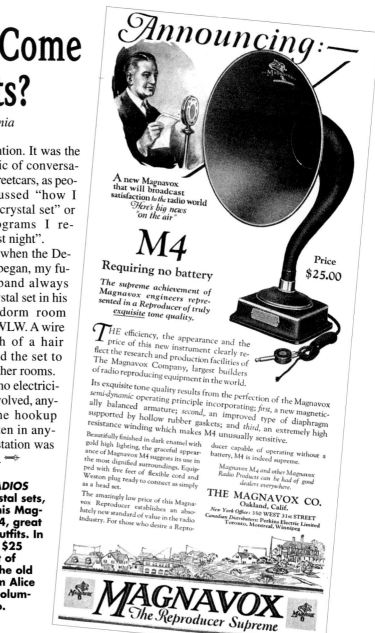

He Bought First Radio for $1 and Three Coupons

MY FIRST "cat's whisker" crystal set was a failure, and I got a subsequent lecture from Dad about wasting my money. Then I saw an ad in the paper. For $1 and three coupons from Mother's Oats, I could receive a completely assembled crystal set. All I would need was an aerial and earphones.

First I had to talk my mother into buying three boxes of oatmeal. But I *hated* oatmeal! Mother decided she'd add a little extra to Dad's bowl each morning so she could use up the oats without him noticing. Of course, she tried to make me promise to eat some, too, but I refused.

I got the coupons and the dollar, put them in the mail and sat on the front steps until the mailman brought that fabulous radio. The aerial was already up, and I'd borrowed some earphones. The set, built right on a Mother's Oats box, was easy to run. But there wasn't much daytime radio, so at first I heard nothing.

Then, about 7 p.m., I heard music from KDKA in Pittsburgh! I called for Dad to come up to my room. When he saw that I had another radio, he practically turned blue.

I quickly held an earphone up to his ear, and he heard the music. Dad was skeptical. He stuck his head out the window to see if there happened to be a parade passing by. Then he called downstairs to ask Mother if she was playing the Victrola.

Finally he simmered down enough to listen for a bit, and I was spared any punishment. Lucky for me he didn't notice the hole I'd bored in the window sash for the lead-in wire!

—*Norbert Young, Tonawanda, New York*

First Crystal Set Made Warm Memory

ONE SATURDAY in February 1924, Dad was all smiles when he came home from work clutching a mysterious parcel. When we asked what he'd brought, all he'd say was, "Oh, you'll see soon enough—right after dinner."

Dad seldom smiled when he came home from work—he was always too bushed. So I knew whatever was in that parcel was something really special. I could barely wait, and probably ate more than usual, trying to speed things up!

Finally the table was cleared and Dad got to work. He drew out a coil of wire, then went to the back porch to string it on the clothesline. Mom helped by fastening the wire onto the line with wooden clothespins.

Dad came back in and clamped a shorter wire onto a cold-water pipe that he'd shined up. That done, he seemed satisfied to just rest, savoring the moment.

While we waited, Mom lit a second gas mantel light that jutted out from the wall and placed a kerosene lantern in the center of the table. The kitchen in our "railroad flat" was cozy and warm, and bedtime had been postponed for us kids.

At last, Dad withdrew what we had been waiting to see—some sort of elec-

By Cornelius Hogenbirk
Waretown, New Jersey

trical gadget mounted on a board. There was a coil, something we couldn't identify with a knob on it, and two pairs of connecting posts.

Dad connected the makeshift clothesline aerial and the water-pipe ground wire to two of the posts, then hooked up

ONE-TUBER. A Dutch Cleanser container was used for the coil on this radio built by Park Gregory of Belleville, Michigan.

a headset to the remaining posts. As he put the headset on, he explained, "This is what's called a crystal radio set. Just wait and see." He fiddled with a springy

wire called a "whisker", telling us he was looking for "a sensitive spot". I moved in close, holding my ear near one of the headphones.

Dad adjusted the knob again and began to look doubtful, when suddenly I heard sounds. Dad smiled broadly, and I was so excited I jumped up and down!

Dad asked Mom for her biggest soup kettle and put the earphones inside it. This amplified the sound, and all of us crowded over that old pot to hear it. What a picture that must have been! Then we all took turns wearing the headset while Mom made hot cocoa and fetched her stenciled tin of iced cookies.

I don't recall what we heard. Perhaps it was Billy Jones and Ernie Hare, "The Happiness Boys". Or it could've been the comedy team of Weber and Fields on *The Eveready Hour*. Whatever we heard, the experience was something really special, and I've never forgotten it.

Mom added more coal to the stove before banking it and took the heated flannel-covered bricks to place at our feet as we snuggled into bed. There was no heat in the bedrooms of those railroad flats, but I didn't care. Tomorrow I'd tell the gang at school all about our new radio! ⇥

Earliest Radios Allowed For Only One Listener

By S.A. Muirhead, The Dalles, Oregon

MY FATHER built our first radio, which consisted of bare wires, a hand-wound tuning coil and a galena crystal laid out on a board. An earphone, plus a long antenna wire strung from the peak of the house to a tree, completed the setup.

The nearest station was 200 miles north in Portland, Oregon, and its programming was strictly impromptu. Once, a Western Union messenger came by the station to deliver a telegram. The announcer spotted a harmonica in the boy's pocket and persuaded him to produce a musical interlude!

The next radio at our house was more advanced. Father built that one with two tubes that cost $7.50 each. The cost represented a week's wages, but, with a rubber tube inserted into each of the two earphones and dividers placed in each tube, eight people could listen at once.

Alas, we children seldom got the chance, because the house was full of neighbors every night! We had to remain utterly silent so our visitors could hear. Since we weren't getting to listen and we weren't getting much sleep either, Father dismantled the radio! ⇥

H. Armstrong Roberts

FOUR-TUBER. Each tube in an old radio like this cost a week's pay.

BABY MAKES THREE. Everyone got to listen in on the old crystal set...if there were enough headphones. If not, you waited your turn.

have to rate that program from the '20s as the one I remember most because of the entertainment it brought my dad.

—*Norton Salis*
Darlington, Wisconsin

Mom Tuned in to Byrd's South Pole Expedition

MY MOTHER was an invalid, so we kept our crystal set next to her bed so she could listen. One night, she was working the cat's whisker trying to get a program. Lo and behold, we realized she was listening to Admiral Byrd at the South Pole. She was so excited!

Mother was especially interested in the expedition because her third cousin, Norwegian explorer Roald Amundsen, had discovered the South Pole in 1911.

—*Elizabeth Frischmon*
Fridley, Minnesota

Manners Made Her Worry About "Two-Way" Radio

MY UNCLE built a radio in 1922 and invited our family to come and listen to it one Sunday. Everyone took turns listening on the headset. We spent the whole day listening to the radio, talking, visiting and eating.

I remember someone wearing the headset and listening while crunching on some popcorn. Suddenly she burst out laughing and said, "Oh, I hope the people on the radio can't hear us eating popcorn!"

—*Uva Vernon*
Rimrock, Arizona

She Tuned in to Win Shorthand Contest

IN 1929, my teacher told us station WOR in New York City was sponsoring a contest for shorthand students. On a specified evening, we'd listen to a special broadcast and try to take dictation at 100 words per minute—a real challenge! Then we'd bring our work to school and transcribe it in a timed typing test.

My dear mother kept my five sisters away from the radio that night so I could participate. A couple of weeks later, I learned I had won! I received a certificate from WOR and a beautiful silver pin inscribed "Expert Typist" from the Underwood typewriter company. I wore it proudly and still have it today.

—*Doris Davison*
Summit, New Jersey

They Planned Farm Chores Around Twice-a-Week Show

BEFORE ELECTRICITY came to the farm, my parents' Atwater Kent radio was powered by a 6-volt rechargeable battery. We listened to only a few programs, since the battery ran down quickly and had to be taken 5 miles into town to be recharged.

Our outside antenna ran from the highest peak on the house to the windmill tower. If there was so much as a

cloud in the sky, we had to disconnect the lead-in wire and ground it to protect the radio in case lightning struck.

When the weather was clear, Dad and I arranged our work so we could listen to *Bradley Kincaid*, a 15-minute program that aired two afternoons a week. "The Kentucky mountain boy and his hound-dog guitar" sang such songs as *The Letter Edged in Black* and *When the Work Is All Done This Fall*.

After 60 years of radio listening, I'd

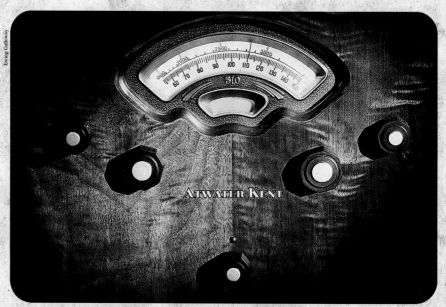

DON'T TOUCH THAT DIAL! No one did when a favorite program came on the old Atwater Kent like this one. Listen close, it's time for...

Bedsprings, Barbed Wire Made Perfect Antennas

By J. Robert Smith, Golden, Colorado

THE MINISTER'S SON at our church in Oklahoma showed me how to build a crystal radio. All it took was an oatmeal box, some copper wire, a galena crystal and a "whisker"—a coiled spring with a sharpened point that could be moved to various spots on the crystal.

When you hit the right spot on the crystal, you could hear music through the single earphone that Hubert had ordered out of a catalog for a dollar.

An antenna was required for decent reception, and Hubert's was 60 feet long, stretched between the church and the parsonage. There weren't many stations in 1920, but Hubert sometimes picked up WBAP in Fort Worth, WLS in Chicago and WLW in Cincinnati.

It was magic. I had to have a radio of my own.

Hubert had an extra galena crystal, and my family always had a Quaker

> ## "It was magic. I had to have a radio of my own..."

Oats box around. Thin copper wire wasn't that easy to come by, but a coil in our Model T had gone bad and it had a bunch of copper wire inside.

But where would I get a dollar for an earphone?

My granddad had a big lawn, and I talked him into letting me cut it for a quarter. After a month, I had my dollar.

Oh, for an Antenna

The next problem was the antenna. I'd have to cut Granddad's grass the rest of the summer to make enough money for the wire and insulators. And Dad was skeptical—a wire strung between the house and the barn might attract lightning.

But I didn't let any of that stop me. I coiled my wire around an oatmeal box and shellacked it into place. I connected it to a homemade whisker and tried it out at Hubert's house. It worked!

Back at home while wearing my earphone, I accidentally touched a small antenna wire to our screen door. Music started coming through the earphone! It wasn't as loud as with Hubert's 60-

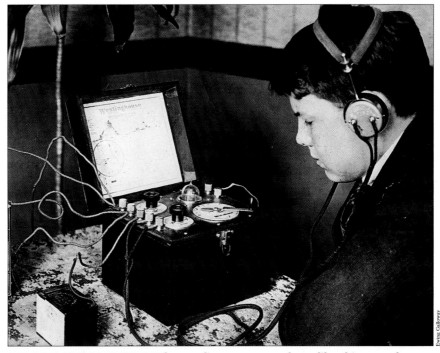

BUDDING BROADCASTER? When radio was young, boys like this one often built them from kits, using any wire handy for that all-important antenna.

foot antenna, but the sound was there.

Of course, Mom wouldn't let me leave the thing connected to the screen door, so I took it to the closest barbed-wire fence. Now the station came in even stronger! But that wasn't very convenient, so I experimented once more.

When no one was looking, I connected the wire to the bedsprings under my mattress. Wow—that worked, too!

"Robert, you'll get us all electrocut-

ed," Mom scolded when she found out. "That may make the lightning come right in here!"

I promised to unhook the wire anytime there was a storm, and we settled on a compromise. "When there are no clouds around, you can listen," Mom said. "But don't go off and leave it on."

Naturally, I sometimes forgot, but nothing ever happened. Those bedsprings made a perfect antenna. ⇒

Was Chaplin the First Mime on the Air?

WOC in Davenport, Iowa was one of only a few radio stations in the United States in 1922. Its announcer was told to speak in a very high voice, as early broadcasters thought a high-pitched tone carried farther.

I believe the first people to really appreciate radio were the farmers, who now could hear market reports at 2 p.m. Someone from the station would run to the cigar store to grab an afternoon paper, then race back to read the reports on the air.

The farmers showed their appreciation by sending chickens and oth-

er produce to the radio station.

One day, Charlie Chaplin was in town to perform at the vaudeville theater and was asked to speak on the radio. It never occurred to anyone to conduct an interview.

They put Chaplin in a room by himself with the big round microphone, closed the door and left. No one heard a sound.

The silent-film star was petrified and said afterward he didn't think he'd ever stand in front of a microphone again!
—Eleanor Conrad
Sarasota, Florida

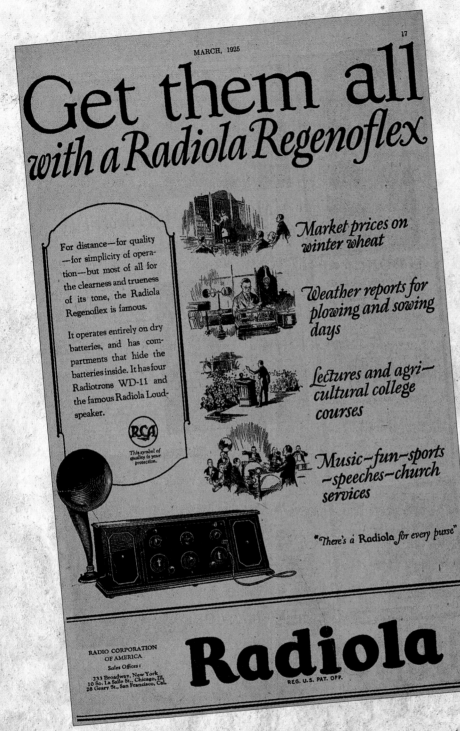

EARLY PORTABLE? Although it ran on batteries, this 1925 Radiola was not exactly a portable. But it brought in music, church services and the farm news. The old ad was shared by Alice Dow of Columbus, Ohio.

Tuning in Faraway Stations Was Evening's Entertainment

IN 1924, we got a battery-powered "RCA Radiola Regenoflex". This was a set with nine batteries and a horn for a speaker. It had a key to turn it on, and four knobs. Two were tuning knobs, which you had to turn at the same time to find a station. This became evening entertainment at our farm.

We lived on the plains of eastern Montana, hundreds of miles from a broadcasting station. But if our radio's batteries were strong and the weather was good, we could pick up stations like CFCN in Calgary, or others from Chicago, St. Louis, New Orleans and San Francisco. Mother kept a log of all the stations we received.

At night, we'd all sit around the radio, sometimes with neighbors, and Dad would see how many stations he could get. It was quite an event when he found a new station in some exotic place like Shenandoah, Iowa or Austin, Texas.

We didn't even have a phonograph, so the radio brought music to our home for the first time.   —*Gilbert Gander*
Spokane, Washington

Men Gathered on Porch To Listen to Prizefights

WE WERE THRILLED and delighted when we got our first radio in the 1920s. It was an Atwater Kent—a rectangular black box with dials and a speaker that sat on top.

We were one of the first families in town to have a radio. Whenever there was a prizefight, Dad would rig it up on the front porch. Every man in town seemed to congregate there to listen, while their wives visited inside with Mom.

If the weather was bad, the airwaves were full of static, and we'd hear one word in five spoken by the announcer. If the weather was good and we still heard static, Dad blamed it on "sunspots".   —*Evelyn Martin*
Lakeland, Florida

Dempsey Match Drew Father, Son to Radio

THE FIRST commercial radio stations in America began broadcasting at the start of the Roaring '20s, when I was 4. I didn't actually hear a radio until I was 9, when my dad took me to a local garage to hear a Jack Dempsey boxing match. We were the first ones there.

The garage's wooden radio was a yard wide and a foot high. Each of its three dials had to be tuned to a certain number to receive a particular station.

Later, I got a diagram from the library, found some parts and built my own one-tube radio on an old board. I listened to Don Ameche from The Little Theater Off Times Square in New York City. It was great—especially for a farm boy with little outside entertainment.
—*Gordon Delsart*
Green Bay, Wisconsin

First Radio He Heard Was Only Static

By James Buchanan, Nashville, Tennessee

WHEN I WAS about 14 years old, the news spread around Simpson County, Kentucky that a man from Indianapolis was coming to visit relatives and bringing a new invention…something called a radio.

My cousin borrowed a pickup and gathered up a whole truckload of us to go see that thing. When we got there, everybody was sitting out in the yard. The man from Indiana was putting up wires between two poles, then running them to a long box with a lot of knobs on it.

The wire was an antenna, he said, and it would pick up sounds from the air. He twisted and twisted those knobs, but all he ever got was some weird noise—what I later learned was static.

I finally saw my first working radio in high school. During winter, I boarded with a family that lived near the school so I didn't have to walk the 5 miles from home.

The Hensons had a radio, a small square box hooked to a car battery. On Saturday nights, their oldest daughter

"On Saturday nights, we'd listen to the 'Grand Ole Opry'…"

and I would listen to the *Grand Ole Opry* in the parlor while she helped me with my lessons.

When I started working after high

school, I saved my money to buy a Crosley table-model radio, and from then on I lost a lot of sleep! Sometimes I sat up all night, just listening to those good programs and performers.

I remember listening to Bluegrass Roy, Cowboy Jack, Texas Jim Robertson, Old Man Perkins and His Boys, and many more. From them, I learned the songs that I would perform on the radio myself in later years when I had my own band. ⚊

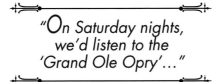

FAMILY HOUR. There might have been a lot of static on the old radio sets, like those the family above is listening to, but it sure beat doing chores. The chores usually got done when the batteries were unhooked.

THE GERALD BROTHERS. That's Oliver (left) and Clifford, back when they were radio stars and once followed another act...Lawrence Welk's!

Musical Brothers Played On 'Drugstore' Radio

By Oliver Gerald, Brookings, South Dakota

BACK IN 1927, my brother and I were radio stars on station KGDY in Oldham, South Dakota. The station was the creation of Alfred Nelson of Oldham, a self-taught electronics whiz.

Alfred had assembled the station's transmitter from discarded generators, meters and switches. The first microphone was an old-time desk telephone, and an old Edison phonograph was used to broadcast and record.

On the air from 6:30 to 9:30 p.m. Monday through Friday, the station was in the rear of a pharmacy. Broadcasts featured local talent, and that's where Clifford and I came in.

"Rowdy" and "Prince", our farm horses, furnished our transportation to the studio. In cold weather, we'd don overalls and sheepskins, ride into town and secure the horses in an empty build-ing. Then we'd head to the pharmacy, pull off our heavy winter wear and perform our favorite songs.

One evening after we'd completed an hour-long show, the druggist gave us "the best box of candy in the house"! Turned out that Charley Becker, a farmer living nearby, had liked what he was hearing so much that he called the drugstore and told them to "treat those Gerald brothers".

After we'd performed a few times, the fan mail and phone calls came pouring in for us. And it wasn't long before we were invited to travel to other towns in South Dakota and Nebraska to perform on other radio stations.

One memorable evening at WNAX in Yankton, South Dakota, Clifford and I waited to go on after Lawrence Welk and his "Hotsy-Totsy Boys" finished their last number. Those were the days!

We weren't paid much, so driving our Model T so many miles—even at 10¢ a gallon—got to be more than we could afford. It all came to an end when KGDY went off the air after a little more than a year.

Ironically, the FCC decided that Alfred Nelson, the man who'd masterminded the transmitter, wasn't qualified to operate his own equipment. Since radio advertising wasn't pulling in a lot of money at that time either, the station was unable to afford an operator who met FCC qualifications.

So the station's equipment was sold and the transmitter that featured so much local talent went silent.

Still, Clifford and I well remember those delightful songs of the '20s, and we look back upon our KGDY days as a once-in-a-lifetime "labor of love".

Many Early Programs Had Loyal Following

MY MOTHER was glued to the radio every afternoon. During baseball season, she followed the games faithfully and knew the batting average of every player of consequence.

If one of my brothers was too sick to go to school, she'd pop a dishpan full of popcorn to aid his recovery and they'd listen to the games together.

The most popular and entertaining evening show was *Amos 'n' Andy*. It became so popular, in fact, that people started staying home from the "picture shows" in droves rather than miss an episode.

This made such a dent in box-office receipts that movie houses let people listen to *Amos 'n' Andy* right in the theater and *then* showed the movie!

—*Helen Riser, Ocala, Florida*

Baby's Unusual Name Paid Homage to Radio

IN THE EARLY 1920s, my grandmother's family moved from a "holler" in the West Virginia mountains to their first house with electricity. Her brother, nicknamed "Lec", was born about the same time. When I asked about this unusual name, Grandma explained that the first electric thing they bought for their new house was a radio—so they named the baby "Electric Music"!

—*Terri Williams
Mechanicsville, Virginia*

RADIO MANIA. Radios became elaborate pieces of furniture, as these old ads from Alice Dow of Columbus, Ohio show. Crosley sold radios, ran a radio station and even owned the Cincinnati Reds, who played at Crosley Field.

Everything on the Air Thrilled New Listeners

IN THE EARLY '20s when our family first acquired a radio, there were no arguments about which programs were our favorites. There weren't all that many stations broadcasting at the time, and we were thrilled with whatever we could get!
—*Carol Smith*
Allegany, Oregon

Dad Skipped Commercials To Conserve Battery Power

MY PARENTS ordered our first battery-operated radio from Sears Roebuck when I was a young girl. Listening to the *Grand Ole Opry* from Nashville, Tennessee was a highlight of our lives.

We'd all gather 'round the radio when the program came on, but my dad was usually the sole operator. He would turn the radio off during commercials to save the battery. Sometimes by the time he turned it back on, the next song would already be half over.
—*Ida Hunt*
Leesville, Louisiana

Opry on the Air Was Fun and Laughs

OUR HUGE battery-powered Motorola radio needed to be recharged after frequent use, so we weren't allowed to run it all day. But every evening at 5:30,

Archive Photos

SWINGING TRIO. Swimming could wait when a chance to listen to that newfangled contraption known as radio came along. This one's portable!

after the chores were done, my sister and I would tune in to WNAX in Yankton, South Dakota and dance to the music of The Bohemian Band.

From WSM in Nashville, Tennessee came the *Grand Ole Opry*, with performances by such great stars as the Carter Family, Roy Acuff, Grandpa Jones and Ernest Tubb. It started on the air in 1925.

One of my favorite comedians on this long-running program was the Duke of Paducah, who ended his routine with this line: "I'm going back to the wagon, boys! These shoes are killing me!"
—*Beulah Wagner*
Cedar Rapids, Iowa

Thrill of Radio Kept Some up Past Bedtime

LONG WINTER EVENINGS were filled with radio during the '20s. We might listen to a favorite program or just twirl the dials to see how many stations we could pull in. Maybe we could receive a more distant station than the neighbors!

The reception was better in winter than summer, and it improved even more after the sun went down. It was easy to become so engrossed that normal bedtimes could be forgotten.

Grandfather had a solution that ensured he'd get to bed on time despite the radio's lure—by using what he called "radio wood" in his stove.

After supper, Grandfather would tune the radio to his favorite program and fill the stove with several chunks of wood pruned from his aging apple orchard. The "punky" wood had many decayed spots, so it burned slowly and gave off little heat.

By bedtime, the living room would be cool enough to make the warm feather bed upstairs far more enticing than the radio!
—*Darwin DeLong*
Eagleville, Missouri

Radio Voices Impressed Toddler

WHEN I was about 3 years old in 1925, my father came home one evening with this strange new contraption and couldn't wait to see how I'd react to it. Mother got me out of bed, wrapped a blanket around me and sat me in my grandmother's rocker.

They fitted some headphones to my ears and asked me if I heard anything. I can recall hearing someone talking. My solemn expression in the photo below might indicate that I was properly impressed.
—*Marian Mossar*
Tualatin, Oregon

He Relished Chance to Tune Superheterodyne

By Laurence Lipsett, Webster, New York

EVERYONE wanted a radio in 1928, but they were so expensive. When Dad bought the superheterodyne, the family marveled.

The console was nearly 3 feet long and 10 inches high. There were five dials—three for tuning, one for volume and one for sound quality.

The speaker on top was shaped like the horn in the classic advertisements showing the RCA dog "Nipper" listening for "his master's voice". What an impressive contraption!

I was in my early teens, so I volunteered to be the chief operator. Just before 7 each weeknight, I tuned in to WGR in Buffalo, the strongest nearby station, for *Amos 'n' Andy*.

I turned the first big dial to approximately 55 AM (there was no FM). Then I turned dials two and three to 55, and adjusted them until the sound was clearest.

When the familiar theme song of *Amos 'n' Andy* came on (I learned later it was *Toselli's Serenade*), the family gathered around the radio, just as most of our neighbors were doing. No one spoke except during the commercials.

LITTLE PICKER. Radio inspired Laurence Lipsett to try the banjo.

In 15 minutes, the program was over. Men went back to their newspapers, and women went back to the kitchen to finish washing dishes.

Having a second radio to use in another room was unthinkable at that time because of the cost.

Another program I enjoyed was Harry Reser's Clicquot Club Eskimos, which advertised soft drinks with a banjo band that inspired me to try playing that instrument.

Radio signals traveled better at night, so I stayed up late Fridays and Saturdays to tune in KDKA in Pittsburgh and WGY in Schenectady, New York, the early "super stations". I also tried to tune in more distant stations, listening to a faint signal through static, sometimes for half an hour, until the call letters were announced.

I picked up stations in Chicago, Boston, Philadelphia and Atlanta, where WSM was a powerful station.

Baseball fans could hear games on many nights. Notre Dame, Michigan, Ohio State and Southern California broadcast football on Saturdays, and Sunday broadcasts featured professional football's Giants, Bears, Packers and Browns. We didn't need television to visualize a game.

Today, I miss radio's Big Bands, innocent comedy and the chance to use our imagination.

EARLY VOICES. Don Ameche (left) was on the radio from the late '20s, as was everyone's favorite "cowboy", Will Rogers.

THE FIRST COMMERCIAL I remember hearing was broadcast over KDKA in Pittsburgh, which was the only station we could receive. It was for Sherwin-Williams paint. At the end of each show, the announcer would say, "Be sure and buy this paint, because it covers the world."

I remember that well, because as a child I thought it was silly to put paint all over the world. —*Muriel Bordis* *Gloversville, New York*

Radio Programs Helped Speed Sisters' Recovery

BACK IN 1927, our family lived 80 miles from Chicago, in Rock County, Wisconsin.

Our family was quarantined then because of scarlet fever, and a local dealer came and installed our first radio. He did this out of the goodness of his heart, as small-town friends and neighbors were wont to do back in the '20s.

My three sisters and I loved listening to that radio—especially station WLS from Chicago. It's possible we all recuperated more quickly because of that radio!

—*Beatrice Shallock, Bakersfield, California*

SHH, I'M LISTENING. The magic of radio was enough to boggle the minds of grown-ups...imagine the surprise of the tyke in this photo sent in by Ruth Paul of Bedford, New Hampshire.

Teen Stayed Mum About Her 'Radio Debut'

By Alice Dow, Columbus, Ohio

AS A TEEN, I longed to sing on the radio. The closest I ever got was an amateur rendition of *Say a Little Prayer for Me*. Evidently no one did, for I never made the big time.

One day I saw a ukulele in Heaton's music store window for $6, and I had to have it. Dad gave me the money, and when I went to the store to buy it, the clerk told me I could take 10 free lessons. It was unbelievable!

The uke didn't come with a case, and I was glad—I wanted *everyone* on the streetcar to see it. I sat down next to an old man and announced, "I get 10 free lessons with this." He didn't respond.

I moved next to a lady with a baby. I told her how cute the baby was, then told her about my free lessons. The baby started crying and she didn't hear me. As I left the streetcar, I tried one more time—telling the conductor.

Got Her "Big Break"

After my third lesson, I was playing five chords and could sing and strum *Bye, Bye Blues*. My instructor at the music store said I could join Heaton's band, which played on a local radio station every Friday at the Fort Hayes

Hotel. What a break! I was going to be on the radio at last!

My parents told everyone. I got a new dress, new shoes and a haircut. I practiced *Carolina Moon*, *Love Letters in the Sand* and *When the Moon Comes Over the Mountain*. I thought I could

> "Tell us what it's like to be on the radio..."

croon like Bing Crosby on *Where the Blue of the Night Meets the Gold of the Day*.

Finally Friday came. My parents let my brother and sister stay home from school and Dad stayed home from work. Mom invited neighbors and relatives and spent the day baking apple pies. The funeral home loaned us folding chairs to set up around our old radio. Everyone was having such a good time that no one even noticed when I left for the studio.

It seemed to take an eternity for the streetcar to arrive. What if I was late?

Finally, I got to the hotel. I ran to the elevator and watched as the floor numbers slowly ticked by. In the distance, I could hear the band playing *Star Dust*—our closing number. I was late!

I hurried into the studio and sat down behind the other band members, tears dampening my sheet music. No one in the band said anything. No one even knew I hadn't been there. No one knew me, period.

What Would She Say?

On the way home, I was filled with dread. What would I say to all those people? How could I tell them I hadn't been on the radio?

As I ascended the front porch steps, everyone shouted, "You were great! How did you learn all that in three lessons?" I just stood there, bewildered, embarrassed, confused...and said nothing. Inside the house, someone put a roll on the player piano—*There'll Be a Hot Time in the Old Town Tonight*.

"Come on, honey," everyone coaxed. "Tell us what it's like to be on the radio." But they were so excited that they didn't even wait for my answer.

So I never told them! ✦

Chapter Three

What a Trip That Was!

What a Trip That Was!

The '20s saw Americans, ever a restless lot, suddenly take to the road in unprecedented numbers. People of even modest means now owned cars, and a few companies were granting *paid* vacations to their work force. The 40-hour work week brought extra leisure time, and slowly but surely, a border-to-border, coast-to-coast network of hard-surfaced roads was taking shape.

Americans decided it was time to get out and see the rest of the country.

When he was 70, Daniel Boone actually walked from Missouri to Yellowstone and back because tales of the area had aroused his curiosity.

By the '20s, you didn't have to walk. You could strap a couple of spare tires on the back of your Ford or Marmon or Packard, throw in a few extra fan belts, tie your suitcases and tents on top and hit the road.

You could visit the uncle who had moved to fabled California. You could go to Estes Park or Yellowstone or Niagara Falls. All those places of your dreams were within reach.

On the other hand, you *did* have to have an adventurous spirit. There was, for example, a stretch of U.S. highway in Nebraska where you had to open and close gates out in the rangeland.

Often Climbed Hills in Reverse

If you owned a Model T and came to a steep hill, it was sometimes necessary to *back up* to the top because the gas flowed into the engine by gravity, and a sharp climb put the gas tank beneath the motor.

Road maps were scarce, and highway signs were unreliable if not dead wrong. It was a long way between gas stations and even farther between good mechanics. Folks had to carry a tire pump, patching kit, compass and toolbox.

One of Mom and Dad's first trips after I was born was to visit one of Mom's college chums in Cleveland, Ohio. I have no personal recollection of it, but the family photo album shows me tentatively dipping my feet into Lake Erie. As Dad told it in later years, most of the trip was over gravel roads.

Every mile was an adventure, as contrasted with today's endless stretches of perfect interstate highways, with clean and comfortable rest stops spaced out every 50 miles or so. (Ask me about Great Inventions of the Twentieth Century and you'll find rest stops on my top-five list.)

People kept detailed trip diaries in those days, both to record the marvelous sights they had seen and also to keep track of their unplanned adventures...the farmer who hitched up a team of horses and pulled your car out of axle-deep mud, the strangers who let you pump a cup of cool water from their well, or the mechanic who worked far into the night to repair your engine.

Travelers depended upon the kindness of strangers, and rarely were they disappointed.

You'll read all about these adventures in the pages that follow, back in the days when people came home and their first words were, *"What a trip that was!"*

—*Clancy Strock*

DINING OUT. More and more families in the '20s loaded the car and headed out into the country to camp and picnic. The car made it all possible, and travel equipment was mostly homemade. This camp box, for example, looks an awful lot like an old suitcase...but who cared? It worked!

My 1928 Auto Race up Pikes Peak

By Robert Talbot, Houston, Texas

NEARLY 70 years ago, a legendary test of man and machine was to drive to the top of Colorado's Pikes Peak. I did it back in 1928.

Six of us, including my father, brother and I, set out from New Jersey in two cars. One was a huge 1926 Packard sedan and the other was a 1927 Ford cabriolet, a two-seater with a rumble seat.

We camped most of the time, driving a wandering route that took us cross-country to North Dakota, where we turned south to Colorado.

Finally we reached Manitou Springs near the base of Pikes Peak. From there you had three ways to get to the top. You could go by cogwheel railway, by nine-passenger open-topped Pierce Arrow touring cars or, if you were brave enough (and dumb enough!), drive it yourself.

Not many people attempted it in their own cars. The narrow dirt road to the top was bumpy and rutted. Even in low gear, the climb was tough and engines constantly overheated. There were barrels of water along the way to refill your radiator, but they often were empty.

The trip up wasn't the worst part, either. Coming down required an experienced driver and even then it was tricky. Much of the braking had to be done in low gear.

Brakes Burned Out

Cars in those days had only rear-wheel brakes. Constant use caused the brake drums to overheat, catch fire and burn out before you knew it. But if you relied on driving in low gear to hold the car back, the engine would dangerously overheat.

Either you stopped frequently to cool the brakes and engine or you risked finding yourself in a runaway car out of control. We saw plenty of evidence of what could happen—there were abandoned cars along the road and the remains of others that had plunged down the side of the mountain.

The Pierce Arrows were specially built for the job, of

H.H. Thomas/Unicorn Stock Photos

NO PEAK PIKER. This 1927 Ford cabriolet made it up Pikes Peak (top) in 1928 with Robert Talbot and his brother. That's their dad in the photo above.

FAMILY TOURIST TRADE. While Great-Grandma sold 10¢ hamburgers, my great-grandfather, William Henry Walker, made his living driving tours up Pikes Peak, says Elaine Graham of Rangely, Colorado. He's in the driver's seat, about to take a group up in September 1928.

course. They took off before dawn so tourists could watch the spectacular sight of the sun coming up over the horizon.

For some reason I still cannot fathom, Dad decided that my brother and I could drive the Ford to the peak. With the brash courage of a 16-year-old, I even made a friendly wager with the drivers of the six touring cars that we could beat them to the top.

They took off first, and we followed in our stripped-down Ford—to make the car lighter, we'd removed everything we didn't need.

Look Out Below!

Soon the steep climbing began and we learned what we faced. The big cars had worn ruts in the narrow dirt road, especially on the curves, which they could manage handily. When you tried to pass, you did it on the outside of the road where the drop-off was only a few feet away. It was scary and treacherous in the dark.

Finally we passed the last car in line, its passengers cheering us on. Then we passed three more, speeding by on the loose gravel at 15 miles per hour and trying not to think about the 1,000-foot drop-offs that were so close.

It took three desperate attempts and 15 minutes to pass the number-two car...and we were nearly to the top. Not much time was left if we were to pass the lead car and win the race.

Suddenly there was a stretch of straight road ahead. (To this day, I suspect that the driver of that number-one car let up a little bit to help us win.) We sped by him and in a couple of minutes reached the little clearing at the top of the mountain.

There was a small block house at the peak, serving as a weather station. The front of it is still there, preserved as part of the splendid new observation area complete with souvenir shop and cafeteria.

I'm close to my 83rd birthday now, but I'll never forget the excitement and the thrill of my 1928 race up Pikes Peak.

SLEEPER CAR. The famous Pullman railroad car company also made autos, like the one Edward Snell (above) rode in with his mother and father on an outing to Liberty Lake near Spokane, Washington. Something about that Pullman name just made you want to snooze.

Travelers' Route Followed "Cow Path", Log Road

ONE OF OUR most memorable vacations was a trip in my grandparents' Ford touring car.

From Spokane, Washington, we drove to Pasco, where we camped in a park with other travelers. Then we took a small dirt road that got smaller and more like a cow path the farther we went. Eventually it was nothing but two tire tracks through the sagebrush.

Just about the time we decided the road wasn't going anywhere, we came out on a little rise above the Columbia River. A cable ferry there took us across to Oregon. We drove down the then-new Columbia Gorge Highway, visited Portland and Astoria, then crossed back to Washington and started for Long Beach.

To get there, we had to cross an elevated log road built over a swamp. The one-track road had a turnout about every half mile so cars going in the opposite direction could pass. If you met a car between turnouts, the driver closest to a turnout was expected to back up.

On this particular day, one driver's back wheels had slid off the track. We had to wait until more cars arrived so there were enough people to lift the car back onto the track. It's a good thing cars were lighter then!

After stops in Tacoma and Seattle, we started back for Spokane. We were driving along merrily when a live cigar ash fell onto Dad's leg. He yelled and grabbed his leg, and the car lurched to the right. Grandpa grabbed the steering wheel just in time to keep us from inspecting the bottom of the canyon about 300 feet down!

As the hills got steeper, the overloaded Ford began to complain. It would run a little, then sputter and almost die. We could've made better time walking!

When we finally got to the top of a mountain pass, the Ford kicked up her heels and chugged happily home.

—*Edward Snell, Edmonds, Washington*

Surprise Visit Backfired—Twice!

By Robert Matsen, Forest Grove, Oregon

IN MARCH 1922, Dad came up with a great idea. "Let's go out to South Dakota and visit my brother Haakon," he said one night after dinner. "We won't let him know we're coming. It'll be a surprise."

We were excited and thrilled. None of us had ever been more than 50 miles from our southern-Wisconsin home. Going "way out West" would be a real adventure!

Motels hadn't been invented, and hotels were too expensive for a farm family of six, so we ordered a tent from Montgomery Ward. One Thursday in August after harvest was finished, we packed our 1920 Nash with bedding, cooking equipment, dishes, clothes and food for a 2- to 3-week trip.

No Gas Gauge

The Nash was a roomy seven-passenger touring car, but it didn't have a gas gauge, so we had to measure how much it needed by taking the cap off and checking with a stick. There were no filling stations then, at least not along our route. When we needed gas, we'd stop at a garage. A man would fill a 5-gallon can from a drum and then pour the gas into our tank.

There were no sanitary facilities, either, but that wasn't a problem. We stopped at country schools, which were spaced at convenient intervals and had outdoor privies fully equipped with Sears catalogs.

We crossed the Mississippi River on a small ferry and drove into Iowa, camping for the night at a park in Mason City. The next morning, leaden skies rained on us, and we spent the first 3 or 4 hours battling mud. Once the rain stopped and the roads dried, we were able to make good time. The old Nash even got up to 35 mph!

That night we reached Sioux Falls, South Dakota and camped in another park. The next morning, we were all excited. We didn't have far to go now. Soon we'd spring our big surprise on Uncle Haakon. But first, we had to cross the Missouri River, on a ferry that did little to inspire our confidence.

Even worse, we were told the barrel of muddy river water on board was *drinking* water. We were told not to worry, as the silt and sediment were "beneficial". Local folks were right when they said the Missouri was "too thick to drink and too thin to plow"!

No Guardrails

Back on land, we drove south toward Uncle Haakon's through the Missouri Breaks. The roads were steep, narrow and winding, with not a guardrail in sight.

We finally pulled up in front of Uncle Haakon's farm machinery shop. What a surprise this would be for him!

Pa went inside, but didn't see his brother. He asked the man behind the counter where he could find him. "Oh, he and his family left Thursday morning," the man said. "They went to visit his brothers and their families in Wisconsin and didn't let them know …wanted it to be a surprise."

Well, Pa certainly *was* surprised, as was Uncle Haakon, who was back in Wisconsin looking for us! ⮞

Family Headed West On Route 66

By Robert Clabots
Lake Havasu City, Arizona

IN 1928, Dad got the itch to move to California. To an 8-year-old boy, going "out West" to the land of cowboys and Indians sounded terrific!

When we left Green Bay, Wisconsin, our brand-new Dodge sedan was loaded down. We packed our gear into a rack on the back and another on the left running board. We hung a canvas water bag from the front bumper and piled the backseat to the ceiling—except for a space for me to sit and hold my little Boston bulldog on my lap. We rode like that all the way to Los Angeles.

After going through Chicago, we rolled onto Route 66. Dad wanted us to

"We drove on plank roads held together by cable..."

see as much of the country as possible, so we made several side trips off that main road.

In the good old days, the nearest thing to a motel was usually a row of one-room cabins. Mother always went in first to check the room. If it passed her inspection, we stayed; if not, we went on to the next town.

LEAN ON ME. Helping his dad hold up the tourist cabin above left, Robert Clabots enjoyed the trip on Route 66, even through the tunnels.

There were few blacktop roads. The slick mud in Missouri made it a job for Dad to keep the car on the road. We often slid off into ditches. The sticky clay built up under the fenders and we'd have to stop and dig it out with our hands. When it rained, Dad would try to find a covered bridge where we could wait it out.

In many areas, the roads ran parallel to railroad tracks. You could drive along for miles on one side, then the road would abruptly cross to the other side for no apparent reason.

Riding the Rails?

Dad was so interested in the scenery that he missed one crossover, turned a bit late and we wound up stuck on the tracks. Hitting those rail ties at cruising speed shook the whole car—and everything in it. We managed to get the car off the tracks just before a train rushed by!

In Arizona and New Mexico, we drove on plank roads held together with cable. Sand sometimes covered the road so thoroughly that Dad had to guess where to drive. Anyone who drove off the road was stuck in the sand until another motorist came along to tow him out.

We met a lot of interesting, good-hearted folks from all over the country. Everyone back then seemed ready to help one another. At gas stations, we could always count on a friendly visit with whoever was there.

During those stops, we not only replenished our gas, oil and water, but found out about the local roads, the weather forecast and how far it was to the next station or cabin. Gasoline came

in three grades then, "low", "regular" and "high". It cost 13¢ to 17¢ per gallon.

Sight-seeing stops took us to the Painted Desert, Petrified Forest, Zion Canyon, Grand Canyon and Carlsbad Caverns, where we had to walk 7 miles to get in and out. (These days, visitors there use an elevator.)

It took several weeks, but we finally reached Los Angeles. I've driven across the country many times since, but that first trip back in 1928 will always hold my most cherished memories.

Couple Honeymooned to Florida Home

By Percelle Paddock
Lexington, North Carolina

AFTER my parents married in Toronto in 1923, they decided to take their honeymoon trip "south of the border".

They were heady with excitement as Dad's first car, a rickety but serviceable 1923 Overland coupe, chugged across the Canadian border and headed south through New York.

Dad didn't tell Mom until they were under way that he planned to keep on going…until they ran out of road, land or maybe both!

The two-lane roads were poor back then, so the going was slow. Dad bought gas at tiny one- or two-pump roadside stations, some of which had a lunch stand attached. At one such stop in Virginia, Dad had to shoo chickens out of the station's outhouse—but returned with two fresh eggs he'd found nestled in the building's floorboards!

The proprietor of the lunch counter fried them up with some country ham and sent Mom and Dad on their way with full stomachs.

Endured Noisy Night

There were no motels, so they sometimes stayed in tiny roadside cabins that held only a double bed and a small nightstand with a wobbly lamp. If they happened to be passing through a town, they could find accommodations at a hotel—usually a barn-like two-story structure with a tin roof.

SLOW GOING. Perc Leidy navigates his 1923 Overland coupe through a muddy stretch of road during his honeymoon trip. He and his bride, Ada, drove from Toronto to Jacksonville, Florida. Before the trip, Perc rebuilt the car in his parents' backyard, the couple's daughter, Percelle Paddock, recalls.

At one such hotel in North Carolina, Mom was awakened by the most awful racket she'd ever heard. Her terrified cries woke Dad, who jumped up and ran to the window, thinking there might be an earthquake. Anxiously surveying nearby buildings, he looked up —and collapsed in laughter.

Unable to speak, Dad pointed at the roof, and mother took a nervous peek. For a young bride from the city, it was an unbelievable sight. A herd of frisky goats had clambered up some low outbuildings and were kicking up their heels on the hotel's tin roof!

Travel became more difficult in Georgia, where the roads were often

LIGHT HEADED. After moving to Jacksonville, Florida in 1923, newlywed Ada Leidy adopted the flapper look, including the short hairdo. "Mom said it was the first time in her life her head had ever felt so light," recalls Percelle Paddock. Ada and husband Perc honeymooned in Jacksonville, where Perc found work and they lived for the rest of the decade.

sandy ruts that would accommodate only one vehicle. In swampy areas north of Florida, Mom and Dad were frightened more than once to actually see the road end, with nothing in front of them but murky water. After a time, a flat raft would appear, poled by a man who asked a small fee to ferry their car across the water.

By now, Mom and Dad were wondering what they'd gotten into. But when they saw their first palm trees in Florida, they realized what an exciting opportunity lay ahead. They settled in Jacksonville, and lived there for the rest of the decade. *(See pages 136-137 for this couple's continuing adventures.)*

Camp Fire Girls Headed for the Hills

By Hollis Smith, Fort Myers, Florida

CAMPING CUTIES. With her fellow Camp Fire Girls, Hollis Smith (far right) enjoyed the Black Hills of South Dakota in 1921. The trip included a ride in a caboose!

AS CAMP FIRE GIRLS, my friends and I honed our camping skills at my parents' cabin on an island in the Missouri River near Chamberlain, South Dakota.

Those weekend outings were fun, but as the summer of 1921 approached, we wanted to expand our horizons. We decided to go camping in the Black Hills.

Our entourage consisted of a trio of Model T Fords, adult chaperones and drivers and 10 teenage girls. How we ever fit into three small cars with all our luggage and camping gear, I can't imagine, but we did!

We attracted a lot of attention wherever we went and became the subject of several newspaper stories. The Camp Fire Girls in Rapid City even had a party waiting for us when we arrived. Bad weather kept us off the roads the next morning, so we rode in the caboose of a freight train to the towns of Deadwood and Lead. The caboose jerked and swayed constantly, but we loved it!

After that excursion, we retrieved our cars and resumed our journey. We camped in beautiful Spearfish Canyon, where the Black Hills Passion Play is now performed on summer evenings.

We visited the graves of Wild Bill Hickok and Calamity Jane, toured a gold mine, saw Bear Butte and Hangman's Hill and admired the fantastic formations of the Badlands. After a week, we returned home to share our experiences with our families, and relive them in our memories for years to come. ✦

HAPPY CAMPERS. Outdoor clothing in 1920 was different than today's styles, as the Camp Fire Girls above show. But when it came time to eat watermelon, girls will be girls, and Dorothy Alexander (standing below) appears to be crowning a champion watermelon-eater and seed-spitter.

Pioneering Mom Led Camp Fire Girls

By Dorothy Smith, Hanover, Indiana

THE EARLY '20s were heady years for young women. They had won the vote and had new worlds to conquer. So why not go camping, too?

In many ways, my mother, Dorothy Alexander, was a pioneer, blazing trails for young women in her hometown of Frankfort, Indiana. In 1921, she became a local leader for the Camp Fire Girls, which at that time was a fairly new organization.

That summer she took her group, including her two high school-aged sisters, Fern and Nell, on a week's camp-out. They were all lively pretty young ladies, and the whole group was ready for some Camp Fire adventures.

They made Indian outfits, earned beads to adorn them and studied the camping arts. Each of them adopted an Indian name. The group of 12 young women put up tents, hiked, swam, learned Indian lore, cooked in the wilderness, feasted on watermelon and spit out the seeds as far as possible.

Some in Frankfort were scandalized, but Mother was blazing new trails for young women. My straitlaced grandmother apparently gave her approval, but drew the line at "bathing beauties".

Mother had recorded the trip with her Brownie camera, and when Grandmother saw Mom's pictures, she took a pencil and scratched out the bare knees of the girls in bathing suits!

The following summer, after her sisters graduated, Mother became the leader of an even bigger Camp Fire Girls group. In addition to camping and other activities, she taught them to embroider quilt blocks. Their original designs depicted cartoon characters Maggie and Jiggs, Kewpie dolls and Camp Fire symbols. Two of those quilts remain cherished possessions in our family.

Mother was a proper lady of the times—she sewed a fine seam and hand-painted delicate designs on china. But she also traveled coast to coast on the Pennsylvania Railroad, seeing Boston, New York, Washington, Yellowstone, the Grand Canyon and California before she met my father and settled down. She was truly a pioneering woman! ⚞

KNEES NOTHING TO KNOCK AT. Times change, and when these Camp Fire Girls (left) exposed their knees in '23, Grandma didn't scribble over the photo, as she'd done in the past! Dorothy (above right, wearing the official headband) had a new group at Tawanka Camp that year.

WHETHER THE WEATHER was cold or warm, the Camp Fire Girls went hiking, as they did on this winter day in 1921 near Antioch, in Clinton County, Indiana.

OUT OF UNIFORM. Dorothy (above center) poses with her sisters, Nell (left) and Fern. Below left, Dorothy displays the rubber boots she wore hiking to Dayton, Indiana in 1920, when she was 20. In full garb, Nell (below right) makes the Indian sign for "fire".

IN COSTUME. The Alexander sisters, Fern, Dorothy and Nell (left to right), line up in their official Camp Fire Girl uniforms. It was 1921, and by then, Dorothy was the local "Camp Fire Guardian" leader. She was a true pioneer, says her daughter, Dorothy Smith.

We Took a Model T to the Mountains

THEN AND NOW. Winifred Miller took a trip down memory lane in the same Model T she and her husband drove to the Canadian Rockies on their honeymoon in '27! The top photo was taken on Winifred's 90th birthday in 1991.

By Winifred Miller
Saskatoon, Saskatchewan

AFTER ED AND I married in 1927, we decided to take a honeymoon trip from Saskatoon to the Rocky Mountains in Banff, Alberta.

I was a schoolteacher and Ed was a farmer, and we'd earned enough so Ed could purchase a new Model T Ford. After loading the car with a tent, gasoline camp stove and two camp cots, we were on our way.

The main highways weren't numbered then; instead, they were designated by colors painted intermittently on telephone poles. Our two-lane gravel route to Alberta was "green".

We had no commitments or deadlines, so we took our time. The little Ford averaged about 20 or 30 mph. Those we encountered were amazed we'd tackle a trip to the mountains in a Model T. Most people who tried this trip did so in bigger more modern cars.

There were no campgrounds along the way, so when we found a pleasant-looking spot, we'd stop and pitch our tent. One morning we found we'd camped in a wild strawberry patch.

For most of the trip, we drove along the flat treeless prairie. The scenery began to change when we descended into the rocky Drumheller Valley. Dinosaurs had once roamed the valley, which we found exciting and interesting. Ed was just as interested in the coal mines, because he'd once worked in such mines in Ohio before coming to Canada.

When we reached Calgary, we pitched our tent in a campground. During the

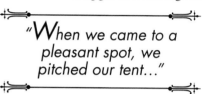

"When we came to a pleasant spot, we pitched our tent..."

night, a terrific thunderstorm struck, and the rain came down in torrents, rushing through our floorless tent. We were thankful we had cots to sleep on!

Once we reached Banff, we had no itinerary. We'd just pick a road and see where it took us. We admired waterfalls, glaciers and the blue-green waters of Lake Louise. We bathed in hot sulfur springs, and marveled at hundreds of snowballs 5 to 6 feet in diameter that were formed by snowslides.

We went to the Banff Springs Hotel and tried to imagine what it would be like to afford to stay in such luxury. At a price of $20 per night, it was out of the question.

We continued camping, and the animals we saw were very tame. The bears were continually looking for handouts, and once we made the mistake of stopping the car to feed a bear.

The bear decided he wanted more and tried to climb into the car alongside me! I stood up on the seat to get away from him while Ed got the car started and drove off. We kept our distance from bears after that.

Our trip took a little over a month, all told. On the way back to Saskatoon, our little Model T never failed us. In rainy weather, bigger cars couldn't navigate the muddy roads. But our Model T with its narrow tires plugged right along.

When we got home, our friends and families welcomed us as though we were returning from an expedition! ⬧

In-Laws Went Along on 1,800-Mile Honeymoon

By Isabel Simmons
Yakima, Washington

THE YEAR was 1927, and we took an unforgettable trip in a 1921 Nash touring car, wide open to sun, wind, rain and dust.

My husband of 3 weeks and I were taking his parents and brother from Everett, Washington to their homestead in Dobie Springs, Oklahoma. He'd promised them this trip long before we married, so we combined it with our honeymoon.

After we drove through Portland, Oregon, the roads were mostly dirt or gravel, with plenty of potholes. Pavement was scarce. After a heavy rain, you picked your rut and stayed in it—or bogged down in the mud and waited for a farmer with a team of husky horses to pull you out.

At night, we stopped in "auto courts" that cost $1 to $2 for a cabin with a lumpy double bed, a wood stove and maybe some plumbing. The cabins ranged from fairly clean to just plain dirty, but they were few and far apart. We took what we could get and made the best of it.

Enjoyed Fellow Travelers

Some auto courts had community kitchens. The women visited while cooking, and the men swapped tales, bragging of driving over 200 miles that day or moaning about bad roads and flat tires. It was fun, and there was a feeling of camaraderie. Traveling any distance by car was uncommon, and we had a shared sense of adventure.

The trip was fairly uneventful until we got to Wyoming, where we battled car trouble, cold rain, flat tires and slick muddy roads. I think we slid most of the way across that state!

At our first stop in Wyoming, in the middle of a thunderstorm, all the cabins

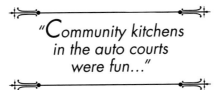

> *"Community kitchens in the auto courts were fun..."*

were full. The owner kindly let us stay in an old building that normally housed sheep. It smelled like it, too!

The next night, in Laramie, only one cabin was available. My in-laws took that, and another kindhearted owner let my husband and me sleep in the laundry.

The third night, in Cheyenne, every-

FIVE'S A CROWD. When Isabel and B.B. Simmons (couple at left) went on their honeymoon in 1927, her in-laws went along! Read Isabel's story to find out why. The quintet is standing in front of the honeymoon vehicle, a 1921 Nash touring car.

thing was full again. We finally rented two dirty rooms in a little hotel—what we used to call a "flophouse".

Through all of this, my in-laws never complained. After all, 23 years earlier, they had driven from Kansas to Oklahoma in a covered wagon, and it took 2 weeks to go 400 miles. We were traveling 1,800 miles in 2 weeks, and they thought it was wonderful!

The next day, we stopped at the home of relatives in Colorado Springs. We'd been unable to bathe in the 3 days it took to cross Wyoming, so we were thrilled to see our hosts' lovely modern bathroom. I made a beeline for it after my husband told me, "You know, your neck is *awfully* dirty." I think that's when the honeymoon ended! ⚓

VERY MOBILE HOME. His family's "house car" might have been the first back in 1925, says H.K. "Lefty" Thurston of Grants Pass, Oregon. These photos, showing Lefty as a 2-year-old tyke, were snapped on a trip from Lockport, New York to Florida. Lefty adds that his mother was mad at his dad for taking some photos in a cottonfield, "where snakes like to hang out"!

Mom, Grandma Took Tot On Trek to California

MOM WAS quite independent, so when Grandmother decided she wanted to visit her own mother and sisters, the three of us set out from Tacoma, Washington for San Francisco, California. Our Model T trip took 3 days.

In 1926, Highway 99 was a far cry from the smooth road it is today, so you can imagine the attention drawn by two ladies traveling with a 4-year-old girl.

The only mishap during the entire trip was a single flat tire—and, believe it or not, we were driving into a service station when it occurred!

The memories of our visit are like a storybook adventure—ferry rides between Oakland and San Francisco…the artists' colony in Sausalito…citrus and fig trees in my relatives' yards…my great-aunt's hillside home near Golden Gate Park…a corner grocery store with an incredible array of penny candy. What more could a 4-year-old want?

After a 6-week stay, we packed everything into our trusty little Ford and chugged back up the highway to Tacoma, with lots of tales to tell Dad and Grandfather.   —Betty Longstreth
Tacoma, Washington

TRUSTY MODEL T. Betty Longstreth, pictured with her father, Charles Foreman, in 1922, has fond memories of the family's Model T. In 1926, she accompanied her mother and grandmother in it for a memorable trip to California.

Newlyweds and 'Lizzie' Climbed Continental Divide

By Violet Dixon, Tullahoma, Tennessee

MY HONEYMOON was a 2-week trip from Missouri to California.

Guy and I were married in 1923, after he and his brother were offered jobs in the Long Beach oil fields. Immediately after the wedding, we set out in a modified Model T coupe. I hadn't seen the car until we were ready to leave, and I was surprised, to say the least!

The rumble seat had been replaced with an open pickup-like bed, and the whole car was packed with equipment and baggage. My brother-in-law and his wife would ride in front.

Guy and I would sit on a padded board stretched across the truck bed. If that got tiring, we could recline on the packed bedding. There was a canvas top for the bed, but because of wind drag, we could use it only when the car was stopped.

We took a small two-burner oil stove for cooking and bought groceries along the way. We usually camped in towns, but had to spend one night on the prairie, where coyotes serenaded us. As a 20-year-old newlywed, I thought that was romantic!

Most of the roads were graded gravel or, in the desert, hard-packed sand trails. There was considerable traffic, and other motorists would come to the aid of those in trouble.

When "Lizzie" couldn't make it over the Rockies, a man with a truck pulled her across while we hiked alongside. To this day, I'm proud to say I walked over the Great Divide!

Liz also broke an axle, so the men hitched a ride to the next town to buy parts while we girls steadied her on jacks and blocks. Later, she blew a gasket and had her innards spread out on canvas in the desert while a new one was installed. Tires went flat so often that Guy spent most of his "riding time" cold-patching tubes so we'd be ready for the next blowout!

In New Mexico, we tried a "shortcut" —20 miles of narrow winding track on the side of a steep canyon wall. We could not see around the sharp bends, and there was no turning back. Twice we had to pull over to the edge so another car could pass. It was one of the few times I've been really scared.

But there was a pleasant surprise at the end of the canyon. A lone woman running a gas station there had a well of the sweetest water I've ever tasted.

We arrived in California dirty but happy, with memories to last the rest of our lives. ➻

STOCK T. Virginia Fulton of Columbus, Ohio sits behind the wheel of her 1927 Model T. It was not modified, as the one Violet Dixon describes in the story above.

HAPPY BIRTHDAY! Elmer Littrell of Wheeling, Missouri stood by his pride and joy, a 1924 Chevrolet touring car, on his 41st birthday, September 6, 1926. His daughter, Ruth Davis of Higginsville, Missouri, still recalls the horsehair robe they used in winter.

Roads Resembled 'Washboards in Swamp Water'

By Jean Quincy, Miami, Florida

WHEN SCHOOL let out for the summer in 1926, my mother, sister and I excitedly began preparing to join my stepfather, who was building houses in Atlanta, Georgia.

We had a "Redbird", a big beautiful open touring car. To ride in style, we each had khaki-colored kicker touring outfits to go with our car.

To prepare for our trip, we practiced snapping the isinglass side curtains in

"Mother gave up on the Redbird and traded for a Plymouth..."

place whenever a rainstorm blew in. Sounds simple, but it was hard work, unfolding the pieces and figuring out where they all went. We usually were soaked and exasperated by the time we finished.

Mother finally gave up on the elegant look and traded in the Redbird, side curtains and all, for a simple blue Plymouth sedan.

I still remember the beautiful drive along the narrow winding road that followed Florida's eastern coast, often with views of bays or the ocean. I thought Sebastian Inlet, with its palms, live oaks and Spanish moss, must be one of the world's prettiest spots.

But when we neared the Georgia state line, the roads were like washboards in swamp water! Whole trees were laid

TRAVELING FAMILY. There were many adventures traveling by car in Florida and Georgia in the '20s, recalls Jean Quincy (above left with her sister, Eileen). Jean's mother (right) was the driver of a Redbird and a Plymouth.

side by side across the roadbeds. For what seemed like miles, we went very slowly, *whump-whump-whump*, over those tree trunks.

One evening after dark, we were stopped on one of those washboard roads by several armed men with flashlights. We were terrified until they identified themselves as a sheriff's posse looking for moonshiners.

"Bird" Landed in Car

The men turned their flashlights on the backseat, where my sister and I had been sleeping with two large dolls. One astonished man said to my mother, "You're a very brave woman, ma'am, to travel these roads at night with four little children!" Mother didn't correct him. Sharp-eyed posse, indeed!

Another night, a soft brown creature flew into the car and landed on top of my foot. "Oh, Mama, you've hit a bird," I cried. I cupped the little thing in my hands, hoping it would revive, but it remained motionless. Minutes later, when we shone a flashlight on it, I found I'd been cuddling a bat! Mother hit the brakes fast, and the bat was unceremoniously tossed from the car.

At the end of the summer, with school approaching, we prepared to return to Miami. The great hurricane of September '26 beat us to it. We traveled the length of Florida after the storm, and I'll never forget the sight of parts of houses and boats hanging in trees. ➤

J.C. Allen and Son

ROUGHING IT. Things weren't *too* rough for these 1926 campers. They had a spacious tent and a reliable car to get them there and back. Back then, there were a lot more places to camp...even in city parks, as the memory below describes.

Twins Celebrated Birthday On Iowa-to-Virginia Trek

DAD MOVED US from Sheldon, Iowa to his Virginia hometown in 1924, a journey that took 8 long days over dirt and gravel roads.

We spent the nights in city parks, where you were allowed to pitch tents and cook with camp stoves. A luggage rack on the running board of our Patterson touring car was converted to a one-person bed, and the other four children slept on the car seats. Our parents slept in a tent, which was set up so it draped over the car.

Most memorable of all, my twin sister and I celebrated our 8th birthday on the road. Dad bought us all nickel ice cream cones—that was a real treat!
—*Marie Arnsmeier, Monroe, Wisconsin*

Travelers Lost Bearings After Spin on Dry Lake

OUR FAMILY decided to leave southern California and move back to Nevada in the early 1920s. We packed up our old Overland and began the slow trek. The miles of sand and sagebrush seemed endless.

Then we noticed that our narrow dirt road was heading straight for a huge dry lake bed. Dad followed the road out onto the lake's perfectly smooth surface. We yelled in delight as he turned the car this way and that. A smooth ride in those days was a real luxury!

Before long, we were in the middle of that dry lake—with no idea which direction to take to get back out! In all the excitement, no one had kept track of which direction we were headed.

So we backtracked to where we thought we'd entered the lake, and finally found that road. Then Dad drove close to the lake bed's right-hand side, watching carefully for another road that would lead somewhere other than the lake.

After about 30 minutes, he spotted a dusty road off to the right that disappeared into the low hills. We took it and hoped for the best. Some 50 miles later, we found we'd made the right choice, and returned to civilization!
—*Robert Jones, Yakima, Washington*

Giant Pothole Sent Her Right Through the Roof!

ONE DAY in 1923, Daddy was driving us in his cloth-topped Oakland sedan to visit friends in Kechi, Kansas. I was alone in the backseat.

The road was very rough. After we bounced over one particularly bad hole, Daddy called back to me, "Lucille, are you all right?"

I answered, but he couldn't hear me. We had bounced so hard that my head hit the car's cloth top and went right through it! My head was actually *outside* the car, with the rest of me dangling inside!

Though I was fine, poor Daddy was convinced my neck was broken. He cried all the way to Kechi. A doctor there said I was okay, although I was scared to get into the car for the trip home. I rode back to Wichita in the *front* seat!
—*Lucille Fulton*
El Paso, Texas

Camping Family Slept in—And on—Their Trusty Car

OUR FAMILY camped in Yellowstone National Park in 1925, during a 3-week trip from California to New Jersey.

My parents slept on a mattress atop our 1919 Franklin, and we four children slept on another mattress covering our supplies inside the car. The supplies we couldn't fit inside the car were stored in cupboard-like boxes Dad had built on the car's sides and back.

My mother cooked with lumpy, strong-tasting powdered milk, using a gasoline stove that was difficult to start. My father had to pump it up first, and the wind would blow out the flame again and again.

When we returned to California in 1927, there were five children instead of four. We had many blowouts and car trouble along the way, but the old Franklin made it.

Later, when our family grew to seven kids, Dad built another "travel car" on the body of a '24 Essex pickup truck. People couldn't believe their eyes when they saw nine people climb out of it!
—*Dorothy Galley*
Banning, California

TOURING THE PARKS. On a 3-week trip from California to New Jersey, Dorothy Galley and her family went through the great national parks, like Yellowstone (above and top) and Yosemite (center). That's their 1919 Franklin parked at scenic Tioga Pass in Yosemite, says Dorothy. On the roof of the car is a mattress. Not only was that a handy place to carry the mattress, but her mother and father slept up there, while the kids snoozed inside! The photo above shows a typical campsite, recalls Dorothy. And, yes, that was the kind of clothing everyone wore while camping. Can't you just smell that bacon frying?

Family Followed Muddy Route to Niagara Falls

By Mildred Weidner, Emmaus, Pennsylvania

THERE WAS A TIME when there were no route numbers at crossroads, just handmade wooden signs. Colored bands about 6 inches wide circled telephone poles to designate specific routes.

The roads were mostly dirt then, so if it rained, they turned into slick sticky mud. I saw plenty of that when my father took us to Niagara Falls in 1926.

If you took a week off work back then, you didn't get paid, so Father was sacrificing a lot to take the family on such a trip. I was 8 at the time, my brother was 14 and my sister 12. We were excited about the trip as were our parents and paternal grandmother.

We started our adventure on a rainy July day. Little did we know that it would rain every day of our trip!

Long Wait for Breakfast

Niagara Falls was about 300 miles from our home in Schnecksville, Pennsylvania, so Grandmother's Buick sedan was packed. Since the car had no trunk, our suitcases were loaded into the luggage rack on the running board. We also packed bedding, a tent, two canvas cots, food, cans of Sterno and a small stove.

There were no fast-food restaurants, of course, and dining out was too expensive. We cooked on our two-burner stove, but it wasn't easy. It took a lot of patience to nurse the

THEY'RE OFF! **With her parents and siblings, Mildred Weidner (center) was ready for an adventure to Niagara Falls in 1926. Even Grandma came along... and it was her Buick they drove.**

faint flame to fry an egg or boil some coffee (no instant then). With six to feed, meals seemed to take forever.

We stopped at campgrounds with outside privies and washhouses, paying $1 to set up our tent. Grandmother had the best accommodations—the Buick's backseat. My brother slept in the front seat, and my sister on the car floor. My parents slept on the cots, which were pushed together so I could sleep on the rails in between.

Every morning, we woke to what seemed like a lake under our tent. While Mother made breakfast, Father and my brother packed the wet tent and all of our gear back into the car. Packing took about an hour every morning, and unpacking took another hour every night.

When we reached Niagara Falls after 3 days on the road, we found a campsite that cost only 50¢ a night and had a concrete-floor washhouse with hot showers and flush toilets. It was heavenly!

The campground was subsidized by a cereal manufacturer. Every day, we received a box of shredded wheat and a pass to visit the cereal plant. After the tour, we were taken to a dining room that had white linen tablecloths and served shredded wheat biscuits with real cream and butter.

We visited the mighty falls on both the American and Canadian sides, and

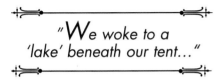

> *"We woke to a 'lake' beneath our tent..."*

took in many of the free attractions. Because of the persistent rain, we did some of our sight-seeing from the car.

The days passed quickly, and soon we were on our way home, following the colored bands and mud roads. We arrived safe, tired and happy, with mountains of soggy laundry from our 10-day trip.

When school resumed that fall, the teacher asked what we had done during vacation. When I said, "We went to Niagara Falls and Canada", I was the school hero. No one I knew had ever traveled so far, and everyone thought I had "seen the world"!

Move from Iowa to Florida Took 2 Weeks

By Ned Dugger, Cedar Hill, Texas

IN 1922, my father decided we should move from Council Bluffs, Iowa to Lakeland, Florida. He sold our home and everything we couldn't pack into our Model T. A wide plank along the outside of one running board created a long, narrow storage space.

Other items were hung in and around the car, leaving just enough room for my parents, brother, sister and me.

Dad had bought a "Blue Book" as a route guide, with instructions like this: "Leave town on Main Street, proceed east to Country School No. 2, turn south for 10 miles to the Lone Oak Tree, then go east again." It was easy to get lost, and we did several times.

The roads left much to be desired. Only a few miles were paved with brick or macadam. Some were gravel, but most were dirt.

Scary Campsite

In southern Iowa, a herd of cattle had churned a muddy dirt road into a quagmire. The old Ford struggled along so slowly that we didn't reach the town where we'd planned to spend the night. We camped in a park next to a cemetery —a scary place for an 8-year-old boy!

In a heavily wooded area of Kentucky, we traveled a road that was little more than a trail. At one point, we found our way blocked by a crude gate. A man came out of a nearby hut and requested a 50¢ toll "for the pike". The trail continued on to a shallow creek. We had to drive through it for half a mile to find the road on the other side.

Dad Loved Dinner

One night we stayed in a tourist home in Tennessee where white-gloved waiters served dinner in a large dining room. I wasn't bold enough to try the squirrel on the menu, but Dad was and declared it delicious.

In another small town, Dad tried to cash some travelers' checks. The merchants, including the banker, were unfamiliar with these and refused to cash them. Luckily, Dad had enough cash to get us out of town.

As we drove the red clay roads in hilly northern Alabama, it began to rain. The car soon was mired in muck. My brother drove while everyone else climbed out to push the car up the hill. We negotiated several hills that way. By the end of the day, the car was a mess!

After 14 days, we finally reached Lakeland. I've driven to Florida many times since, but none of those trips proved nearly as exciting as the first.

THEY'RE STUCK! "After skipping school in '28 for the 'Senior Sneak', Dad and his friends got stuck in the mud on what passed for roads near Cascade, Idaho," says Afton Fanger of The Dalles, Oregon. Canoeing, anyone?

GREAT CAMPERS...That's what her sister, Margaret, called the Chandler family, shown here on a Lake Michigan beach, says Emma Swadling of Naples, Florida. Other favorite spots were Grand Marais on Lake Superior, where the boats brought in fresh fish, and Interlochen, where there were music camps.

Looking Back, Short Trip Was Most Memorable

THE MOST MEMORABLE trip I ever took was in 1924...even though I never quite made it out of our driveway!

My parents were proud of their shiny new Ford touring car. I remember it had bows in the top so the roof could be folded down completely. I was only 14 that year, but had been taught to drive so I could help with chores and run errands during harvest and hay season.

Our garage was a shed attached to our barn. Directly in back of the shed was a big old tree and on one side was a windmill.

One morning when the men were extra busy, my father said he wanted me to take my older sister to a neighboring town for a Civil Service Exam. I told Papa I'd gladly do that if he would back the car out for me (driving in reverse made me very nervous).

"No," he said, "you can do

it," and then he went about his work. So I got in the Ford with its top laid down, started the engine and began backing out...slowly and carefully.

Then, for some unexplainable reason, I gave it the gas instead of braking. I smacked into that old tree and broke every bow in the Ford's top! That shook me up so badly I immediately drove forward, hit the windmill and smashed the radiator!

ROCKY ROOMS. Before motels, many travelers stayed at cabins like these, notes Hazel Balk of Chagrin Falls, Ohio. You could park just outside the door, and your neighbors, while close, weren't right on the other side of the wall.

When the dust settled, I just sat there with my head down, crying my eyes out. Soon, Papa walked up and just stood there, staring at the car. His pride and joy had both ends caved in.

After a few moments, he walked over, patted me on the head and said quietly, "I guess you were right. You really *can't* back up."

That's all he ever said! I would have felt better if he'd yelled at me, but Papa was never one to yell.

—Hildred Feather
Derby, Kansas

Broken Axle Was No Problem to Tackle

IN THE SUMMER of 1927, after my brother and I graduated from high school in Loveland, Colorado, Dad and Mother made arrangements with our Uncle Fred and Aunt Lena to meet us in Wyoming.

Both families would then travel together to visit other relatives in Washington State. Uncle Fred drove a Model T, and Dad a Star. We drove north to Billings, Montana, then turned west, following the Yellowstone River. Everything was going well until one day when we were a long way from any town, or even a farmhouse.

Uncle Fred was following us in his Model T, when he suddenly stopped. We went back and found he'd broken a rear axle! What would we do?

Just as Dad was getting ready to drive to the nearest town to see if he could purchase the part, a farmer drove up in his pickup truck.

When told of our problem, he said, "I've been carrying around a new axle in my truck. If you can put it on, you can have it."

Boy did that sound good! Searching along the riverbank, we found three sturdy trees that had been cut down. These made a good tripod. Dad always carried a block and tackle in his car for just such an emergency.

It was fastened onto the tripod and we hoisted the rear end of that Model T up so we could remove the old axle and put on the new one. Within a short time, we were on our way again.

Try that with one of today's cars!
—*Harvey Marks, Lakewood, Colorado*

Reno to Sacramento Was a Tough Trip

EVERY TIME I drive my car over the beautiful highway from Reno, Nevada to Sacramento, California, I can't help remembering how different it was back in 1928.

Although it was only a distance of 137 miles, the road was steep and narrow with lots of dangerous curves. The journey could be quite an ordeal, and I'll never forget my first trip on that road.

I was 15 at the time, traveling with my 18-year-old sister, my mother and our dog. We packed our essentials and set out on a hair-raising adventure that remains in my memory to this day.

Our old car would bravely chug up a steep grade, slow down to a crawl and finally stop...radiator boiling. Mom would stay in the driver's seat while my sister and I jumped out and quickly found some rocks to put behind the back wheels so the car wouldn't roll backward.

Occasionally, there were wider places in the road where we could stop and let the engine cool down. Sometimes, there might even be a little stream where we could cool ourselves and re-

BIG BEAR BUDDIES. Big Bear Lake in California was still frozen in this photo taken April 7, 1929. "My father, Alvin (holding skis), owned a cabin there for many years," says Mary Kay Evans of Cypress, California. "And I still recall using the toboggan my mother, Louise, is standing behind."

DIG THESE DUDES. Cow-*boy* Richard Brown (left) of North St. Paul, Minnesota says his dad (center) had this shot set up at a Medora, North Dakota dude ranch in '27. That's Mom at right. According to Richard, the only *real* cowboy around was the one who snapped the photo.

fill the radiator. But most of the highway was just one lane in each direction with no place to stop. Trucks would labor up the steep grades at about 5 miles per hour, with a long string of cars behind them.

When a trucker came to one of the wide places in the road, he'd pull out and motion for the cars to go around. Those truck drivers were the real heroes of the road. They could be depended on to help if people had trouble—which was a frequent occurrence. Those old cars weren't very dependable and their skinny tires were always going flat.
—*Marie Lipera, Sparks, Nevada*

Ewing Galloway

Potatoes for Winter Required All-Day Excursion

By John Hirsh, Fort Lauderdale, Florida

THERE COULDN'T have been a more excited 7-year-old as I anticipated my first car trip alone with my father.

After much discussion between my parents, they decided that just Dad and I would drive out to Water Mill on Long Island. He knew somebody on a potato farm there, and our mission was to get two large bags of potatoes to see us through the winter.

At long last, the day dawned bright and clear. Father dressed for the outing in a wool visored cap, his usual bow tie and "plus fours", those baggy knickers made famous by golfer Bobby Jones.

After an early breakfast and a round of good-byes to my mom and sister, we loaded a laundry rope, bag of sandwiches and a thermos of lemonade into our new Studebaker and started off down the hill.

That 1927 sedan was my father's pride and joy. Our last Studebaker had been a convertible touring car, and Dad didn't like it when he had to hook on the isinglass side panels when it rained. Now he only had to roll up the windows.

After stopping for oil and gas and checking the tires and radiator, we headed for Clason Point. This was the Bronx

end of the ferry ride to College Point before the present-day Whitestone and Triborough bridges existed.

We waited for the ferry to dock and unload, then reload. Our car was about the fourth one aboard, stopping just abreast of the engine room. I was torn between staying there to admire the engine and going to the front deck so I could see where we were going. I chose the front deck.

Fun Aboard Ferry

The ferry swung way out into the East River, with me hanging on the front gate across the two lanes of cars, and my father hanging on to *me*. It was a warm day, and we stayed there until the last possible minute, watching the ferry glide gently past the telephone pole-sized pilings and finally nudge into the loading ramp. Then we went back to the Studebaker and all the cars started up again.

We followed the main road through towns, villages and duck farms. There was no such thing as a highway, and our top speed wasn't very fast…but we were in no hurry.

We finally pulled off the road in the town of Water Mill. My father got the lunch bag and thermos from the back-

BOATLOAD OF BOATERS. Before big bridges, these straw-hatted commuters took the ferry, just as John Hirsh did.

seat and handed me my favorite sandwich—egg salad with tomato and lettuce—plus a paper cup of lemonade. Dessert was an orange, and I felt like a king as my father showed me how best to peel this rare treat.

From there it was just a short drive to the potato farm. I got out to stretch my legs and check on all the mysterious farm equipment while my father spoke to his friend and selected two large sacks of potatoes, which they tied on each

> "*Our top speed wasn't very fast—we were in no hurry…*"

front fender and running board with the laundry rope.

Our Indian summer day had begun to cool, so on the drive back, I climbed into the backseat and pulled the heavy blanket off the blanket rail to snuggle in for a nap. What bliss! Only the excitement of getting back on the ferry woke me.

When we got home, my father shouldered those big bags down into the cellar, then told my mother the events of the trip. It's difficult now to believe we could spend all day just getting potatoes, but there was no hurry in that leisurely time. Now I wish that trip had taken longer.

Chapter Four

Cherished Photos

Cherished Photos

A man named George Eastman is the one we have to thank for most of the wonderful pictures on the next 17 pages. He not only was a pioneer in the whole field of photography, but in the '20s, his new, light-weight and relatively cheap cameras turned the country into a nation of amateur photographers.

Suddenly everyone could make "Kodak Memories" of picnics, pets, new cars, family gatherings, trips to the beach, Grampa snoozing on the porch swing with a tiny grandaughter nestled in his arms, or Mom enjoying a happy moment with her children.

Until then, photos were made by professionals in their studios. The poses were stiff and smiles were forced. No one looked like they were having much fun.

I still have the very first picture I snapped. Our family had one of those "Box Brownies" with a cheap lens and a single shutter speed. It was primitive by today's standards, but it took surprisingly sharp photos.

After a lot of begging on my part, Dad loaded the camera with a fresh roll of film and I set out to photograph the scenic marvels of our farm. My first target was a black barn cat that was a special favorite of mine. It walked toward me and I snapped the shutter.

First Photo Wasn't the "Cat's Meow"

Well, live and learn. If you want a sharp picture of nothing but a cat's tail, I've got *just* what you're looking for. The cat's spiky black tail juts straight up from the bottom of the picture, and that's all you see—except for a fence in the background. Apparently, I'd forgotten to adjust for the speed with which the cat was approaching.

I've taken thousands of pictures in the years since then, but for some reason, I just can't part with that one of the cat's tail.

I have priceless pictures of both sets of grandparents and a whole album filled with snapshots Mom and Dad took during their 1920 honeymoon trip. Others show my newlywed parents, laughing as they tried out their new wringer washing machine.

There are pictures of the old homestead...snow scenes, playing croquet on the front lawn, roses in bloom on the fence. Now the house is completely remodeled, the barns are gone and a subdivision thrives where the corn once grew. The trees Dad planted are the only landmarks I recognize. It's nice to have photographs of how things were in my childhood.

I also have photos of Dad sitting on a cellar door, holding his newborn son. Recently, one of my daughters was startled to discover how much her son Andy looks like his great-grandfather. I'd never noticed until she pointed it out.

Yes, I can revisit a childhood I now only dimly remember...little fraction-of-a-second glimpses of my early life and the wonderful people who loved me as much as I loved them. Those photographs are like a time machine, permitting me to scoot back in years whenever I choose.

Memories sometimes blur and fade, but the pictures are there forever.

So turn the page and enjoy several dozen intimate glimpses of life in the Twenties. Our thanks goes out to the many readers who shared these precious records of their early years with all of us.

—*Clancy Strock*

1. Birds of a Feather

1. JUNIOR BIRDMEN. Birdhouse-building competition was held in Helena, Montana, recalls Elmer Rothfus, Sun City, Arizona (far right in middle row).

3. Quiet Time

2. Instant Patches?

2. HOLEY EMBARRASSING. When Grandma saw her boys' long underwear showing through their holey britches on this photo, she tried to color it out, says Karen Nelson of Burket, Indiana. That's Karen's dad, Walter, front and center.

3. CHILDREN'S HOUR. Betty Jane Blanton of Dowagiac, Michigan sent the photo of herself (on the right) and her sister, Marjorie Lee, reading *American* magazine with their mother, Flossie May Archer, in 1925.

4. Crank 'Em up

5. Batter up

4. *ROCKY ROAD.* Anna Belle Wilcoxson was behind the wheel in 1920 when this decked-out bunch took a Sunday drive in the Denver mountains. Her grandson, Paul Wilcoxson of Arvada, Colorado, sent photo.

5. *THE CHAMPS.* The Calvin, North Dakota nine reigned in their region in the early '20s, beating teams from as far away as Canada, says Alice Thomas of Santa Clara, California. Her husband, William, is in the middle of the back row.

6. *MADE IN HEAVEN?* This 1928 make-believe "womanless wedding" was a church fund-raiser held all in good fun, explains Lucille Stamper of Danville, Indiana.

6. Here Come the Brides?

7. Dressing Down

7. **LAST LESSON.** Edward Midgley and twin brother Louis were put in the front row after they "forgot" the last day of school in 1923 was dress-up day. Edward, Orem, Utah, remembers being embarrassed.

8. **HOMEMADE GOWN.** Decked out in a red wool dress she made without a pattern, Goldie Marrs of Rockford, Iowa had her portrait snapped and tinted when she was 18, in 1928.

9. **TAILGATERS.** Backseat driver Charles Gable of Columbia, Pennsylvania peeked out of a Model T with his sister, Mae (left), and their friend Gertrude Siegrist in 1921. The car belonged to Gertrude's dad.

10. **PIG-TAILED PAL.** Doris Tonry of Elyria, Ohio sent the photo of her cousin, Martha, feeding a pet pig. Doris, a city girl, loved to visit Martha at the farm. Both recall swimming in the horse trough!

8. Lovely Lady

9. Peek-a-Boo

10. Don't Hog It!

11. Gym Dandies

11. *TEAM OF TURNERS.* This 1924 gym team was based in Madison, Wisconsin, says Lucille Dobe of West Allis. Lucille (seated, center) was on the team and competed in national meets.

12. *FLYING HIGH.* Deneesa Christenson was a happy newlywed after her June 1925 marriage to Harold. Yvonne Horvath of Milwaukee, Wisconsin shared the photo of her parents.

13. *MUSICAL MOTORMAN.* The violinist in this swinging quintet was not only the motorman on her local streetcar, but later became her husband, says Harriet (Mrs. Emil) Padrta of Solway, Minnesota.

12. Uplifting Experience

13. One Hot Band

14. Say "Boo!"

15. Fashion of the Times

14. QUEEN FOR A DAY. Joe Lanaghan, Clinton, Iowa, says his wife was treated like a queen as far back as her first year in school. Erma was the queen at the 1920 kindergarten Halloween party at Kirkwood School in Clinton.

15. MYSTERY LADY. Sara Pora of Windsòr, Maine doesn't know the name of this intriguing lady, but she well remembers the 1920s, when such elegant clothing was in fashion. Sara especially recalls button shoes and fur neck pieces.

16. PICK IT, MOM! Doris Lynch of Modesto, California remembers the LeClaire Rhythm Roamers, who performed Saturday nights at the Roof Garden, high atop the LeClaire Hotel in Moline, Illinois. Doris' mom played the banjo.

16. Making Music in Moline

17. Do I Hafta Smile?

17. NOW, DON'T MOVE. Pop was quite a camera buff, as this photo attests, reports James Oswald of Chicago, Illinois. James was about 5 then. So who took the photo of Dad taking the photo? One of his brothers, says James.

18. MY BUNCH IS BIGGER! "Mom told us to pick some wildflowers. I picked a lot, but my sister, Mary, only picked a few. She was pouting because I wouldn't share," explains Dorothy Robinson of Bluffton, Ohio.

19. WEDDING FOR A FLAPPER. Virginia Bouckaert's parents were married on June 6, 1923. Virginia, St. Louis, Missouri, says her mother left her flashy beaded dress at home in favor of a more conservative wedding gown.

18. Biggest Bouquet Wins

19. The Flapper Bride

20. Baby Rides in Style

21. Listening in

20. REGAL CARRIAGE. Maxine Ludwig pushed a plush pram while baby-sitting back in 1921. Maxine's daughter, Barb Oskowski of New Castle, Pennsylvania, says she dug through her "prized box" of old photos to send this one.

21. CUTE CONSTITUENT. When "Silent" Cal Coolidge gave his inaugural address, Taye Waldron of Carson City, Nevada listened on a crystal set (above). It happened in 1925, when her family was living in Stockton, California.

22. NEIGHBORHOOD BUNCH. "This was our 'gang' in the '20s," informs Phyllis Sukalec of Sun City Center, Florida. Phyllis (fourth from left) says this happy group from Joliet, Illinois had a lot of fun and didn't need store-bought toys.

22. The Gang's All Here

23. Serene Scene

24. Touchdown Hero

23. *"THE DUCHESS"* was what Elizabeth Merkel was called, relates granddaughter Rosemary Greinke of Milwaukee, Wisconsin. She earned that nickname because of her stately walk and posture. In this photo, she's reading a letter from her husband, who was in the Army.

24. *SIGNAL CALLER.* Art Sullivan was quarterback of the Black Hills Normal School "Yellowjackets" in 1925. Marlys Sell of Billings, Montana says her dad "lettered" 4 years at his school in Spearfish, South Dakota.

25. *BOTTLE MAN.* In 1927, Keith Outland was delivering Coca-Cola in bottles in Zanesville, Ohio, reports James Gebhart, Highland, California. This was Zanesville's first Coke company.

25. Refreshing Pause

26. Right in Fashion

27. Little Drummer Boy

28. Hair of Gold

26. PRETTY NANNY. Lisa Legg of Yardville, New Jersey sent a lovely photograph of her grandmother taken in 1929, 3 years after she'd come to America from Germany. Young Ellen Christian worked as a nanny and learned English from the children.

27. PASS THE DRUMSTICK. John Kester was only 5 when he got his first set of drums and started to teach himself to play. Not many years later, John, of Elkhart, Indiana, was an accomplished drummer, getting $2 a night for a "gig".

28. UNCUT BEAUTY. Betty Crowell of Montecito, California says her sister, Gretchen, still has long golden locks, just as she did in 1927. Betty also recalls that their aunt made Gretchen's nightie with a hand-tatted hemline.

29. Hang on!

29. *LET'S GO!* There weren't many cars in the neighborhood when Mary Meyrick of East Hardwick, Vermont climbed on the running board of her uncle's flivver in Philadelphia in '23 when she was 2.

30. *WICKER WONDER.* When her mother, Grace Budish, was just a tot, she rode in splendor in this wicker buggy, says Mary Ann Koebernik of Franklin, Wisconsin.

31. *BOWL BEAUTIES.* When the Hollywood Bowl opened in the early '20s, Millicent Bolton of Pasadena, California (seated second from right) was one of the colorfully dressed usherettes.

30. Buggy Baby

31. Usherettes

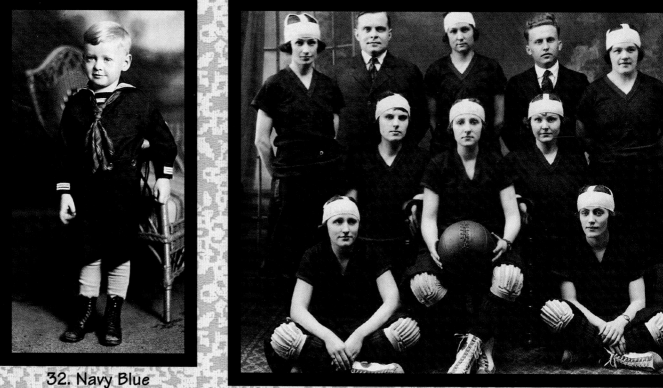

32. Navy Blue

33. Basketball Beauties

32. *AHOY!* It must have been a sign when her brother, Herbert Heath, dressed up in a sailor suit, says Mable Bole of Carmichael, California—he later became a sailor!

33. *HALL OF FAMER.* Olive Wolcott, Enfield, Connecticut, notes this photo of her team, which played in Kent, Ohio, is in the Basketball Hall of Fame along with her uniform. She's seated on the floor at right.

34. *STEP CHILDREN?* Rachel Blouse (right front) and pals posed in front of the church where her dad was minister in Dallastown, Pennsylvania, where she still lives.

35. *BUTTONS 'N' BOWS.* Strapped shoes and hair bows were in style when Marie Newell was confirmed in 1926, says daughter Patti Astle of Baraboo, Wisconsin.

34. Step by Step

35. Just Confirmed

36. Snowy Stroll

36. *DOLL AND BUGGY.* Marie Perrine of Jackson, Michigan recalls that she loved playing with her dolls and buggy in the '20s. That's her brother Wayne joining the fun.

37. *SIS' BIG DAY.* Dorothy Anderson of Hayward, California sent the 1923 wedding photo of her sister, Katherine Lindsay, with one of her brides-maids, Nelly Thompson.

38. *DAD'S STORE.* It was "The Biggest Little Store" in Chester, Nebraska, says Norma Haist, who lives in Hastings. Her dad's wearing the cap.

37. Bridal Flowers

38. Ready to Serve

39. Hoosier Honeymooners

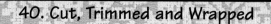

40. Cut, Trimmed and Wrapped

41. Dolly and Me

39. NEWLYWEDS. Tom and Anna Miller were married in Summitville, Indiana in the 1920s. Bettina Miller of Milwaukee, Wisconsin says her grandparents made their home there for 60 years.

40. PRIME CUT. He was still learning the business when this photo was taken, says Newton MacDonald of Montauk, New York. But he learned well and later managed an A&P store.

41. HELLO, DOLLY! Laverne Stevens of Mission Viejo, California was one excited little girl when she got her Minnie Lane doll for Christmas in 1926. She named her "Vernie".

42. "TRY TO SINK!" Read the legend on the "float", which was in the buoyant water of Great Salt Lake, at "Saltair" resort in 1924. Hugh Shira of Alta Loma, California is the young boy standing on the float.

42. Water's Fine

43. Scouts' Honor

44. A Day with Dad

45. Mighty Angler

43. *BADGE EARNERS.* The Canandaigua, New York Girl Scouts gathered for a photo in 1926, says Helene Hammond of Auburn, New York (standing third from the right).

44. *ME AND POP.* A 1927 boat ride with his dad on Chesapeake Bay still brings back fond memories for Walter Graves of Hollywood, Florida. He still has the name tag he's wearing.

45. *FISH STORY.* No, James Oswald of Chicago, Illinois didn't catch this muskie that was bigger than he was, but he had fun posing with it in Eagle River, Wisconsin in '24.

46. Got Her Goat

47. Attractive Aviatrix

46. "I WANT TO DRIVE!" While brother Rolland was grinning, she was pouting, explains Donna Balcombe of Escondido, California, because he wouldn't let her hold the reins on the goat cart. The siblings were 4 and 2 back in 1927 in Whittier, California.

47. MOM'S AWAY! Lula Mae Adams loved to get dressed up and go to town, says her daughter, Audrey Lambert of Brentwood, Tennessee. On this particular trip during the 1920s, Lula Mae climbed aboard a biplane at an airfield near San Antonio, Texas.

48. SAM'S HARDWARE. Nail kegs stand next to the loafers' bench at Sammy Funkhouser's store. He posed for this photo in December of 1928, says Dean White, whose father rented land from Sammy in Shelby, Nebraska. Dean lives in Shelby today.

48. Sit a Spell

49. Dance School Darlings

50. Spring Chores

51. Bathing Beauties

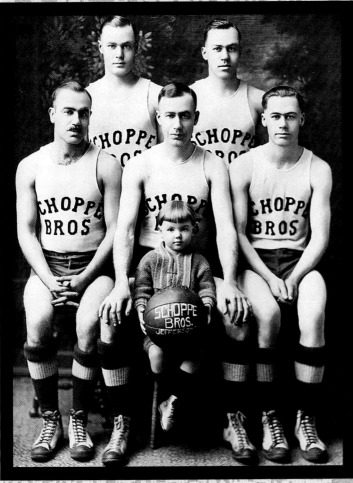

52. Bucket Brothers

49. POINT THOSE TOES! Alice Risio (far left), Seekonk, Maine, and her pals posed in '24. Alice recalls their moms made the dresses.

50. SPRING CLEANING. The stove was on the porch and Mom took a break, while little Mildred and Ordean got some fresh air. Chuck Halla of Hartford, Wisconsin sent photo of his mom and siblings.

51. TESTING THE WATER. Lillian Zellman (second from right) of Oak Park, Michigan remembers the hot summer day she and her girlfriends had this photo taken.

52. FIVE OF A KIND. The Schoppe brothers were just enough for a basketball team. Charles Schoppe (right front) of Des Moines, Iowa notes they didn't have any subs. "If one fouled out, we played with four."

53. Easel Does It

54. Strummin' Away

53. **BRUSHING UP.** The ladies of a Gloucester, Massachusetts art colony took advantage of a fine day on a waterfront street. Photo's from Janet McDermott of New York, New York.

54. *UKULELE BABY.* Mom played the "uke" as Taye Waldron of Carson City, Nevada displayed the dress and pants her mother made. Though it was the style then, Taye says she was a little shy about showing her underwear!

55. *COOLING IT.* Stopping the Model T to let it cool down was common back in the '20s. It gave James Oswald of Chicago, Illinois time to pick a few rocks for the running board while the rest of the family stretched their legs.

56. *COUPLE O' COUSINS.* Her North Dakota cousins, Muriel and Elton Peterson, were patient enough on this day in 1925 to have their photo taken, says Ruth Merritt of Yakima, Washington. Elton doesn't seem to mind the "Little Lord" outfit.

55. Running Bored

56. Hi, Cuz!

Chapter Five

'The Silents' And Other Fun

KOMIC KOPS. The Keystone Kops didn't *need* sound for their slapstick comedy and wild chases. Movie audiences loved them— and made enough noise of their own laughing at the Kops' antics! Keystone was the name of the movie company run by Mack Sennett, the "King of Comedy" in the '20s.

'The Silents' and Other Fun

When I tell my grandchildren that there was no television when I was growing up, they gasp and ask me, "Grampa, what did you *do*!" I suspect they have a mental picture of my mother knitting while Dad read the Bible aloud by the light of a flickering candle as my sister and I sat on little stools at his feet. You know, sort of a *Little House on the Prairie* setting.

Ah, I wish I could take them back to the Twenties for a few days. They'd be astonished at how much they're missing in this TV-Nintendo age.

I wish they could know the excitement that started when posters appeared all over town, announcing the circus was coming in a few weeks. Elephants! Lions! Tigers! Death-defying high-wire walkers! A man shot out of a cannon! Pretty girls in spangled tights!

Endless Wait for the Big Top

Imagine seeing real live tigers and elephants...and the Bearded Lady.

We knew we would be there when the circus train unloaded before dawn. We would go to the airport and watch as they put up the enormous tents. Maybe we'd even carry water to the elephants. Later there would be a parade through downtown, and then the thrilling afternoon and evening performances.

Looking back, I know that much of the thrill was in the sheer *anticipation*...days and days and days of sweet agony. Nowadays, you're cheated out of that when instant entertainment comes at the push of a button.

I vividly remember the first "talkie" I saw. It was *Rio Rita*. We had now seen—and heard—the future, and it was dazzling.

Chautauquas, the variety shows of the era, came to town each summer and offered everything from musical performances and magicians to patriotic oratory or fire-and-brimstone gospel preachers. The audience sat on wooden benches and women fanned themselves with palm leaf-shaped fans that carried advertising for the local mortuary.

Occasionally barnstorming pilots would turn up at the local airport. Soon a crowd would gather to watch the daring aerobatics. Then a few brave souls would pay for a brief ride over the town, and we'd crowd around afterward as they described how the world looked from a thousand feet up in the sky.

Local Park Became an Oasis

From early spring until the autumn leaves dropped, Lawrence Park was our favorite community gathering place. It was *the* place for reunions, church picnics and threshing ring picnics, as well as for individual families just enjoying an outdoor breakfast or lunch where the kids could run off steam and parents could meet with their friends.

The park was on an island in the Rock River, reached by a bridge. It had a community swimming pool, a shelter house with gas stoves, outdoor grills, lots of picnic tables under the big elm trees, a gazebo-like bandstand where the municipal band played Sunday afternoon concerts, a few baseball diamonds, and a World War I cannon aimed up the river, perhaps to fend off an invading armada.

Yes, our lives in the Twenties were brightened with all sorts of fine entertainment that cost very little. Good times were usually shared in the company of family and friends, and we certainly didn't lack for fun.

No, kids...we didn't have television. But we had grand times, as the memories on the next pages make clear.

—*Clancy Strock*

Harold M. Lambert

My Brother Danced for Babe Ruth

By Marie Vincent, Salt Lake City, Utah

BACK IN '26 when this "roaring" decade was in full swing, the Charleston was the latest craze.

I learned the Charleston in my dance class and taught it to my younger brother, John. He was only 6, but he was a natural, mastering not only the basic steps but at least six difficult variations. Could that boy dance!

We lived in Provo, Utah then, and one day our father was going on a business trip to Salt Lake City. Often he'd take one of us children along, and after he completed his business, what a thrilling day we'd have!

We'd enjoy lunch at the Hotel Utah and an afternoon of vaudeville at the

> *"The orchestra leader gave the downbeat and John did his routine..."*

Pantages Theater. On one unforgettable day, Father took little John to the Pantages.

Babe Ruth was appearing on the vaudeville circuit then. His program was to ask people from the audience to get on stage and entertain, for which he'd give them an autographed baseball.

As father entered the theater, he saw a couple from Provo. They'd seen John do the Charleston, and they persuaded Father to let John dance on the program.

He Was Skeptical

When it was John's turn, Babe asked him what he could do. When John told him he danced the Charleston, Babe looked down skeptically at this small, adorable boy in his three-piece suit.

Babe asked John what music he danced to and John replied, "*Yes, Sir, That's My Baby*". Babe asked the orchestra if they knew the song, and the leader enthusiastically said they did.

Shaking his head doubtfully, Babe told the audience, "This young man says he can Charleston. Let's see what he can do."

The orchestra leader gave the downbeat and John went into his routine, dancing like a little professional. The audience went wild!

They screamed, shouted, whistled and stomped. As they said in vaudeville, he brought down the house!

Babe was so impressed that at the end of the program, he came back to John with a big grin and said, "This young man will have to give us an encore!" Again, the audience went wild.

I'll never forget the proud look on Father's face that night as he told us all about it. John just stood at his side, listening quietly, happily clutching an autographed baseball from Babe Ruth.

SHALL WE DANCE? John Morgan, 6, was wearing this new three-piece suit when he danced the Charleston for Babe Ruth in 1926. Marie Vincent says her brother brought down the house.

Neighbors Gathered 'Round the Organ

MY MOTHER'S beautiful Story & Clark organ was a wonderful source of fun and entertainment for our rural family before we had radios or electricity.

My grandfather had bought the ornately carved instrument (left) in 1889 so his nine daughters could learn to play. After it became my mother's, we often gathered around it in the evenings with our neighbors.

I especially remember an evening in June 1926, when I was 7. A group of neighbors arrived with a carnival glass dish in honor of my parents' 25th anniversary.

Everyone gathered in the living room to sing as Mom played favorite old songs and hymns before serving the refreshments our friends had brought. Back then, there was time to relax and enjoy life after a day's work, unlike the hurrying pace of today.

My two most cherished possessions today are that old organ and Mom and Dad's lovely anniversary dish.
                                                              —*Mrs. Golden Reinart*
                                                              Hopkins, Michigan

ALL THAT JAZZ. The "Flea Hop Dance Orchestra" performed around Brady, Nebraska in the 1920s and toured the Western states in 1928. The combo included Jocelyn Schmidt's parents, C. "Roy" and Cecilia Stryker (center), and her aunts, Gladyce Thompson (far left) and Bernice Britton.

Jazz Combo Practiced in Our Living Room

By Jocelyn Schmidt, Arroyo Grande, California

A RED-HOT jazz orchestra often practiced in our living room during the 1920s, while friends and neighbors danced on the front porch.

The "Flea Hop Dance Orchestra", composed of my parents and my mother's two sisters, often played for dances near our home in Brady, Nebraska.

My father was the manager, saxophonist and drummer. My mother played ragtime and jazz piano. Aunt Bernice played a wild fiddle, and Aunt

Gladyce could make her soprano "talk"!

All three sisters were typical flappers, with short skirts and bobbed hair. They sang like larks, danced a mean Charleston and put on hilarious shows. Sometimes they hired local musicians to jam along with them.

They had great fun, and so did everyone who heard them.

In the summer of 1928, they went on tour, performing in the Black Hills and from Seattle, Washington south to Ti-

juana, Mexico. After that, they drove east through the Sonoran Desert on Route 66, then a wooden plank highway, where they were stopped by hundreds of tarantulas crossing the road! They also played in New Mexico and Colorado before heading home.

Our musical heritage played an important role in our lives, and we'll always remember that wild, wonderful orchestra. If anyone remembers seeing them perform, I'd love to hear about it!

For Chicago Couple, Dancing Was Part of Their "Ritual"

WE LIVED in a Chicago suburb during the '20s, and every day when our work was done, there seemed to be another adventure.

Dancing to Wayne King at the Aragon Ballroom or Lawrence Welk at the Trianon was a ritual. On weekends, we traveled to Lake Geneva or Lake Delavan in Wisconsin, where small dance bands played until 1 o'clock in the morning.

Despite Prohibition, liquor was available at speakeasies all over Chicago. We never knew where they got

their supply, but bourbon and gin were $1 a pint. Canadian whiskey was trucked in by "rumrunners".

Roosevelt Road was one of the bootleggers' favorite routes to the city, and it ran through a small town called Broadview. Its sole policeman, "Indian Joe", rode a big Harley and was the bane of the rumrunners. Several attempts were made on his life, but he was tough and always got his man. He was our Tom Mix on a motorcycle.

—*George and Edna Biringer*
Bella Vista, Arkansas

Entertainers Enlivened Small-Town Life

By Paul MacElwee
Shamokin, Pennsylvania

THERE WAS NO TV during the early 1920s, and radio was in its infancy. But we had plenty of entertainment right in the middle of downtown Shamokin, Pennsylvania—and it was free!

In addition to circuses and carnivals, we were visited regularly by Arizona Jack, who toured the country selling the "snake medicine" that he claimed cured everything from athlete's foot to dandruff.

Under the light of kerosene lanterns, Jack would snap a big black whip to attract the attention

> *"The 'Human Fly' would scale a town's tallest building..."*

of passersby. Once he had an audience, he'd do amazing tricks with his lariat, usually "snagging" a blushing young woman in the crowd with his rope. After the show, he'd start a sales pitch for his "snake oil". Many people bought it.

Another popular entertainer was the "human fly". He traveled from town to town, climbing each community's tallest building. In Shamokin, that was

ANOTHER TOP ACT was screen legend Harold Lloyd, seen here in his usual tight spot.

the National Dime Bank in the center of town, and people crowded into the intersection to watch.

He made use of ledges and windows as he scaled the building, and when he reached the top, the relieved spectators would applaud and shout their praise. Then he'd climb down to the street and circulate among the crowd to collect contributions.

A local music store occasionally sponsored a pianist who would stage an endurance test, playing nonstop for hours in the store window. Every now and then, he'd sprinkle powder on the keys to soothe his tired fingers.

But the most exciting day of all came when Borax's famous 20-mule team came to town. This, presumably, was the team that ventured far into the desert to bring Borax to market. The driver showed unusual skill in handling the team of 20 animals, especially when it rounded an intersection.

Whenever one of these "acts" came to town, the news spread like wildfire. Young people especially would flock to the areas where the performers set up their stages.

None of the television shows of today comes close to providing the thrills we got from those "free shows" we saw during the 1920s in downtown Shamokin!

J.C. Allen and Son

Forbidden Game of Chance Yielded Family Treasure

By Edith Landfried
Spokane, Washington

WHENEVER I see a carnival, I'm reminded of a sunny summer day in 1928, when I was 11.

A carnival had come to our little town of Davenport, Washington, and my brother and I were anxious to go. Our mother, a strict Methodist, looked askance at anything so worldly, but told us we could go—as long as we did not play any games of chance.

The first attraction to catch our

STEP RIGHT UP! The carnival meant a chance to play games and win prizes.

attention was a booth filled with dazzling prizes won by spinning an arrow mounted on the counter. The man in the booth was persuasive, I was weak, and before I knew it, I had the arrow spinning.

My brother and I watched with bated breath as it slowed and then stopped at the best prize on the counter—a beautiful carnival glass bowl!

We carried it home with some trepidation, but when I gave it to Mom, she was so taken with its beauty that she didn't think to scold me.

It was given a special place in the china cabinet, and is now one of my most prized possessions.

INFLATION. Movie tickets had gone up to 25¢ when this photo was taken, but lucky Jack Bedwell remembers when they were a dime...for everyone but him.

Projectionist's Son Was Luckiest Kid in Town

By Jack Bedwell, Manzanita, Oregon

REMEMBER WHEN a dime would get you into the local movie house to watch the antics of Our Gang, Charlie Chaplin and Harold Lloyd? Remember cheering for the good guys like Hoot Gibson and Tom Mix as they swooped down on the bad guys in black hats?

I sure do—and I didn't have to pay a dime to see them. I had a balcony seat, on a 4-foot stool in front of a square opening where I could look down on the crowd. My father was the guy in the projection booth, and I was the luckiest kid in town!

Watching a film from the booth had its drawbacks. The movies were made of highly flammable acetate, and the

> *"When the film broke, everyone booed and stamped their feet..."*

two projection machines used carbon-arc lamps that generated lots of heat.

Since there was always the risk of fire, the booth was lined with tin sheeting, with no outside windows or air-conditioning. It got mighty hot in there before the movie was over, and our only relief came from an old General Electric fan.

The projectors were equipped with a series of thick magnifying prisms that projected the 35-millimeter film into life-size images on the screen over 100 feet away.

It was exciting to watch Dad fire up those big machines by turning on the electricity and moving two 8-inch-long carbon rods together, making a bright flash. He slowly moved them apart until a brilliant blue-white light was ready to shine through the prisms.

Dad Made Shining Impression

Prior to each show, Dad would lift the heavy metal film cans up into the booth, remove the 18-inch reels, make sure they'd been rewound by the previous projectionist and put them on the machines in proper sequence. Sometimes a comedy short or newsreel would be part of the program, so he had to keep close watch to ensure continuity of his show.

To do so, Dad had to start and stop his machines right on cue. Near the end of each reel, a cue sign would flash, indicating it was time to turn on the other projection machine and close its shutter.

A second flash signaled it was time to turn off the first machine and open the shutter on the second. I got pretty good at spotting the signs, and would tell Dad when to start and stop the machines. I can still hear the sprockets clattering as the film raced through them, and smell the acrid odor of acetate.

It was fun to watch the crowd be-low when the film occasionally broke or burned. The screen would go blank and Dad would turn off the machine and turn up the houselights. Everybody would boo, holler and stamp their feet. The pianist would play a tune or two, hoping to quiet the crowd until the film started again.

Meanwhile, Dad was unthreading the machine, pulling the two broken ends together, making a temporary splice with tape, then re-threading the machine. After the show was over, he'd put the reel on a rewind machine, hand-crank the film onto another reel and cement the broken ends together with a smelly liquid called acetone. A guy could get woozy breathing that stuff!

Dad had to constantly be on the alert for anything that would make the film or machines break down, and he repaired and maintained everything himself.

Today, projection booths are automated. An operator need only place a high-tech cassette in a machine and push a button to get images to the screen. The film is no longer flammable, there are no sprockets and there's no acetone smell. The days of "the silents" are over ...but the memories will stay with me forever. ⚊

Children Saw Vaudeville Matinee for 7¢

I BEGAN attending vaudeville shows in 1920 and never missed a week. We lived in Chicago Heights, Illinois, about 30 miles south of downtown Chicago. Our Lincoln and Dixie Theaters drew many of the name acts from that big city.

The kids' show every Saturday afternoon included a feature picture, a comedy, short subjects, one installment in a 20-chapter serial and seven vaudeville acts—all for 7¢!

We saw all the best, including Will Rogers and Harry Louder. My feet still tap when I hear *The Sidewalks of New York*. I also enjoyed a group called The Chinese Jugglers, who used to sing *My Old Kentucky Home*.

—*Eugene Weishaar Pacific Beach, Washington*

Silents Were Super for Page-Turning Participant

By Adrian Nader
River Edge, New Jersey

FOR US KIDS of the 1920s, the silent movies allowed an escape from our limited lives into a world where we joined brave heroes and beautiful ladies in fantastic adventures.

For a time, I was even a participant, working as a "page turner" for the pianist, my sister Gladys.

The two small theaters in our town of New Lexington, Ohio seemed like temples of magic. Every couple of days, my buddies and I would check the "Coming Attractions" photos in front of both theaters, hoping for a Western featuring our heroes William S. Hart, Tom Mix, Buck Jones or Hoot Gibson.

We also loved Douglas Fairbanks as the *Thief of Baghdad* and, of course,

> *"My job was to turn the pages. We practiced at home..."*

Charlie Chaplin, Harold Lloyd and the Keystone Kops.

To those who grew up watching "talking" movies, the old silents may seem boring or even ludicrous. Such exaggerated acting! How could anyone be taken in by such antics?

One Look Told All

Well, it helped carry the story. With the help of only a few words on the screen now and again, those skillful pantomime artists helped us understand the story line.

The actors and actresses were carefully cast and costumed so that merely one look at them would let you know who were the virtuous ones, the funny ones, the brave, the industrious, the lazy, the cowardly and the wicked beyond redemption.

In the 1920s, theme music was being written for the better shows, and these songs became best-sellers as sheet music. Our family library still contains many of them.

A local theater manager hired my sister Gladys to play piano, and as soon as a film was booked, she'd receive a set of cue sheets describing each scene or sequence and the "mood music" to accompany it.

The sheet might say something like: "Jim and girl walk to balcony. Play Dvorak, Opus 16, 10th measure; continue to end of balcony scene."

My job was to sit on a stool next to Gladys, turning the pages. When it was time for a new song, I'd snatch the sheet music away and plop a different piece in its place, opened to the marked measures. This was no easy task, so we practiced at home before opening night.

And opening night was scary!

There we sat, in front of all those people, straining our necks to watch the movie for the next cue. We were always afraid we'd miss it and ruin the effect! But after a showing or two, we relaxed and enjoyed the experience.

The first movie we accompanied was a World War I film, *The Big Parade* with John Gilbert, Slim Summerville and Karl Dane. But

my memory of turning pages for another such movie are more vivid.

In one scene, The Red Baron, Germany's top flying ace, streaks across the sky in his small red triplane. The plane seems to shimmer as it darts about in combat. After it is shot down, the Baron crawls from the wreck.

Was Plane Really Red?

The hero lands his plane and walks toward him. The Baron holds up his billfold, and we see a close-up photo of his loved ones (*Hearts and Flowers*, Sis!). The hero indicates he'll send the billfold to them, and the Red Baron dies peacefully.

By the 1940s, I began to doubt my memory of the red plane when the thought struck me that the early '20s silents were black-and-white.

Aboard a Navy ship in the Pacific, the mystery was solved. I often played cribbage with the ship's doctor, and one day he happened to mention he'd been a movie projectionist in Chicago in the '20s. I told him my Red Baron memory.

"Was the plane red or wasn't it?" I asked.

"It sure was," he said. "The plane was hand-tinted in each frame on the film. The color shimmered on the screen

because the edges of the painting on each frame didn't match exactly the edges of the frames that followed through the projector."

End of mystery!

My career as a page turner had ended near the end of the '20s, with the advent of talking pictures. But for me, no movies will ever be more memorable than those early silents.

SING ALONG. Songs that were played for silent movies often became hits on their own, as this sheet music from Adrian Nader's collection shows.

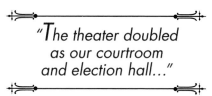

THE BOYS. Even after sound came to movies, Ollie and Stan needed only the minimum of dialogue to produce belly laughs from audiences.

Pianist's Job Was No Work, All Play

By Grace Frost, Red Creek, New York

AT AGE 13, I started playing piano to accompany the silent movies in our upstate New York village on Saturday nights. I was paid a whole dollar, but I didn't consider it "work". As far as I was concerned, I was going to the movies!

The Powers Theatre was on the second floor of a block-long brick building, up a wide flight of stairs between a grocery store and the post office.

It was a large room, lined with about 100 straight-backed chairs, and it doubled as our courtroom and election hall.

The projection booth was built out over the alley, next to the fire escape. That must have been a chilly perch on winter nights!

The stage, draped with an elegantly painted canvas curtain, was used for school plays and traveling road shows. But on Saturday nights, the curtain was replaced with a silver screen. My perch was a balcony off to one side.

The boys liked to sit on the tops of the chairs in the back row so they could see over everyone else's heads. They sometimes shot a paper wad or two at me, but the suit-jacketed constable kept things from getting too rowdy. An enterprising young lady often brought popcorn to sell until the movie began.

Show Time!

First we saw slides advertising local businesses, such as F. M. Douglass Gift Shop and Stationery Store, Perkins Market and the Brynsneth Restaurant. Next came short previews of coming attractions, and finally, the main feature, a cliffhanger serial and comic shorts.

Typical fare from the mid-'20s might include Colleen Moore in *When Dawn Came* and Charles Hutchinson in *Go Get 'Em Hutch, Part One*. (Part Two

> *"The theater doubled as our courtroom and election hall..."*

would be shown the following week.) The shorts and serials were always very worn and had to be repaired during the show, amid loud clamoring from the audience.

My job was easy. Each film came with a cue sheet, suggesting appropriate music for the accompanist to use. But I didn't have any sheet music, so I simply improvised or played something familiar as the action (or lack of it) dictated.

My only regret was that the Powers didn't have a big theater organ, like the one my Aunt Molly played in Rochester.

With the advent of "talkies", the Powers Theatre went out of business, and I was out of a job. But at least I was saved from a permanent crick in my neck from craning to watch the movie from my piano bench every Saturday night!

Rural Theater Had a Charm All Its Own

MY MOTHER played the Victrola for the silent films at our movie hall in Round Hill, Virginia. The music had nothing to do with the movie—it was just a little noise to break the silence.

Sometimes Mother fell asleep and the record would end, making a scratching sound as the needle went 'round and 'round in the last groove.

"Wake up, Mrs. Larrick!" someone would yell, and the music would start again.

We also had a lady who always read the subtitles out loud. That would bring another yell: "Shut up, Miss Hal-lie!" Then things would be back to normal for a few minutes...until she started up again.

The hall got pretty hot in summertime, so the owner put in a fan. It made a lot of noise, which didn't matter since the movies were silent. But the fan was a really big one—it practically blew our hair straight out from our heads!

Round Hill was a small farming community, and most of the movies shown were Westerns. When city folks visited our movie hall, they often joked afterward, "That was the first time I could see the horses and smell them, too!"
—*Charley Larrick, Alexandria, Virginia*

Ewing Galloway

GOOD GUY. Tom Mix was always a valiant hero, and he wore the white Stetson to prove it!

Attendance at Cowboy Films Was "Boys Only"—Almost

OUR "THEATER" in Newburgh, New York was really just a tin shed, and it got so cold in winter that we all kept our coats on. We could hear someone shoveling coal for the furnace, but I think it was just being moved from one pile to another to give us the *illusion* that we were getting heat.

Cowboy movies were very popular then, and most of the time the entire audience was made up of boys. Hoot Gibson, William S. Hart (who was originally from Newburgh), Ken Maynard, Tom Mix, Bob Steele and Buck Jones were our heroes.

The tin screen, painted white, was much larger than the average theater screen. Some of the boys would shoot metal staples at it before the show began.

We knew the movie was about to start when the pianist walked down the aisle to the upright piano. This brought an immediate chorus of hoots, whistles, screams and stomping. She played only two songs—one for tender love scenes, and another for when the Indi-

ans were attacking the wagon train.

It wasn't unusual for some boys dressed as cowboys to walk down the middle aisle with toy guns in holsters. They'd stand there shooting blanks at the screen or ceiling. No one, including the manager, seemed to mind. To us kids, this seemed perfectly normal behavior.

The only adult in the theater at those times was the piano player. I hope she was well paid.

—*Marshall Balfe*
Santa Rosa, California

Chaos Often Reigned at Saturday Matinees

THE SATURDAY silent movie matinees I attended with my sister were anything but silent.

Big kids tried to read the captions to little kids, who were constantly asking, "What are they saying?" Other kids kept changing seats, running to the rear of the theater to buy popcorn, and leaving to get a drink or go to the restroom. It's a wonder we could follow the movie at all.

Sometimes the film caught fire. The operator would have to put it out and splice the film back together before the show could go on. Meanwhile, there were about 80 little kids ready to riot. The manager would come down and tell them to be quiet or he'd take them outside.

Before "talkies" started, the theater bought a machine that played records with such common movie sounds as trains and galloping horses. We thought it was a great invention. —*Gene Bond*
Worthington, Iowa

Toddler's Trips to Movies Left Indelible Impression

MY FIRST MEMORY dates to 1925, when I was 3 years old. My mother was a good pianist, and she played for weddings, civic organizations and church in our hometown of Wakefield, Michigan. When the first silent pictures

came to town, it was only natural for her to play for them, too.

Three times a week, she'd take my brothers and me with her. She'd put me in a wicker clothes basket next to the piano. I could clearly see her, my two brothers and all the townspeople who packed themselves into a small lodge hall to see the latest wonders from the magic city of Hollywood.

Soon the lights would turn off and the projector would start, clickety-clacking as it projected a pure-white cone of light toward the white screen.

Cigar smoke filled the room with an acrid smell. I looked up at my mother, but she ignored me, playing intensely to match the action on the screen.

I was too young to understand the concept of "motion pictures". I couldn't even see the screen. But the sensation of darkness, sounds, flickering lights and cigar smoke was so ingrained in my young mind that I've never been able to forget it. Even today, I can close my eyes and clearly see, smell and hear this unforgettable experience.

—*Larry Stevenson*
Seattle, Washington

Theater Thwarted Youth's Daring Kiss-and-Run Caper

IN 1925, I earned my 10¢ admission to the theater in Ocean Bluffs, Massachusetts by selling the *Saturday Evening Post*, cashing in tonic bottles left behind by tourists and setting pins in a bowling alley.

I usually went with my best friend, 12-year-old Alec, who was crazy about girls. Before the show started, we'd sit at the rear of the theater, listening to the piano music, as Alec sized up all the young females in the aisle seats.

As soon as the lights went out, Alec would dash down the aisle, kiss the prettiest girl on the cheek, then run back to his seat. No girl ever cried out. There were only loud giggles from the victims and their friends.

After this kiss-and-run episode had occurred several times, a notice flashed on the screen. It read: "If the young man who is annoying the young ladies in the audience does not stop, he will be permanently barred from this theater."

This *made* our summer. We were just as famous as if our names had appeared on the most-wanted list at the post office!

—*LeRoy Hebert*
Lexington, Massachusetts

Blue Hawaii

WALTZ SONG
With Uke & Banjo Uke

Played by
BILLY WRIGHT
Featured Organist

Words & Music by
ABEL BAER
Writer of "HELLO ALOHA"
IRVING CAESAR
and
IRA SCHUSTER

POPULAR EDITION
LEO. FEIST INC. NEW YORK
CANADA, LEO. FEIST, LIMITED, 193 YONGE ST. TORONTO
FRANCIS DAY & HUNTER LTD, 138-140 CHARING CROSS ROAD, LONDON W.C.

MOVIE ROMANCE. When Bill Wright (inset above) played the movie organ, his usherette wife-to-be (far right below) came to listen...twice. They went out for a couple of White Castles afterwards, and thus was born a marriage of 60 years.

Rival Theater Workers Found Matrimony at The Movies

By Bill Wright, Monrovia, California

IN ONE WAY or another, my organ playing kept me "in show biz" for 75 years. In fact, I met my wife of 60 years while I was working the keys at a silent movie.

It was 1927, and Loew's Midland Theatre in Kansas City was ready to open. They needed an organist to accompany a 32-piece symphony on this big occasion. I auditioned with six other organists and somehow got the job.

The biggest thrill of my life (next to meeting my wife, Irene) was rising from the pit with that big symphony orchestra to do *Overture*, which opened every show.

Irene was the cashier at a competing theater just down the block, The Pantages. One night, a bunch of the "Pan" usherettes and their cashier came to the Midland to take in our show.

The usherettes sat in the front row so they could flirt with the orchestra boys, but Irene sat right in front of the organ.

I was busy playing for the Marion Davies' film *When Knighthood was in Flower*, so I didn't notice too much about the girl sitting near the organ that night. But when she showed up in the same seat the next night, she really caught my attention!

When I asked her if she liked the picture, she said, "No, I was so interested in watching you play that I missed the picture."

I fell for that one hook, line and sinker. "Meet me after the show and we'll go out and have a couple of White Castle hamburgers," I offered.

She sat through that awful flick three times, but she did meet me. Six months later, we were married!

Serials Kept Moviegoers Guessing

By Don Jones
South San Francisco, California

TELEVISION hadn't been invented in the '20s, and the few radio stations that were operating then weren't on the air for many hours.

For us kids, the silent movies were our primary entertainment. In my hometown of San Jose, California, my friends and I frequented theaters like the Hippodrome, T&D and the Liberty.

As soon as we got to the theater, we'd head directly to the front-row seats. When we saw *Way Down East*, starring Lillian Gish, I sat right behind the organ and noticed that the music was marked as the property of the studio that produced the picture. The music also had cues and other marks to tell the organist when to play.

Some of the minor characters had their own musical themes. For example, every time the crabby old busy body appeared, the organist played music from Tchaikovsky's *Humoresque*. To this day, whenever I hear it, I picture that mean woman marching down the street to spread some more malicious gossip!

The serials were always exciting. These full-length movies had the same cast every week, and each episode usually ended with the hero getting himself in dire straits. You had to come back the next week to find out how he extricated himself.

One episode I recall ended with the hero imprisoned in a small adobe cell. As the reel ended, the cell walls started to close in, threatening to crush him.

Naturally, we were lured back the next week, and found our hero pressing against the walls with his shoulders and feet. He was so strong that he pushed a hole through the outer wall and escaped!

I remember vividly the first movie I saw with sound. I deliberately went to see what this "sound" business was all about. The first part of the film was silent, and I was

LILLIAN GISH starred in *Way Down East*, which Don Jones saw from a seat right behind the organist.

used to that, so I almost forgot about it. Then there was a scene where a woman was setting a table, and I heard the tinkling of knives and forks and the scraping of moving chairs.

I could hardly believe my ears. There were these natural sounds, coming right out of the screen in front of me! I could hardly wait to get home and tell my family about the miracle I had witnessed.

Pianist Mom, Projectionist Dad Made Sure Show Went On

By Calvin Canniff
Junction City, Kansas

AROUND 1927, when we lived in Haven, Kansas, my mother played piano and Dad operated the projection machines at the movie theater.

This was before the day of baby-sitters, so Mom had me sit beside her on the piano bench. I still have some of the sheet music she used.

While Mom played, I watched the movies and began learning to read. Some of the first words I recognized were "help" and "I love you".

Before the show, local merchants advertised with glass slides that Dad

placed in front of the projector lens to flash the image on the screen. Sometimes a slide was accidentally put in upside down, which was always good for a laugh from the audience.

At least once during the show, the film would break and Dad would have to stop the machine, splice the film, rethread it and start the machine again. Mom would break into a lively rendition of *Maple Leaf Rag* to keep the audience entertained.

In a "Hot Seat"

Sometimes I sat with Dad in the projection booth, a small enclosure at the rear of the theater. The large bulbs in the projectors generated a lot of heat, and

there was little ventilation, so the temperature often topped 100° by the end of the movie. When it started getting hot, Dad would start shedding his clothes. Often by the end of the movie, he'd be working in his underwear!

Sound for early "talking movies" was on a record and had to be synchronized with the picture. The needle on the turntable traveled from the center of the record to the outer edge, and sometimes it skipped a groove.

When that happened, the film might be showing a woman talking, but the sound was that of a dog barking! Dad quickly adjusted the needle until sound and picture were synchronized again.

Silent Film Organist Enjoyed View from the Pit

A FEW years ago, I met a gentleman who began his music career as an organ accompanist for the silent movies.

J. Paul Mellott got his start at age 18, working for the Victory Theater in Findlay, Ohio. He played in an organ pit just below the edge of the stage.

The 1920s was the era of the grand movie palaces with ample stages to present the numerous and popular vaudeville shows. "Most of these theaters were owned by the California movie studios during the Roarin' 20s," Paul told me.

Two weeks before each new movie started showing at the Victory, Paul received a cue sheet suggesting back-

"He played Western music for Tom Mix and his horse..."

ground music for each scene. This gave him time to rehearse, because it was up to him to make the songs correspond to the proper scenes. Sometimes it worked …sometimes it didn't.

"Now and then my sheet music would stick together and I'd end up playing the wrong accompaniment for a particular scene," Paul recalled with a laugh. "Whenever that happened, the audience wasted no time booing me!"

On other occasions, Paul would play thunderous organ music to underscore a

By Shirley Kaminski
Westfield, Massachusetts

dramatic moment…then, in the quiet pause that followed, a woman in the audience could be heard reciting a new recipe or sharing a bit of gossip.

A Ticklish Experience

Paul chuckled as he told me about a live Hawaiian show at the theater in 1926, with about a dozen dancers doing the hula. While the dancers swayed to his exotic music, their long grass skirts were tickling the top of his head in the organ pit.

He also recalled playing Western music for an appearance by Tom Mix and his horse, "Tony".

"Tony walked onto the stage so quietly that I didn't even see him," Paul remembered. "I found out later he was wearing sponge rubber covers over his hooves to prevent the horseshoes from scratching the polished stage floor. And they prevented him from slipping."

Tom Mix's performance showcased his prowess with a six-shooter and lariats. His finale was a "standing rope" act, and the famous cowboy's prop fell right into Paul's lap!

But most of the stars Paul saw were on the screen above him…Buster Keaton, Wallace Reid, Marie Dressler, Mack Swain, Francis X. Bushman, Lillian Gish, Colleen Moore, Mabel Normand, Vilma Banky, Clara Bow. He considered Mary Pickford and John

Barrymore the best dramatic actors, and Charlie Chaplin the top comedian.

Paul's theater career ended when Vitaphone Records began making recordings to accompany the movies. These records were placed on a "reproducer" with special care to synchronize each record with the film. At first, the sound and pictures were often mismatched, leaving the audience confused.

Paul went on to become a church organist, but he never forgot those days of playing for silent films.

MARIE DRESSLER had no trouble being heard when talkies arrived.

RUDOLPH VALENTINO thrilled girls as "The Sheik" in heyday of silents.

She Had a Front-Row Seat for Every Show

MY FATHER played pipe organs in theaters in Los Angeles, California during the silent movie era. The organ was in the center of the pit, and Mother and I sat right behind it in the front row so I could watch Dad work.

That grand instrument had three or four keyboards, plus loads of stops, tabs and pedals. This was before stereo was invented, but the sound came from both sides of the stage. The organ could mimic the sounds of church bells or a lion's roar.

I watched Dad and imitated his every move, my hands flying across imaginary keys and my feet kicking imaginary pedals. No wonder no one sat near us!

When the talkies came, they ended the age of theater pipe organs. No more concerts during intermission.

Once wonderfully ornate, theaters, too, have become plain and are no longer places where you dress up to go. Grandly uniformed ushers no longer escort you to your seat, and somehow, the glamour is gone.

But I'll always have my memories of the days when Lon Chaney's mask was removed in *The Phantom of the Opera* or when Tom Mix rounded up the outlaws. Whether the movies were scary, thrilling or touching, Dad made music for them all.   —*Ruth Bishop*
Yuba City, California

GANG'S ALL HERE, and so is their director, Bob McGowan. The *Our Gang* group of child actors changed over the years, but there was always "Pete" the dog.

Ewing Galloway

Burkhardt, our principal, standing in the middle aisle! He pointed his finger at us and told us to get back to school, which we did—pronto! —*Frank Giordano Potomac, Maryland*

Machines on Theater Seats Sold "Kisses"

WHEN I WAS 8 years old in the '20s, I often went with my mother and grandmother to a movie house in Philadelphia, Pennsylvania called Nixon's Grand. The show featured vaudeville acts along with a movie and assorted shorts.

The show was of little interest to me, really. What I most cared about were the candy machines attached to the back of each seat that dispensed Hershey's Kisses!

When a nickel was inserted in the slot and the handle twisted, out rolled a cardboard tube filled with eight or so chocolate drops, individually wrapped in shiny tinfoil. I always had a nickel saved for the candy machine, and sometimes I managed to get an extra nickel from Granny. —*Walter Ribeiro Sr. Pennsauken, New Jersey*

Dad Read Titles to Tot During Silent Movies

MY DAD took me to see the silent films at "The Dust House" in Cambridge, Massachusetts when I was very young. He would read the subtitles to me so I knew what the actors were saying. My favorites were Our Gang and Charlie Chaplin.

The pianist played galloping tunes for the Westerns and slow songs for the love scenes. One night at the movies, we saw a cat wander onto the stage. It sat down, watched the picture for a few minutes, then nonchalantly walked off!

When the "talkies" arrived, the sound at first was so distorted that only a word or two could be understood. But we still thought it was a miracle to hear something. After a few months, the sound improved and everyone enjoyed it so much. —*Jim Boleyne Dallas, Texas*

Chaplin's Pratfalls Drove Budding Musician to Tears

HOLLYWOOD was a great place to grow up in the 1920s. Movies were shot right on the streets and in the neighbor-hoods, and back then I saw Clara Bow and many other old-time actors.

My fondest memory is of watching from the playground at my school on Sunset Boulevard as Charlie Chaplin climbed a steep set of stairs carrying a double bass. He'd walk up a dozen steps, trip and fall down the stairs. Then he'd pick up the bass and try again, with the same results.

To a future symphony orchestra player, this was very upsetting. I was in tears until the teacher explained the bass was made of rubber.

Funny, but I wasn't worried about Charlie Chaplin! —*Ruth Lowder Calabash, North Carolina*

It Was "Curtains" for Truant Movie Fans

IN THE MID-1920s, my friends and I would often "bag" school (play hooky) and go to one of the two movie houses in town. Admission was only 6¢.

One afternoon we didn't return to school after lunch and went to the matinee instead. About a half hour into the show, the screen went blank and the houselights came up.

Imagine our surprise to see Mr.

HIGH HOPES. Evelyn Brooks of Jensen Beach, Florida wore this outfit when her parents entered her in a local theater's *Our Gang* contest in 1929. The 4-year-old came in second. "Since I wailed and cried when the audience began clapping wildly, I lost my one and only bid for fame," Evelyn recalls wryly.

Attendants Kept Air Fresh By Spraying Disinfectant

MOVIE THEATERS were different in the 1920s.

Mama and Pap would take my sister, Dotty, and me to the movies. Their favorite movie house was the Chester Theatre. Admission was a nickel per person, and the first movie that I remember seeing was the *Thief of Baghdad* with Douglas Fairbanks Sr.

Theaters weren't air-conditioned then, so during summer, attendants walked through the aisles with a spray gun, squirting disinfectant to freshen the air.

Refreshments were sold during the movie, and you could hear voices calling out, "Ice cream! Five cents a cone!" It wasn't unusual to hear a parent's distraught voice, either, usually calling something like, "Michael, where are you? It's time to come home!"
—*Barnet Chernick, Brooklyn, New York*

Unmasked "Phantom" And Marvelous Music Made Memories

SILENT MOVIES were our biggest entertainment. I'll never forget Lon Chaney in *The Phantom of the Opera*. I walked into the theater just as the mask was pulled from his horrible face, and I turned around and dashed right back out. They almost didn't get me back in! After all these years, I still remember that awful face.

Then came the wonderful Saturday afternoon in autumn 1927 when I traveled 40 miles to Terre Haute, Indiana to see the first "talking picture", *The Jazz Singer*. It was pure heaven to hear Al Jolson sing *April Showers*, *Mammy*, *Sonny Boy* and *Rainbow Round My Shoulder*.

Sound wasn't heard through all of this picture, only in parts. Soon "all-talk" pictures were coming out. These first talking movies were musicals, and we loved them. —*Maxine Myers Dugger, Indiana*

THE PHANTOM gave Maxine Myers a real fright. Read her tale at left.

Valentino Fans Wept At News of His Death

RUDOLPH Valentino was admired by everyone during the '20s. Who could forget him as the sheik who swept a beautiful woman off her feet, carrying her away on his horse to his desert hideaway?

Valentino's intensely romantic roles stirred the imaginations and hidden longings of every woman who saw him. He wore his dark hair slicked back, in the popular style of the time, and had hypnotic dark eyes.

I learned of his death while riding home on a streetcar with my aunt, who saw the headline in a newspaper someone else was reading. While pointing it out to me, she burst into tears.

She was not alone—others in the car sobbed openly. People closely identified with their idols in those days.
—*Helen Riser, Ocala, Florida*

Player-Piano Operator Was Paid 50¢ a Night

IN 1920, I was hired to operate the player piano at the local movie house for 50¢ a night. I'd walk a mile to the theater every night, through rain, cold, snow and heat. The walk back to my home in the country was dark, long and lonely.

At first I pedaled the piano, but later it was powered by electricity. However, I still received 50¢ a night, to the envy of all my friends. —*Willmuth Crook Providence, Utah*

LITTLE ANGELS. Clyde Clark (far right, front row) began singing with the Boys Choir of Grace Episcopal Cathedral in Topeka, Kansas at age 8—even though his family was Presbyterian! "We lived across from the cathedral, and singing in the choir was fun—thanks to organist George Barnes," says Clyde. "We always raced to the cathedral grounds after school for some touch football or baseball. 'Barney', as we called our leader, participated in the games, too—what fun! Thanks to Barney's influence, I've been singing all my life—and still do today, at the First Presbyterian Church in Bradenton, Florida."

Ain't We Got Fun!

"HARD TIME" party held in my folks' attic provided cheap fun in '24, says Jan Amundsen, Horseshoe Bend, Ark. Mom is "Chinaman" in second row; Dad is "Charlie Chaplin" in derby (left rear).

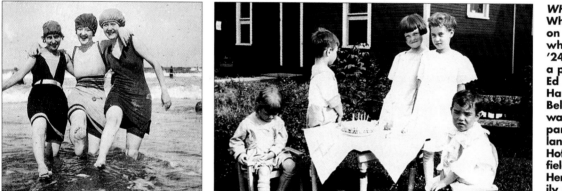

BURNING BEAUTIES. The writing on the back of photo above left notes these '20s bathing beauties got dandy sunburns. Jane Ettesvold of Tucson, Arizona sent photo and wonders *how* in those suits?

WHOOPED IT UP. When all us kids on the block had whooping cough in '24, Mom threw us a party (left), says Ed Adams of Gig Harbor, Wash. Below: Cedar Point was an amusement park near Cleveland, explains Mary Hoffman of Mayfield Heights, Ohio. Her husband's family posed on trackless train in '21.

MELON HEADS. My cousins got caught in a neighbor's melon patch in 1920, laughs Georgia Presley of Little Rock, Arkansas. The owner, a photographer, let them keep the loot if they'd pose for this shot.

LEAVING CEDAR POINT AFTER A BIG DAY

COMING HOME BROKE

Trip to Circus Swept Tot Off Her Feet

By Elizabeth Towzey, Tampa, Florida

IT WAS Circus Day in our small city of Johnstown, Pennsylvania, and the year was 1923.

I was 4 years old and too young to understand what all the excitement was about as my older brother and sister talked about the big show.

My father and grandfather had been looking forward to the circus, too, ever since the huge posters went up all over town. Grandpa wanted to treat his grandchildren to the fun, and Daddy wanted to relive the excitement.

As a boy, he'd earned his admission by doing odd jobs around the circus

---

> *"The loud barkers made me want to run to the gate..."*

---

lot. When he couldn't get a job, he usually succeeded in slipping under the edge of the tent.

Now Daddy and Grandpa were ready to take the kids to the Greatest Show on Earth. Mother thought it was a good idea—until she realized they planned to take *me*.

"Betty's too little," she said. "You'll get interested in the performance and forget to keep an eye on her. The other two can go, but I won't let you take the baby."

Mother Gave in

Unfortunately for my mother, I'd been eavesdropping, and walked into the room in heartrending sobs. "Now look what you've done," Grandma said crossly. "How are you going to tell her she can't go along?"

Mother knew it was a losing battle. "You two men keep her between you," she said. "And don't you dare let go of her hand. If anything happens to Betty, I'll never forgive you."

We walked the few blocks to the trolley, Gwen and Billy in front, and Daddy and Grandpa obediently holding my hands. In 20 minutes, we were at the park.

The music, sounds of the animals and the loud voices of the barkers made me want to run to the gate.

Once inside the Big Top, we found seats halfway up the bleachers. Daddy carried me so my feet wouldn't slip between the boards. Daddy and Grandpa sat me between them, where they were sure I'd be safe.

Loved the Elephants

We had good seats, right above the center ring. I loved the horses and their trick riders. Then came the dancing bear and a dog act. I covered my eyes as the tigers jumped through flaming hoops, but I loved watching the lumbering elephants and the clowns.

Then Daddy pointed out the people climbing high ladders. "Those are trapeze artists," he told me. "In a minute, you'll see them flying through the air and catching each other!"

But I didn't. At that moment, I went flying through the air myself—straight down between the boards of the bleachers! I landed on my back in soft saw-

dust, wondering how I'd gotten there. I wasn't hurt, but sure was frightened—all I could see were legs and feet!

Before I could make a sound, a man in a circus uniform picked me up.

"Hey, up there!" he yelled to the people above us. "Did someone lose a little girl?"

I saw my father's startled face looking down, then he and Grandpa pulled me back up. My rescuer explained he'd been chasing a boy who'd sneaked in without paying. The boy ran under the bleachers and reached up and grabbed my feet as he tried to climb up and scramble away from his pursuer.

"I'm sure he didn't mean to hurt her," the man said. "I don't think he even knew she fell."

We didn't stay to see the trapeze artists. Grandpa and Daddy agreed there'd been enough "flying" for one day.

When the circus returned the next summer, the whole family went—and *Mother* never let go of my hand! ⚞

BIG TOP. The circus was a big attraction to kids like Elizabeth Towzey in '23. Read how she missed part of the show when she did a "flying act" of her own.

Harold M. Lambert

AUDIENCE PARTICIPATION. When a band like this heated up in the '20s, the dancers got right in with the boys. One is even being served dinner by the clarinet player...and on bended knee, at that. *Hot diggety!*

Cab Calloway and Band Performed in Bathrobes!

I WORKED at the Fox Audubon Theatre in New York City during the 1920s. In 1929, after a performance by Cab Calloway, we started to show a film, but discovered there was no sound. The Vitaphone was broken.

While repairmen were being summoned, I went backstage and asked Mr. Calloway if he and some of his band would go back on stage with the emcee. They hurried right out—still wearing their bathrobes—and sang, danced and told jokes until the sound was repaired. Not one person left the theater. Now that's what I call showmanship!
—*Arthur Pinkerton*
El Paso, Texas

Tune from Victrola Days Is Still a Hit with Her

BACK IN 1921 when I was 4, my parents bought a Victrola. When Dad got paid each week, he'd buy a new record for 25¢. Soon we had quite a selection of popular tunes.

I wasn't tall enough to reach the turntable, so Grandpa built a stool that allowed me to put on records. How I loved that Victrola!

I played my favorite, *Ragtime Cowboy Joe*, so often that my mother got sick of it and starting hiding it. I always managed to find it, and eventually learned the words so I could sing along.

I still sing along with *Ragtime Cowboy Joe*, but now it's on a player piano roll. I suspect my neighbors have the same reaction to it that Mom did, and wish they could hide the piano roll!
—*Maxine Van Tornhout*
St. Petersburg, Florida

Loud Music from Piano Muffled Conversations

WHEN I HEAR tunes like *My Wild Irish Rose* or *Smiles*, I'm reminded of the player piano in the home where I boarded during high school. Three other country girls boarded there, too, so we had lots of fun—but little privacy.

When one of our boyfriends called on us and it was too cold to sit in the porch swing to talk, we'd sit on the piano bench, put on a roll, turn up the volume to "loud" and pedal away, conversing in perfect privacy.
—*Marie Freesmeyer, Jerseyville, Illinois*

"I Got Guy Lombardo's Autograph on My Purse!"

ON A BEAUTIFUL summer night in 1927, my date and I went to the Gunter Hotel roof garden in San Antonio, Texas to dance to the music of Guy Lombardo, "the most beautiful music this side of Heaven".

The evening was just as wonderful as I'd anticipated. I not only got to hear the lovely music, but was privileged to meet Mr. Lombardo and get his autograph. I didn't have anything for him to sign, so he autographed my little beaded evening bag—which I still have!
—*Sug Querner, San Antonio, Texas*

GUY FAN. Back in '27, Sug Querner (above and at right) got to meet Guy Lombardo. He signed her beaded evening bag, which she's kept all these years.

UNION GIRL. When she started playing the cello on radio in 1927, Elizabeth Smith was paid union wages and rode the streetcar home. Elizabeth, seen here in her 1929 high school graduation picture, also enjoyed strumming the ukulele on her front porch.

Teen Played Cello on Radio and at Theater

I STARTED playing the cello on radio stations in 1927 when I was still in high school. I earned union wages—$3 for the first hour, $1.50 for each additional hour. There was no "canned music" for stations to use then.

One of my jobs was performing with a string trio for a station's sign-off at midnight. Then I rode the streetcar home alone.

I also performed with the pit orchestra at the Coliseum Theater in Evansville, Indiana, playing for everyone from Liberace and Lily Pons to Marian Anderson. Minnie Pearl brought groups like "Sons of the Pioneers" to the Coliseum every week.

I had a ukulele, too, and played *Yes, Sir, That's My Baby* and other songs while sitting on the front porch with friends, drinking lemonade.
—*Elizabeth Smith, Claremont, California*

College Girls Enjoyed Era's "Silly Songs"

DURING COLLEGE, I sometimes played my banjo ukulele and sang while my female house mates danced. Often we just all sang together, mostly popular songs. There was a host of silly tunes, like *There Is a Tavern in the Town, Willy the Weeper, My Name Is Samuel Hall* and *The Night That Willie Died.*

Some of the popular collegiate songs were *Varsity, The Maize and Blue* and *Sweetheart of Sigma Chi.* Just one of our favorites was a tune called *Collegiates.* I still remember the words:

Collegiates, collegiates,
Yes, we are collegiates;
Nothing intermediate—no, ma'am!
Trousers baggy, all our clothes are raggy—
But we're rough and ready—Yea, hot dog!
Garters are the things we never wear.
And we haven't any use for
RED HOT FLANNELS!
Seldom ever, ever in a hurry
Never, never worry
We're collegiates—RAH, RAH, RAH!
—*Helen Riser, Ocala, Florida*

Dancers "Cut a Rug" to Popular Musician's Tunes

MY MOTHER'S COUSIN, Obie Utterback, was a natural musician. He and his partner kept the residents of Monroe County, Missouri dancing for 15 or 20 years.

If you were going to a dance during the 1920s, you were going out to "cut a rug". When you "got your nickel's worth" there, that meant the musicians were rotating, and the dancers didn't have to wait while the musicians took a break.
—*Louise Foster Moberly, Missouri*

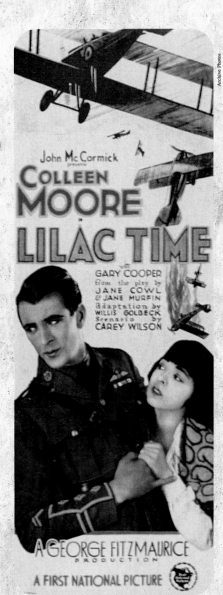

John McCormick presents
COLLEEN MOORE in LILAC TIME
with GARY COOPER from the play by JANE COWL & JANE MURFIN adaptation by WILLIS GOLDBECK Scenario by CAREY WILSON
A GEORGE FITZMAURICE PRODUCTION
A FIRST NATIONAL PICTURE

"COOP". By the time Gary Cooper made *Lilac Time* in 1928, he had played in 17 movies...and made seven of them that year alone! Coop would continue to star in movies until his death in 1961.

SHARING THE SPOTLIGHT. Musician Obie Utterback couldn't resist posing with a movie star while visiting his sister and brother-in-law's theater in Blodgett, Missouri, jokes second cousin Louise Foster.

This Orchestra Made Music With Kitchen Utensils

By Roger Sherman, Redmond, Oregon

MY MOTHER was part of our church's hilarious Kitchen Cabinet Orchestra in Hurffville, New Jersey. They first performed in October 1925, raising $57 for the church.

Congregations in other towns asked the group to perform for their fund-raising efforts, and they were happy to oblige. They became quite popular and played for several years.

The orchestra was fun to watch, and it was fun for the participants, too. The women's red jackets had tin ice cream spoons sewn to the front, and their stylish hats were made from brown paper bags decorated with bows made of spoons.

All their "instruments" were household articles, mostly kitchen utensils. A covered washtub served as a drum, a carpet sweeper became a bagpipe, and an ironing board and scrub brush doubled as a bass violin and bow. Clothespins, sieves and funnels were also used, although I can't recall exactly what was done with them.

All the members played kazoos, except when one of the women played a "violin solo" on a baking pan. The audience always marveled at the beautiful sound she got out of that thing. That was because someone else was playing a *real* violin well out of sight!

The orchestra played old favorites like *Down by the Old Mill Stream* and *Let Me Call You Sweetheart*. Their show sometimes included a Tom Thumb wedding, and my mother drafted me to play (rather reluctantly) Tom. I was the only male in the bunch! ✐

COOKING UP TUNES. The "Kitchen Cabinet Orchestra" used household items and kitchen gadgets to make music in New Jersey during the '20s. Roger Sherman's mother (back row, fourth from left) was a member, and Roger himself was drafted to play the groom in a Tom Thumb wedding. He's wearing the top hat in the front row.

Chapter Six

How We Got Around

How We Got Around

TROLLEYS and trains, T's and planes...those were some of the ways we tooled about in the '20s. Of course, real horsepower was still popular, but "Old Dobbin" was about to give way to cars and tractors for good as the auto began making us a mobile society.

RURAL ROAMERS. A trip to the country was suddenly no big deal in the '20s. On a warm spring day, this couple had only to start up the Model A and drive out of town a little ways to find a nice shade tree to park under. Sitting on the running board and having a chat was a great way to spend the afternoon.

Americans suddenly had new ways to scratch their "wandering" itch in the '20s. They put the horses out to pasture for good and cranked up the Tin Lizzie. They built new and better roads hither and yon. And, wow! They grew wings.

No single event dramatized it more than Charles Lindbergh's solo flight from Long Island to Paris. "Lindy" became a national hero—and my first hero. Not that people hadn't flown across the ocean before, but dauntless Lindy did it *alone*, fighting weather and sleeplessness and mind-numbing discomfort.

What a guy! That same year an aunt gave me a pony for Christmas, and without hesitation I named him Lindy.

I even built my own little model of the *Spirit of St. Louis* out of scraps of lumber, whittling a propeller that spun when I ran around the yard making my own airplane noises.

And, of course, I *had* to have a "Lindy" aviator cap complete with earflaps and isinglass goggles.

Lindbergh's feat had such an impact on an entire nation that air travel increased by *400%* in the year after his flight. The popular passenger plane of the era was the Ford Tri-Motor (the "Tin Goose"), equipped with wicker chairs and big windows. They even served sandwiches to the passengers.

Meanwhile, new makes and models of automobiles proliferated. The most spectacular car in my town was a Cord, a low-slung sportster with huge chrome pipes coming out the sides of the engine compartment. The rich banker drove a Packard.

"It Was Owned by a Little Old Lady..."

An elderly lady who attended our church owned an electric auto. A mysterious, stern-lipped dowager, she came to church garbed in black from hat to shoes. After services, she walked outside to the car, which looked somewhat like a giant black phone booth on wheels, and silently drove away.

I suggested to Dad that we should get one. He explained we couldn't because we lived in the country and it would require too long an extension cord to drive to town. *Oh.* Of course.

Locally, the ultimate test of a car was whether or not it could make it up Lord's Hill outside of Dixon without shifting into low gear. (Apparently, they shaved the hill down considerably in the last 60 years—so it's no longer a tough challenge these days.)

I can't remember much about our family car of the '20s...not even what make it was. But it had four doors, a window shade for the back window, and small flower vases on the post between the front and back doors. A jack and other essential tools were stored behind the backseat, where they rattled and clanked with every bump.

It was a sturdy brute, eagerly plowing through winter drifts and the deep-rutted muddy country roads that could be counted on when spring thaws came.

But those who couldn't afford cars weren't left in the lurch, either. Streetcars and city buses provided cheap reliable transportation for working people. Best of all were the double-deck "rubberneck" buses in downtown Chicago. A ride atop one of those is the only clear memory I have of my first visit to the Windy City.

The memories that follow will take you back to this exciting decade when America took to the skies and highways. And it's easy to get there...just turn the page.

—Clancy Strock

Harold M. Lambert

ALL TIED UP. Fitzgerald Harder wasn't going far on this pony, as it's tied to a tree, but his memory below tells of fast-paced adventure on a trolley.

Ballpark-Bound Boy Saw a Bargain He Couldn't Pass Up

I WAS 9 years old in 1927, growing up in Hammond, Indiana. The prospect of going into Chicago alone on the streetcar was real adventure.

A newspaper, *The Chicago Herald and Examiner*, had selected me and some other boys to attend a major league game in Chicago. Both my parents worked and couldn't go to the game with me, so they said I could go with a group of friends, providing I stayed with them so I'd make the right streetcar connections—I'd have to transfer twice.

They counted out the correct number of tokens and gave me 50¢ in spending money. My mother walked with me to the corner, and as I boarded, she made me sit near the motorman.

I made my first transfer without a hitch. But then we passed a butcher shop, with a sign advertising neck bones at 5¢ a pound. What a bargain! I yanked on the cord, the motorman stopped and before my friends could talk me out of it, I was running to the butcher shop!

After making my purchase, I was more than a little confused about how to get home. I backtracked several blocks, lugging my 10-pound package. Finally, a policeman helped me get on the right car. By the time I got home, my friends were already back from the game! Both Mother and Father were waiting for me at the corner. One of my friends told them I'd left the streetcar and never made it to the game.

I wasn't allowed to travel alone again, but that 10-pound sack of neck bones established me as the thrifty shopper in the family, and our larder was in much better shape for a few days.
—Fitzgerald Harder
Arkansas City, Kansas

Tall Trestle Took Travelers to Terminal

IN 1927 and '28, I commuted daily to the Normal School in Newark, New Jersey, taking the trolley car over a high trestle to the terminal in Hoboken.

I boarded at the last stop in Jersey City, and by then the cars were full, so I rode on the rear platform, squeezed in among the other commuters. There was nothing to hold on to, so with books in one arm and briefcase in the other, I just swayed as the car traveled the mile to the terminal.

Everyone left through the front door, paying the regular fare of 5¢ or student fare of 3¢.
—Margaret Criswell
Whiting, New Jersey

Streetcars Supplied Mining Towns' Link to the City

THE RUMBLING swaying orange streetcar was often our only means of transportation. We thought little of walking a mile to catch the trolley for our occasional trips to town for shopping or, if we were very lucky, a movie.

Uniontown, Pennsylvania was surrounded by coal mines and many glowing, smoky coke ovens. A network of streetcar lines went out like spokes on a wheel to the various "patch" towns.

The cars often were filled with babushka-wearing women of various ethnic backgrounds, chatting amiably with friends in the language of their native lands. As I rode with them, I often wondered what they were saying. Were the smiles because of a productive garden, a new baby or an upcoming wedding?

The front of each car had a board listing all the little towns on its particular route. I always read and re-read these signs, and sometimes even asked the conductor if a particular car was the one for me. I always feared getting on the wrong car, although I never did.
—Mary Barr
Farmington, Pennsylvania

Elevated Road to Jersey City Heights, N

STEEP RIDE. Three trolley car lines converged to take passengers across this tall mile-long trestle over Hoboken, New Jersey. Margaret Criswell, who provided the photo, said she often made the trip standing on the rear platform because the trolley was full.

ON TRACK. Eleanor Riddle's father, Fred Williams (left), worked as a trolley conductor in Peoria, Illinois in 1921. The money changer around his waist held nickels, dimes, quarters and tokens. The fare was one token, or 10¢. That's the motorman, Jess Pierce, on the right.

Trolley Had Charm All Its Own

By Eleanor Riddle, Port Charlotte, Florida

DURING the Roaring '20s, the *clang, clang, clang* of the trolley was a familiar sound. Streetcars, as we called them, were the principal means of transportation in cities then. Very few families were affluent enough to own an automobile.

My father was a streetcar conductor in Peoria, Illinois. He was young and handsome, and proud of his natty uniform and important job. But there were frustrations, too.

The cars ran on a tight schedule and were supposed to be at each corner at a specified time. Dad often heard cries of "Here comes somebody else!" as a latecomer raced to catch up to the car before it pulled out. Sometimes Dad waited, but to keep to his schedule he often had to leave dawdlers behind.

Another frustration was the mischievous boys who sometimes disconnected the cars from their overhead lines. Those lines supplied the cars' power source, so if the lines were unhooked, the cars didn't run.

The pranksters often struck while a car sat idle at the end of the line, waiting for the return trip. While the operators were relaxing and eating their lunch, the boys would sneak up and disconnect the trolley. It was easy to disengage, but could be difficult to reconnect, especially in winter.

Advertisers, realizing they had a captive audience, posted colorful signs above the windows all around the interior of the cars.

Lydia Pinkham's Compound, Morton's Salt, Sloan's Liniment, Carter's Little Liver Pills, P&G Soap and Quaker Oats are just a few of the names I remember.

We lived a short distance from the streetcar route. Mother often sent my sisters and me to meet Dad's car at lunchtime with a hot meal.

As a special Christmas Eve treat, the whole family always rode on his streetcar to the very end of the line, where the wealthy folks with grand homes tried to outdo each other with their holiday decorations. We "oohed" and "aahed" all the way.

In the early '30s, buses began to replace the trolleys. Perhaps they were more efficient, but they'd never come close to the charm of streetcars. ⇒

Little Traveler Thrilled by Train

By Ann Reeves, Richardson, Texas

PLATFORM PERFORMER. Already a seasoned traveler at 5, Ann Reeves (above) enjoyed tossing pennies from the end platform, like the one below.

BY THE AGE of 5, I was a veteran train traveler, and each trip I took in the late 1920s was sheer delight.

It didn't matter where we went. The atmosphere of the crowded station was enchanting—the pungent odor of coal cinders and smoke, the clamor of baggage carts, the hissing steam, the colorful red caps, the surge of humanity.

Train men scurried about among the "seeing-offs" and "welcome-backs", filling the air with more excitement.

There was such expectancy as the train prepared to pull out of the station. Each tentative jerk, lurch, groan and shudder told us something momentous was about to take place.

The flagman waved his lantern, the conductor shouted, "All aboard!", and I clutched my doll and ran to keep up with Daddy.

Drew Friendly Waves

We waved from our window to anyone and everyone, always getting a response and a grin. I especially remember smiles and waves from a woman shelling peas on her rickety front stoop …two barefoot, blue jean-clad boys

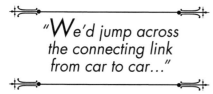

"We'd jump across the connecting link from car to car…"

with fishing poles…even a bunch of kids skinny-dipping in a woodland creek. Wow! How they ducked into the water when we came around the bend!

My sister and I usually bunked together in a lower berth, sleeping with the soles of our feet touching so each of us had a window to peer out. We inched the green shades up just enough to watch the scenery rush by as we were lulled to sleep to the *ding, ding, ding* of bells at crossings.

During the day, we played double solitaire on a small table the porter placed between us. And we always welcomed the "news butcher", though why he was called that we never knew. He had a basket filled with oranges, grapes, candy bars, comic books and little train lanterns filled with candies.

Going to the dining car was an adventure. With squeals, we'd sway toward the heavy doors between the cars, then jump quickly over the connecting link. How bold we felt when less-experienced travelers seemed to pale at this!

In the diner, we were so enchanted with the way the waiters balanced their trays and elegantly presented steaming food with a flourish. They even gave us finger bowls!

Sis and I loved the observation platform at the tail end of the train. It was a neat little back porch tacked onto the last car. While standing there, we'd throw pennies onto the tracks for other children to find. It was delightful to imagine their excitement at finding "treasure" on the tracks. ⚒

Lyman E. Cox

Boxcar Bottleneck Made Children Late for School

I GREW UP along a main railroad line in southeastern Pennsylvania. There were at least six sets of tracks for passenger, mail and freight trains. We watched as mailbags were snatched from their posts and incoming mailbags were tossed out. I gazed at the passenger trains in awe, waving to people sitting at white-draped tables in the dining car.

Nearby, the trains stopped at a depot to take on water and other necessities. A long line of boxcars would block the crossing, often making us late for school. Our mothers signed our tardy slips: "Held up by freight at RR crossing."

While we waited, we passed the time by playing or jumping rope. It was fun to read the slogans on the cars, too, like "Pride of the South" and "Great White Way". —*Mrs. Johnny Johnston, Crawfordville, Florida*

Train Ride Was Boy's Dream Come True

By Edward White, Santa Rosa, California

AS A BOY of 7, I gloried in the tales of the Pine Tree Limited, which ran between Portland, Maine and Boston, Massachusetts. It was a "crack train", which meant it ran on a strict timetable, always arriving within 120 seconds of its posted schedule.

She was the pride and joy of the Boston and Maine Railroad. New Englanders were proud to boast they had ridden the fabulous Pine Tree Limited, and spread her lore of speed, comfort and punctuality.

The Pine Tree made regular stops in my hometown of Portsmouth, New Hampshire, but they were brief ones. Nothing was allowed to impede its schedule. Two minutes—120 seconds—was allotted before the sound of *"Board!"* echoed down the track and the train once again rolled.

I'd stand and watch the steam billow forth as the engineer blew the cylinders clear with a charge of steam. The huge driving wheels slowly began to turn in smooth acceleration.

A blast on the steam whistle let the freight yard ahead know the Pine Tree was moving out of the station. Her giant Baldwin 6000 Series engine was headed for Boston.

Ran Like Thoroughbred

I always dreamed of someday riding that train. The local trains were slow and stopped at every hamlet along the way. But the Pine Tree wouldn't poke along at 30 mph. She sped through the countryside at 70 mph—faster if she was making up time. Riding it would have been as thrilling as riding a fire engine!

One night in November 1926, my mother, sister and I went to the station to take the slow "milk run train" to Concord, New Hampshire. Our train was waiting there, so we boarded.

As we walked to our seats, I noticed the appointments were nicer than I remembered. We'd barely seated ourselves when the train started moving.

It quickly gathered speed, moving at least twice as fast as usual. I told my mother, "This train is moving out just like the Pine Tree does!"

When the conductor came by to punch our tickets, he told my mother we were on the wrong train. We *were* on the Pine Tree…and bound for Boston!

The train made a fast unscheduled stop at Greenland, 10 miles from Portsmouth, so we could get off. The conductor quickly told the station manager to flag down another train to take us home, and then he was gone. The Pine Tree Limited sped down the tracks and disappeared into the night, making up time.

It was only a 10-mile ride, but being on the Pine Tree Limited was all I'd imagined. It was a dream come true. ⇥

Newlyweds' Train Trip Left Them Stuck in Snow

I WAS MARRIED March 19, 1929 in Durango, Colorado. That evening, my bride and I boarded a train for Rico, Colorado, near the town where I was working for a lumber company. About halfway into our trip, the train came to a jarring stop. We had run into a snowslide!

The conductor told us what had happened, but said not to worry—there was plenty of coal for the potbellied stoves in both cars.

There were no telephones or CB radios, although the conductors all had telephone headsets for emergencies. It was pitch-black and snowing, but the conductor climbed the nearest telephone pole and called for help.

He returned to assure us help was on the way, although he couldn't say how long we'd be stuck. The 22 passengers shared their food, sang songs and told stories by the light of the oil lamps to pass the time.

About 11 a.m. the next day, the snowplow and work train arrived, bringing sandwiches, fruit, milk and coffee. The engine was put back on the track, and we went on our way.

When we arrived in Rico at about 9 p.m., the one hotel in that small town was full. When I told the owner my wife and I had married the day before and had been on the snowbound train, he had two male guests double up so we would have a room!

—Clyde Proctor, Santa Rosa, California

SNOWBOUND STEAMER. Train travel in the mountains, like Colorado's Durango & Silverton above, often meant delays because of snowslides. Clyde Proctor shares his snowy experience from 1929, which also happened in Colorado.

THE DASHING PILOT at left looked dapper in his flying helmet. This brave aviator stole the heart of little Gertrude Ward, a 12-year-old tomboy who took a memorable flight with him in the '20s.

An Air Ride to Remember

By Gertrude Ward, Fort Myers, Florida

MY DAD was Chief of Police in the small Indiana town where I grew up during the '20s. Nothing exciting ever happened there—that is, until an incredible afternoon when I was about 12.

This day started out like any other. Mother was baking pies and had run low on fuel, so Dad and I started up our old Chevrolet and headed downtown to buy kerosene for the cookstove.

Driving down Main Street, we heard a strange loud noise. When we saw people running out of their houses and looking up at the sky, we knew it must be an airplane. Dad stopped the car so I could get out and look (it was the first plane I'd ever seen).

The plane kept circling low, then headed for a field outside of town to land. By the time Dad and I reached that field, a large crowd had gathered—our town hadn't had this much excitement since Dad caught some chicken thieves the year before.

We made our way to where the airplane stood and I was instantly spellbound. What a thrill to be so close to such a magnificent flying machine!

I heard someone speak and I looked up. My heart turned a flip-flop. There,

standing before me, was the most handsome young man I'd ever seen. Dressed in a flier's suit, goggles and boots, he sported the most beautiful smile. Wow! Two thrills in one day!

The pilot approached Dad with an air of confidence and introduced himself. Dad shook hands and introduced me as "my tomboy". It wasn't the introduction I'd wanted, but I swallowed my pride, gave the pilot a big smile and said hello.

Oh, for a Ride

While the two men talked, I walked around the plane, touching it very gently. Oh, just to sit inside or, better yet, go for a ride, I thought. Suddenly, my daydreaming was interrupted when I heard my dad ask me, "Would you like to go for a ride?"

I assured him I would and gave him a big bear hug. As I ran to the cockpit, my heart was thumping so fast I could hardly swallow. "Hold on and don't fall out," cautioned the pilot as he helped me aboard.

Then he twisted the old wooden propeller and the engine responded with a roar. Jumping into the cockpit, he adjusted his goggles, gave a carefree wave

to the crowd and we were off!

As we bumped along the rough ground, I said a short prayer (I knew Mother would never forgive Dad if I got killed). Before I knew it, we were airborne. For a moment, all was calm, then the plane shuddered and we climbed higher and higher.

Enjoyed Bird's-Eye View

As we flew over the town, I mustered the courage to look down. Everything looked different and I wondered how Mother and her pies were coming along—and was thankful she had no idea where I was.

Going up in the plane had been fun —coming down was scary. It seemed like we were coming down too fast. When the wheels touched, we bounced a couple of times and rolled to a stop. Whew—what a ride!

The pilot helped me to the ground, patted my shoulder and said, "You're a brave little girl." Dad had said I was a tomboy and now this aviator was calling me a "little girl". Here I'd fallen in love with him and he hadn't even noticed. Before he could turn away, though, I snapped a mental picture of him so I could remember his handsome face forever.

When Dad and I finally got home, Mother didn't believe where I'd been. When we finally convinced her, she was so stunned she forgot to bawl us out for being late with the kerosene. Though we didn't have any pie for supper, we sure had a lot to talk about.

The final chapter of this story takes place on May 21, 1927. My dad came rushing home that day with a newspaper. Sputtering excitedly, he handed it to me and asked, "Have you seen this fellow before?"

The story was about a young man who'd flown solo across the Atlantic to Paris. Alongside was a huge picture of the pilot who'd accomplished this remarkable feat. I took one glance at the picture.

Of course, I recognized him! How could I forget that big smile? It was my hero! I let out a squeal, kissed the picture and then—it dawned on me: I had taken my first airplane ride with Charles A. Lindbergh!

Flight with Barnstormer Thrilled 8-Year-Old

By Phil Gabler
Deerfield Beach, Florida

MY PARENTS, sister and I were enjoying dinner at our home in Hagerstown, Maryland, when Dad casually mentioned, "I hear that an airplane has landed in a farmer's pasture on North Potomac Street on the edge of town. Would you like to go see this barnstormer?"

My mother and sister weren't interested, but I couldn't wait. It was 1923, I was 8 years old, and airplanes were few and far between.

While riding to the field in our four-cylinder Chevrolet coupe, I asked, "Dad, why do they call them barnstormers?"

"Well, they generally fly these contraptions from one farmer's pasture to

---

"The craft was made of welded bicycle tubing and canvas..."

---

another and sleep in the barn overnight. But how they came to be called barnstormers, I never have heard."

By the time Dad and I arrived, a crowd had gathered. The pilot and mechanic were trying to talk the more courageous visitors into taking a 30-minute ride at $2 a head.

The plane was an open-cockpit two-seater with a World War I surplus Liberty engine. The radiator was mounted over the engine between the two wings, where the wind could cool it. The craft's fuselage was made of welded bicycle tubing covered with canvas.

Planes Were Novelties

Airplanes in the 1920s were mostly made by bicycle shops and boat-builders, and were considered more of a risky novelty than anything practical.

The upper wing of this biplane was made of spruce spars and ribs, also covered with canvas. It was held in place with struts and wires.

Soon a woman stepped forward and bought a ride. The pilot said he needed one more person. Dad looked at me and said, "How about it, son? Would you like to go?"

I was up on the wing and climbing in before the pilot could even give me a hand! The pilot gave us goggles and buckled us in, then climbed in behind us. The mechanic stood waiting, hands on the propeller.

"Switch off?" he asked. "Switch off," the pilot replied. The mechanic turned the engine over with the prop a time or two, stopping on a high compression point.

"Switch on?" the mechanic asked. "Switch on," came the reply. With a quick spin of the prop, the engine roared to life.

Off They Went!

We taxied down the field and turned into the wind. With a roar, the plane moved faster and faster until we lifted up and into the sky. The wind howled over our heads and our hair flew every which way as we looked down on the houses that now resembled toys.

The pilot leveled off and we turned and banked and turned and banked, soaring over the city. The wind whistled through the wing struts and wires.

After a bit, the pilot did a long dive with a quick pullout. I felt a little queasy and looked over at my seat partner. She was somewhat green.

The pilot throttled back the engine and we were able to converse for the first time. It didn't much matter, though, because all I could say was, "Wow!"

PORCH SITTER. After he took his first exciting airplane ride, this must have seemed a pretty dull seat for Phil Gabler.

Afterward, I felt like someone special, a member of a small set of exclusive adventurers. I couldn't wait to get home and tell my mother and sister and all my pals at school about the flight.

I was so excited I momentarily forgot it was summer and there was no school, so I'd have to wait a bit before I could brag to my schoolmates about this thrilling accomplishment.

Mother wasn't too pleased with Father for letting me take a ride in that "foolish contraption", but I was happy beyond belief.

A few years later in 1927, when Charles Lindbergh stunned the world with his solo flight across the Atlantic, I felt part of that historic event. ✈

SENSIBLE SWAP. When a local businessman needed a place to store his airplanes, the flying club Nick Vuyosevich (above) belonged to offered its hangar in exchange for flying lessons, says Nick's daughter, Nina Anderson of East Canaan, Connecticut.

Ewing Galloway

Flight Left Boy with Astonishing Souvenir

I OFTEN RODE my bike from our home near Omaha, Nebraska to a racetrack to look at the horses. On one visit in 1925, I noticed biplanes taking off and landing there. To a 12-year-old boy, that was really something. Then I found out they were giving rides over the field and back for $2.

That evening, I begged my dad to let me take a ride. After I promised to do all kinds of extra chores for the rest of my life, he gave me the $2.

The next morning, I was at the track bright and early and was the first to go up, wearing a white sailor's cap pulled over my ears for a makeshift "helmet".

When we landed, I handed the pilot a black Crayola from my pocket and asked him to write his name on my cap. Later, my mom put it in a trunk with outgrown clothes and stashed it in the attic.

In 1945, I was going through that trunk and found the sailor's cap—with the name "Chas. Lindbergh" written on it!
—*L.F. Leonard*
Englewood, Colorado

Theater Patrons Prayed For Lindbergh's Safety

ON MAY 20, 1927, a group from our church was attending a show in New York City. During the intermission, the manager came out and asked everyone to say a silent prayer for the safety of Charles Lindbergh, who was flying solo across the Atlantic.

The next day, we heard that Lindbergh had landed near Paris, France. It was nice to know that maybe, in some small way, our prayers kept him safe and helped him achieve his goal.
—*Margaret Criswell*
Whiting, New Jersey

Schoolchildren Sang Praises of "Lucky Lindy"

I WAS 8 when Lindbergh flew to Paris. Our teacher told us what a great accomplishment this was, and said Lindbergh was a hero. We were sent home early that day, but first we sang a song: "Lucky Lindy flies alone, in a little plane all his own." I can't remember the rest, but we sang our hearts out.
—*Muriel Bordis, Gloversville, New York*

Children Were Baffled by News of Historic Flight

I WAS PLAYING ball with my cousins one Sunday morning when my uncle came out on the porch, waving a newspaper. "Hey, kids," he yelled excitedly, "This guy named Lindbergh just flew an airplane across the ocean!"

We just stood there and looked at him, as we had no idea what he was talking about. My uncle said, "Oh, well, you'll read about it in your history books someday."
—*Leona Lamon*
Adamsville, Alabama

VIVE LINDY. Charles Lindbergh is feted at a reception at the Hotel de Ville in Paris after his historic solo flight across the Atlantic. There would be more of this when he got home.

SOLO NO MORE. The "Lone Eagle" was no longer alone when Lindy got home to his wife, Anne, pictured here at Long Island.

Ewing Galloway

Boy Was Proud to Shake Lindbergh's Hand

By Marvin Thrasher
Portland, Michigan

"DID HE MAKE IT?" I asked Dad as he tucked a blanket around me.

"He made it," Dad assured me, tousling my hair. "Go back to sleep."

I'd dozed off while we waited for word of Charles Lindbergh's safe arrival in Paris. We'd been sitting in the car outside the local newspaper office, where folks without a radio often awaited the latest news.

Men had died seeking the $25,000 prize for the first nonstop crossing of the Atlantic Ocean, so interest was high in Lindbergh's attempt. It seemed that grown-ups talked of nothing but Lindbergh. His flight was their generation's equivalent of a man walking on the moon.

That Christmas, I received a "Lucky Lindy" hat. It was sheepskin inside, brown leather outside and fit tightly over the head, secured by a strap under the chin. Mine was the deluxe model, complete with eye goggles. My baby sister received a "Lucky Lindy" doll.

What Had Teacher Planned?

The following spring, our teacher asked us to wear our Lucky Lindy hats to school, and sent our parents a note explaining why. She wrote in script instead of printing, so we children couldn't read it. That was a good thing, because if we had, we'd have been too excited to get a wink of sleep!

The next day, classes were dismissed so we could watch Lindbergh land at the airport across the street. The crowds were so big that none of us

---

"Lindy smiled and held out his hand..."

---

could get near him, but we did see him get in a car and drive away.

Years later, in sixth or seventh grade, my class took a field trip to Greenfield Village in Dearborn, Michigan. As we got off the train, I saw Lindbergh talking with someone at the other end of the platform. My enthusiasm knew no bounds and I ran straight for him.

"I saw you land your plane once when I was just a little kid," I called out to him.

Lindbergh smiled and held out his hand. I took it, and he placed his other hand over mine and smiled more broadly. At that moment, my teacher arrived and quickly led me by the shirt collar back to my classmates, where I received a stern lecture about staying with the group.

Lindbergh overheard it, and when she paused for breath, he came over and spoke to her. She just nodded, red-faced. Then Lindbergh shook hands with every kid in my class!

Today, whenever I meet someone who boasts of once meeting the Prince of Wales or Marilyn Monroe, I extend my hand and say, "Shake the hand that shook the hand of Lindbergh!" ✈

FOREVER AIRBORNE. The *Spirit of St. Louis,* Lindbergh's historic airplane, still "flies" at the Smithsonian's Air and Space Museum in Washington, D.C., where it continues to thrill flying fans of all ages.

Children Saw Lindbergh's Plane—from the Inside!

VERY EARLY one morning in September 1927, my father woke my two brothers and me and told us to get dressed. I was only 3, and could not imagine why Dad was getting us up at 4:30 a.m.!

Dad told us we were going someplace very exciting, and herded us into our 1922 Chevrolet. Fifteen minutes later, we were at what is now called Lindbergh Field in San Diego, California.

We pulled up alongside a hangar, and a gentleman opened the huge sliding doors so Dad could bring us inside. I was immediately lifted up and placed in the cockpit of an airplane—the *Spirit of St. Louis*! The plane had been brought there after Charles Lindbergh's historic flight.

I remember my father saying, "Son, this is something you should always remember." It wasn't until years later that I appreciated the magnitude of it all.

After each of us kids sat in the plane, we were hurriedly escorted out of the hangar and the doors rapidly closed behind us.

The "event" had been planned the evening before. The security guard had eaten in the restaurant where Dad worked, and when their conversation turned to the plane, Dad talked him into carrying out our secret escapade.

In 1978, when my wife and I visited Washington, D.C., we headed straight for the Smithsonian Institution, where the *Spirit of St. Louis* is now enshrined. When I saw it, I couldn't believe how small it was—in my memory, it seemed so big!

As I stood there, flooded with nostalgia, I felt proud and thankful that my father had given me such a rare experience. It's a moment I'll always remember.
　　　　　　　　　　—*Clarence Duke, Modesto, California*

Family Greeted Lindbergh On His Return to States

AFTER Charles Lindbergh's historic flight, we decided he was a hero we had to see. When we learned he was appearing in St. Louis, we went to see him.

GETTING READY. It was May 20, 1927 and a young pilot was preparing to fly solo across the Atlantic. By the next day, Charles Lindbergh (left background with head down) would be known all over the world.

He stood tall and handsome in riding pants, leather jacket, leather helmet, black spats and brown high-top shoes. His mother stood at his side, wearing a long dress and a hat. She was a beautiful woman, and there was a striking resemblance between mother and son.

The crowd stood at a respectful distance as Lindbergh thanked everyone for coming. Then he invited us to come up, one at a time, to have a good look at the *Spirit of St. Louis*. We queued up in orderly fashion; no one pushed to be first in line. It was a thrill to actually touch the plane.

A man was selling pencils with a picture of Lindbergh, and my sister and I each wanted one. Our parents thought 10¢ was too much to pay for a penny pencil, but we won the argument. I wish I still had that pencil today.

—*R. Lucille Crawley*
Sunset Beach, California

Mail Plane Crash May Have Taught Lindbergh a Lesson

BEFORE Charles Lindbergh became world-famous, I could look into the sky from our central-Illinois farm and see him flying the mail from St. Louis to Chicago. He always stayed between Route 66 and a set of railroad tracks, taking him directly over our farm.

Sometimes, he'd dip his wings, fly low and wave to whomever he could see below. Once he yelled out jokingly, "Is this the way to St. Louis?" I always enjoyed waving back. One day in No-

---

Youthful Imaginations Took Flight in Grounded Plane

By John Hoover, Lebanon, Oregon

WHEN THE local newspaper reported an airplane was coming to town to take up passengers, it caused quite a stir. It was the early 1920s and few people in Chambersburg, Pennsylvania had even *seen* a plane.

A cow pasture near our house would be the landing field. We sat on the porch as the townspeople streamed past, many carrying picnic baskets.

The plane arrived on schedule, but instead of landing, the pilot just flew back and forth, waving as if trying to tell us something. He circled a couple more times, then flew away. We later learned there were so many people on the field that he was afraid to land.

We were disappointed, but an incident a few months later *more* than made up for it. A big two-engine Army bomber made a forced landing a mile from town and broke a propeller on a rail

fence. It was in a remote spot, and the plane sat there for a week, unattended.

It was a golden opportunity for my friends and me. We couldn't resist playing "aviator" in a real airplane—especially one with three open cockpits!

There were plenty of things to investigate. The forward cockpit was

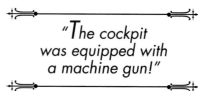

"The cockpit was equipped with a machine gun!"

equipped with a machine gun, and we took turns manning it, pretending to be in an aerial duel with the Red Baron.

What a noisy station that must have been, with two big engines pounding away on either side, not to mention the blasting from the machine gun.

The bombardier sat in the middle cockpit, behind the wings. My buddies

and I found no bombs in the plane, but the notches where they hung were small and not far apart. In the floor was a square hole that was covered with leather and laced shut with rawhide. Bombs were apparently dropped by hand through this hole.

Behind the bombardier sat the pilot, who required few controls. There was a "joystick" that controlled wing flaps and tail elevators, a foot-operated "rudder bar" that moved the tail, and a throttle lever. That was it.

So with a full crew of kids on board and everyone at their "battle stations", we'd pretend to start the engines and take off on a bombing raid over enemy lines. The "pilot" would mimic climbs and dives, banks and turns, and even take a loop or two.

Our fun ended when the Army people returned to make repairs on the plane and flew it away. But they left us with memories to last a lifetime. ✈

POP 'N' JENNY. Byrd "Pop" White ran a garage in Des Moines, Iowa, but his first love was flying a JN4-D, the famous "Jenny" used to train World War I pilots. Jack Boyce of Theodosia, Missouri says his dad, Merrill Boyce, got his pilot's license in the late '20s, thanks to Pop White.

vember 1926, cold rain turned to sleet, and a heavy fog blew in. As Lindbergh was returning to St. Louis, he became disoriented, got off course and ran out of fuel.

He circled, looking for a spot to land, but found nothing. He had no choice but to bail out, tossing the mailbags with him, and let the plane crash.

Lindbergh's parachute brought him down in an Osage hedgerow bordering a field of cornstalks. He was shaken but unhurt except for a few scratches. Trudging through the muck and stubble,

he spied a light in a farmhouse window. Luckily, it was one of the few homes in the area with a phone.

The plane came down near the small community of Covell, damaging a hog house. One wheel and part of the landing gear had crashed through the roof. The mailbags were recovered later.

The following May, I was plowing a field when my uncle drove out and shouted that "Lindy" had just crossed the ocean to Paris nonstop. When I read about his flight, I noted that on *this* trip, he had fuel to spare. Maybe he learned

a lesson from that crash at Covell!
—*Myles Myers, Winter Haven, Florida*

Flag-Waving Students Hailed "America's Hero"

IN MAY 1927, every pupil at P.S. 156 in Brooklyn, New York paraded down nearby Howard Avenue and lined up along the curb. Each of us was given an American flag, with instructions to wave it when "America's hero" drove by. We stood there for more than an hour.

Suddenly, a thunderous ovation erupted. The motorcade sped by and Charles Lindbergh waved to the crowd. "Lucky Lindy" remained my hero for many years. —*Barnet Chernick Brooklyn, New York*

Boys Built Plane to Mark Historic Flight

MY FRIENDS and I in Waterloo, Iowa decided to build an airplane after Lindbergh's memorable flight. It was large enough for one boy to ride in—providing it was pushed, of course.

We used cheesecloth for the wings and fuselage, and had two large "L's" printed on the latter. We told everyone they stood for "Lucky Lindy".

That summer, Waterloo had a parade, and I got to ride down Fourth Street in the plane. I remember the kids crying out, "Look, there's Lucky Lindy!"
—*Gene Katoski, Cleveland, Ohio*

LINDY FANS in Waterloo, Iowa built this plane to honor their hero. From left are Kenny Koch (in cockpit), Chuck Gloor, Russ Boeger, Bob Koch and Gene Katoski, who shared the photo. At far right is Kenny's brother, Paul, who ran into the house in tears when he wasn't allowed to sit in the plane!

High-Flying Duo Was Always Ready for Takeoff

IN THE EARLY '20s, Daddy would take us on Sunday drives in his Chandler. No matter which direction he started out going, we inevitably ended up at the airfield in Dayton, where a few aircraft and pilots were always around.

Mother got bored with this routine, but I loved talking to the pilots with Dad. We inspected every parked craft —usually flimsy open-cockpit biplanes.

We often saw barnstormers who put on daring shows for a small fee. They also took up paying passengers for a penny a pound, and Daddy often took me along on these flights.

I was a skinny fearless tomboy, so I squeezed into the front seat beside him. As the pilot gave each of us a helmet, we trembled with anticipation.

"Contact!" yelled the mechanic.

"Contact!" the pilot yelled back.

With a quick twist of the propeller, the engine sputtered and roared into action, taking us down the field, then gently we would rise into the sky.

There were absolutely no restraints to keep us in the seats, but I never had a moment of fear. I loved looking over the side of the plane and seeing cows grazing. The fields looked like patchwork quilts, and the rivers like ribbons.

I felt like a bird. It was a thrill I'll never forget.

—*F. Jane Clark*
Dayton, Ohio

Adventurous Youth Talked Sister into First Flight

MY BROTHER and I were driving through Rapid City, South Dakota, when we spotted a fair where a pilot was giving 5-minute rides for a penny a pound. My brother wanted to stop, but I was nervous. I'd never flown before, and had heard our neighbor say he never would. "If the plane ever stopped," he reasoned, "how would you get out to crank it?"

My brother finally talked me into it and climbed in front with the pilot. I sat behind them with another passenger.

We didn't go very high, but I remember the other passenger saying, "Look at the Model T's down there. They look like men's shoes running down the road!"

—*Dolores Brady, Gillette, Wyoming*

Tickets to Stage Show Dropped Out of the Sky

IN OUR small town, we rarely saw an airplane. One hot summer day in 1920, the whole town woke to the sound of a plane buzzing back and forth overhead. Most of the kids ran outside to take a look. It was the first plane I'd ever seen.

To our amazement, some papers came fluttering down. They were advertisements for a stage play at the local theater, with "Admit One Free" printed on the bottom. There was a wild scramble to pick up all the tickets.

For years afterward, every time an airplane flew over our town, all of us kids would run into the street, yelling, "Drop some tickets down!"

—*William Fitzgerald*
Manitowoc, Wisconsin

SPECIAL DELIVERY. Back in the '20s, airmail was a big deal because airplanes were relatively new and few. So when a mail plane came to town, people were more interested in the airplane than any letters it carried.

Youngsters Played Prank On Horse-and-Buggy Rides

WHAT FUN we had hitching up our horse, "Lottie", to the buggy and heading off to church three times a week. Dad used to say Lottie could run so fast that she outran the raindrops!

My brother could make a sound like a car horn, and we loved sneaking up behind a slower-moving buggy so he could "honk" at it. The other buggy would practically end up in the ditch trying to get out of the way!

In winter, Lottie pulled our little sleigh over the shortcut across the fields. Sis always got the coveted seat next to Dad, and one of my brothers rode on the horse's back. Mom rode with a lap robe and parasol umbrella.

Gasoline shortages in more modern times bring a wonderful thought to mind: Why don't we just return to those glorious horse-and-buggy days? I'd say, "Glory hallelujah!" —J.K. Walton
Patoka, Illinois

Graf Zeppelin Flew Past School Window

THE ONLY SOURCE of daylight in our small classroom was one tiny window. One day, that light dimmed suddenly, as though night had fallen! We turned toward the window and saw a flying object so big that it blocked the entire window.

The craft moved slowly, but we finally made out the word "GRAF" printed on its tip. It was the famous *Graf Zeppelin*, which had just arrived for a visit from Germany.

The Graf was a hydrogen-inflated commercial airship that made many successful transatlantic flights. The *Hindenburg* came later and was even larger, but airships were no longer built after it was destroyed in an explosion.
—*Barnet Chernick, Brooklyn, New York*

"Sardine Can" Ferried Children to School

WE RODE to school in North Dakota in a horse-drawn bus. In fall and spring, it was a homemade, canvas-roofed bus mounted on a buggy chassis. After the first snow, we changed to a homemade bus mounted on sled runners. We were packed in so tightly we called it the "sardine can".

Tin covered the bus' sides and roof,

and there was one door made of pine boards in the rear. About a foot of straw covered the floor, and we huddled under World War I Army surplus blankets to stay warm. The only window was a small one in front for the driver, with the reins squeezed through a narrow slit underneath.

There was no road maintenance, so the driver simply drove his team whichever way seemed best, avoiding as many large snowdrifts as he could. Sometimes, though, the horses floundered. Then the bigger children would get out and shove the sardine can through.

Sometimes, when blowing snow hampered the driver's vision, the bus would lurch sideways into a drift and tip over. We considered this no catastrophe. We'd simply scamper out, push the tin bus back into place, count noses and be on our way.
—*Erling Rolfsrud*
Farwell, Minnesota

Horse-Drawn Sled Pulled Them to School in Winter

THERE WERE NO snowplows in North Dakota, and after a heavy snow, our road was obliterated. Travel by car was impossible.

To take us 2-1/2 miles to school, my father would put the wagon box on sled runners and hitch up the horses. Then we didn't have to keep to the roads— Father selected the shortest routes across the fields, and off we'd go.

We children bedded down in straw, bundled in horsehide blankets, with hot bricks under our feet. When Father

ON THE FARM. Doris Shepley (right) posed with her little sister in front of the family's first car at their North Dakota farm. The car wasn't usable in winter, however, when snow blanketed all the surrounding roads. Then the family went everywhere in a horse-drawn sled.

got too cold, he jumped down and ran alongside the horses to keep warm. One winter, even sled travel was difficult, and school was canceled for 4 weeks.

I remember traveling to our country church on Christmas Eve in a horse-drawn sled. Everyone's horses were housed in a barn during the service. Afterward, we went to our grandparents' for presents and hot oyster stew.

It was great when the snow melted in spring and we could travel by car again. But the big puddles left behind sometimes forced drivers to detour across the fields—just as we'd done all winter long!
—*Doris Shepley*
Falls Church, Virginia

EDUCATION TRANSPORTATION. This is how Erling Rolfsrud and his friends got to school in 1920s North Dakota. They called it the "sardine can" because it was packed so full. In the winter, the bus was mounted on runners to go over the snow. When it got stuck, the bigger kids had to get out and push.

Mom's Driving Was A Real Washout

By Lorraine Irwin, Long Beach, California

IN THE SUMMER of 1928, Grandma got a new gasoline-powered Maytag washer. It sounded a lot like today's lawn mowers and belched pungent exhaust, but with some shaved yellow soap and a bit of bluing, it cleaned laundry miraculously.

Grandma soon invited all her children to use her marvelous new machine. Mother's turn was scheduled for Tuesday, but Father would be working out of town with a threshing crew. "No problem," he told Mother. "I'll just teach you how to drive."

Grandma lived only a mile and a half away, so Mother reluctantly agreed to give it a try.

My sister Phyllis and I watched from the parlor as Father walked Mother around the Model T, giving her instructions. Then Mother got behind the wheel, and Father pointed out the levers on the steering column and the three pedals on the floor.

Soon Mother was driving in circles in the backyard and then out onto the gravel road. She was laughing when they returned. It seemed she had mastered the Model T.

On Tuesday, Mother looked a bit nervous as she loaded the laundry, Phyllis and me into the backseat. "I want you to sit still," she told us sternly, "and don't say a word!"

She got the car started and took one tentative spin around the yard before pulling onto the road. Everything was fine until we came to a turn, going about 15 mph. We slid around the curve, a back door swung open, and the clothes basket full of laundry flew right through it!

Phyllis grabbed me as I slid toward the open door. Mother reached behind the seat, trying to hang on to us and stop the car at the same time, and inadvertently threw the car into reverse. We jerked to a violent stop, but at least *we* were still in the car. The same could not be said for our laundry, which was strewn all over the road behind us!

After climbing out and making sure we weren't hurt, Mother stood up straight, smoothed her hair and breathed a sigh of relief. We calmly picked up the clothes and drove on to Grandma's and back without incident. But Mother never got behind the wheel of any car again! ⇥

FAMILY PHOTOS can attest to the fact that autos were considered part of the family. Jeanne White of Sayville, New York also mentions that no one spoke to her mother for 2 days after she bobbed her hair.

WEIGHTY PROPOSITION. Grace Anderson of Markesan, Wisconsin says her very modern mother drove this sturdy Buick in the late '20s. She and her brother thought both the car and their mother were just wonderful.

WHAT A BARGAIN. Juanita Hoeffner of Stuart, Florida reports her cousin paid $25 for this yellow jalopy. They were thought to be wealthy to have a car like this to take them to picnics and for rides in the park.

New Traffic Light Left Mom Stalled at Corner

MY MOTHER was one of the few women we knew who drove a car in the 1920s. One day, on her way to pick up Dad from work, she discovered our town had installed its first traffic light. She'd never seen one before, and wasn't sure what to do.

Mom wanted to turn on to Main Street, but the light was red, so she stopped—just as she was supposed to.

But when her light changed to green, she noticed that now the light on Main Street was red—so she waited some more!

Soon her light turned red again. She knew she couldn't turn now, so she stayed put. (Luckily, there wasn't much traffic in those days, so no one was waiting behind her!)

Mom sat through four or five light changes, growing more and more impatient. Finally, she waited for the Main Street light to turn green and shot out into the intersection—even though *her* light was red.

When Dad got into the car, Mom complained that she couldn't get a green light on both streets at the same time!
—*Edward McDaniels*
Albertson, New York

First Solo Drive Was Her Last!

By Mary Jane Strand, New Richmond, Wisconsin

AFTER DRIVING me into town one day in 1923, my brother learned his Glee Club was to sing at another school. Albert never passed up a chance to sing, so that meant I would have to drive the car home—even though I'd never driven the Model T, or any other motorized vehicle for that matter.

Albert gave me a few hasty instructions, pointed the car toward home and went on his way.

I was fine for the first two blocks. My first turn brought the car to a dead stop, facing a ditch. Now what? Albert had only showed me how to *stop* the car, not how to start it.

I knew where the starter was, so I put my heel on it and pressed hard. Nothing happened. I'd seen Albert use the crank, so I got out and cranked, with no result. I pulled a nearby wire and cranked. Nothing. Then I turned a key on the dashboard and cranked again. The engine snorted and shook. The Ford was running!

Now I had to turn around, so I pushed the pedals…clutch, brake, *something*. The car lunged forward toward the ditch. In my confusion, my foot slipped, sending the car backward into a sign on the other side of the road.

I tumbled out, sure some damage had been done, but found nothing worse than crumpled fenders and some cracked sign boards. That wasn't so bad, and besides, the car was facing toward home!

Cheered, I got the car started again and bounced triumphantly homeward. I stayed in the middle of the road, and other motorists gave me plenty of room. I began to feel the confidence of an experienced driver.

After the first 4 miles, I neared a small one-lane bridge. An approaching Buick had already started across it. I sped up, hit the bridge with a bound and made for the Buick, which hesitated only a second before hastily backing off the bridge just ahead of me.

I smiled at the driver, thinking he was a nice man to accommodate me so agreeably. But what I heard him say *wasn't* very nice, and the look on his face changed my opinion entirely.

The last leg of my trip took me up a steep hill toward our driveway. I had the car going full force to get up the hill, staying in high gear. I turned on to our lane, anticipating a grand entrance, but I'd asked too much of the tired machine. It sputtered and died a quarter mile from the house.

That was my first and only venture in the Model T—and the only time I ever drove *any* motor vehicle unsupervised!

By the way, Albert is 86 years old, and he still loves to sing. ⚞

Learning to Drive Was a Real Adjustment for This Farmer

IN 1923, the farmer next door bought a new Model T touring car. The salesman delivered it and had George practice driving it around the pasture. Just one problem—George couldn't stop the car! He finally drove it into a pond, where it became mired in the mud. George waded out and vowed he'd never get in that contraption again!

The next day, he decided to give it another try. The road that passed our house was a two-rutted lane, and when George drove past our house, he stopped to talk to Dad and me.

Dad noticed the two front fenders on George's new car were missing and asked if he'd lost them. "No," George replied. "I couldn't see the front wheels well enough to drive this thing, so I took them off!"

The following week, George took his wife and children out for a drive and stopped at our house to chat with Mom. Their three children had large red bandannas covering their faces, knotted in back. When Mom saw this, she asked George's wife if the children had sunburns.

"No," the woman said. "George thought we were going by the fence posts so fast that it might make the children dizzy, so he blindfolded them!"
—*Earl Caldwell, Silver Cliff, Colorado*

HOUNDED FOR A RIDE. "My great-aunt and uncle, Lura and George Bunker, must have loved their hounds," says Elizabeth Terrell of Concord, New Hampshire. "They've not only taken a backseat to give the dogs a better view, but, if you look closely, you'll see each one is wearing protective goggles!"

TOOL OF HIS TRADE. Benjamin Bucher demonstrates the tool he invented for removing tires from the Model T. Benjamin's daughter, Betty Becker of Waterville, Ohio, says her dad created the tool after breaking his arm during a tire change—a common mishap in those days. Benjamin owned a garage and Ford dealership in Waterville during the '20s and '30s.

Car Ensured They Could Picnic Every Sunday

OUR FAMILY was the first in the neighborhood to have a car. My grandmother bought it for us. She figured that if she paid for it, whenever it left the garage, she'd be in it. And she was right!

Every Sunday in summer, rain or shine, we piled into that big old Dodge touring car and went on a picnic—whether Dad wanted to or not.

Around 10 a.m., here would come Grandma on the streetcar carrying her huge picnic basket filled with fried chicken or pork chops, homemade noodles, a big jar of olives, a jar of red beets and some hard-boiled eggs.

When it was pouring rain and we couldn't have a picnic on the schoolhouse or church steps, we'd just eat in the car! —*Maxine Van Tornhout*
St. Petersburg, Florida

Boy Had to Peer Through Steering Wheel to Drive

THE '20s were not very "roaring" in South Dakota as far as travel was concerned. There even remained some sections of ungraded dirt trails that had been impressed onto the land by the wagons of the first settlers pushing westward in search of free land.

The car that carried us through these rugged conditions was a 1923 Willys-Knight three-door coupe. In those days, "three door" did not mean a car with a hatchback. The third door was on the right side for access to the backseat.

Another feature on that Willys was one that I prized—a hand throttle on the steering post. It allowed me to learn to drive at age 8, even though I was too small to reach the foot feed.

On my 10th birthday, I was allowed to take the car alone to the nearest village to buy some ice cream. I was small for my age, so I had to look through the steering wheel to drive. (We didn't need driver's licenses then.)

On a subsequent trip to the store, a neighbor met me on a downhill slope and couldn't see me behind the wheel. He thought it was a runaway car and almost drove into the ditch!
—*Forrest Dannenbring*
Fort Dodge, Iowa

Judge's Verdict on Driver's Examination: No, Thanks!

IN LANCASTER, New Hampshire, driver's licenses were issued by the local magistrate. His office was on the ground floor of a building on Main Street, with a big plate-glass window in front. When court wasn't in session, he could usually be seen sitting at the window, nodding to passersby.

The day my dad stopped in to apply for his license, the judge told him to drive his "machine" around the block for the driver's test. When the judge made no move to get up from his chair, Dad asked, "Aren't you coming with me?"

"No!" the judge shot back. "I wouldn't ride in one of those things for all the money in the world!"

Dad dutifully drove his car around the block. When he returned, the judge told him, "Well, you got back, so I guess you passed the test."

By the way, when I last saw the judge, he had given in to progress and was being chauffeured around town in a Packard limousine! —*Richard Long*
Marstons Mills, Massachusetts

Even Train Collision Couldn't Stop This Car

IN 1929, my grandparents' old Willys-Knight got hit by a train. Miraculously, my grandparents survived and lived to celebrate their golden wedding anniversary. What's more, they weren't the only survivors!

In a photo taken after the wreck (top right), the car looked like it was be-

COMPANY CAR. Richard Long was 3 in 1924 when he posed with his dad and his dad's company car, which looks like a new Ford Model T five-window coupe. Richard's dad was manager of the telephone company in Lancaster, New Hampshire. In later years, the company car was an Essex, then a Nash.

WHAT A WRECK! Even a train couldn't stop this Willys-Knight! Glenn McCloskey's grandparents, who owned the car, had the frame and many of the parts replaced after the crash and continued to drive it for years. The experience even prompted them to open their own garage business.

yond repair. But my grandparents hauled it to a dirt-floor garage, where all the body parts were pulled off. A new wooden frame was built, many of the parts were replaced and before long, the car was drivable again.

The car ran for a good many years afterward, probably because of its old sleeve-valve engine, which was hard to beat. More modern mechanics claimed it wasn't efficient, and the engine was discontinued. It was certainly durable enough to survive a train wreck, though.
—*Glenn McCloskey*
Laguna Hills, California

Driving up Hill Backward Kept Gas Flowing

OVER THE YEARS, my parents owned two Model T's. The first was a 1914 touring car with rakish fenders that stuck straight out. The second, a 1923 sedan, had doors in the middle and split front seats.

Back in those days, women had to be nimble to ride in a Tin Lizzie. Early Model T's had no left front doors, only an impression of one molded into the body. The passenger had to get out to let the driver exit.

Also, the gas tank was under the front seat, and I recall my mother having to hop out so dad could measure the fuel with a stick.

Once, during a family trip in Oregon, our car stalled because the engine was higher than the level of gas in the tank. (Model T's didn't have fuel pumps.) So we *backed* up the hill to keep the gas tank above the engine. That way the gas continued to flow.

The early models didn't have batteries, either, so the headlights worked on a magneto system. When my father approached another car at night, he'd slow down—which meant his headlights would dim. If the other car had a battery, its lights would remain bright. "Doggone cars that won't dim their lights," he'd mutter. "Just wait till I get a Buick!"
—*R. Wellington Madsen*
Yacolt, Washington

Bright Driver Shed Light on Road Signs

ROAD SIGNS were difficult to read at night in a Model T. The car had no battery, so the headlights were powered by a magneto that depended on the engine's rotation. In high gear, the headlights were dim, but adequate. That is, unless you needed to read a road sign!

When Father had to read a sign at night, he'd drive up as close to the sign as possible, depress the brake pedal, and race the engine to generate enough power to make the headlamps bright.
—*Ralph Rice, Vista, California*

READY TO RIDE. Donald Meyer of Albuquerque, New Mexico shared this cherished photo of himself (right) and his brothers, Tom (center) and John, with their inseparable companion, "Spot". Their dad, Joseph Henry Meyer, took the photo in 1922 outside the family's home in Wapakoneta, Ohio (also the home of Neil Armstrong, first man on the moon).

Ewing Galloway

KNIGHT OF THE ROAD. A 1928 Willys-Knight, like this one, brings back fond motoring memories for Kathryn Miner. See her story below.

"Air-Conditioned" Oldsmobile Gave Them Years of Service

WHEN WE MOVED to a farm in Kansas in 1921, our car, an "air-conditioned" Oldsmobile, served us well—except when the roads turned to mud or were covered with snow. Then Father took us the 2 miles to school in the wagon, or we rode in a buggy and tied the horse in the school yard until it was time to go home.

By 1927, the Oldsmobile with its flapping curtains was getting worn. A car salesman was a frequent visitor that summer. Once he even hiked out to our most remote meadow to talk with Father while he was cutting hay.

Finally, the salesman brought us a beautiful blue 1928 Willys-Knight. It had an inside mirror, a vase on each side and a two-tone musical horn! No more flapping curtains, either—this was a *sedan*. Father paid $1,700 cash for it…he never bought anything until he'd saved up enough to pay on the spot.

I was sure that a more beautiful car would never be built. My brother had different feelings about the car—he still recalls the many patches that accumulated on the tires' inner tubes.

Despite frequent blowouts, that Willys-Knight did perform well on the roads. My sister once confided that she drove it an unheard-of 50 mph one day when coming home from town!

—*Kathryn Miner, Gerry, New York*

Sporty Stutz Bearcat Fueled Girl's Dreams

WHEN I WAS 5, my teenage cousin had a red Stutz Bearcat roadster and took me everywhere in it. I had always loved red, so that car really impressed me.

In fourth grade, when I won $500 in the citywide spelling bee, my father suggested I put the money in the bank, where it would draw interest. By the time I finished school, he said, I'd have enough money to take a nice trip or buy a car. The word "car" convinced me. I could just see me, all grown up, in my own red Stutz roadster!

I put the money in the bank and returned faithfully every posting period to get my interest. Then in 1929, the banks went broke. There went my money and my red Stutz roadster. To this day, I'm still looking for a nice guy about my age who has a red Stutz Bearcat and will take me for an occasional ride in it!

—*Maxine Van Tornhout*
St. Petersburg, Florida

Crossing the Delaware On Ferry Was a Thrill

I'LL NEVER FORGET taking the ferry across the Delaware River from Pennsylvania to New Jersey.

We'd wait on the dock in Philadelphia for what seemed like hours in our black Model T touring car. There was no trunk, so our luggage was packed on the fenders and the rear of the car. (The driver's side had no door, either, so the driver couldn't just step out to crank up the car and get us started.)

While we waited, the ice cream man would make his rounds. He was dressed completely in white and walked from car to car, selling nickel ice cream sandwiches from the box on his shoulder.

If it happened to rain, that was a big thrill. Then we got to put up the isinglass windows, or curtains. If I'd been

MOTOR MEDICS. Where there's cars, there's mechanics. Sandell's Garage was at Clark and Ashland in Chicago. That's my uncle, Hjmar Sandell, behind co-worker in the '20s, says Grace Frizane, Mount Prospect, Illinois.

CHEVROLET FANS. Audrey Thibodeau's parents, Mr. and Mrs. Roy Shuler, stand in front of the general store in Tincup, Colorado—surrounded by Chevrolets. The cars belonged to the Shulers' friends, who joined them for an annual fishing trip. Mr. Shuler owned the first Chevrolet garage in Springfield, Colorado.

READY TO CHARGE! Margaret Asselin, Port Huron, Michigan, and her Aunt Eugenia posed with Eugenia's electric car.

Family Got Charge Out of Electric Car

MY MOTHER had an electric car during the 1920s. It could go a distance of about 30 miles, then it would slow to a stop.

We charged the batteries every night in the garage, running our electric bill to around $2 per month. We added distilled water to the battery cells (25¢ per gallon) and used castor oil for lubrication.

—*Elizabeth Smith*
Claremont, California

very good, I was allowed to twist the little locks that held the windows in place.

After a long wait, we finally boarded the ferry—a trip that seemed magical to a 4-year-old. That was the first leg of our journey to Wildwood. If we were lucky, we'd have only one or two flat tires on the rest of the 60-mile trip, which took most of the day. What a joy to finally arrive at the beach!

—*Barbara Hockett, Vista, California*

Grandpa Had No Use For "Newfangled Machines"

MY FATHER owned the first Chevrolet garage in Springfield, Colorado, and we lived in an apartment over the garage for several years.

One of my earliest memories is of sitting on the edge of the concrete grease pit, my short legs dangling over the edge, to watch my father work on cars. In those days, there was no lift to raise a car above the mechanic's head. The car was driven over the grease pit, and the mechanic walked down a few steps to work beneath it.

Daddy was not just an ace mechanic, he was an excellent salesman, so business was good. Every farmer in the county was anxious to have motor transportation in those days. Every farmer, that is, except one—my grandfather!

Grandfather was adamantly opposed to those newfangled machines. He would much rather ride his beautiful black stallion. And when it came to transporting his family, he put more trust in the good old horse and buggy or wagon than in anything that made such loud

noises and had to be cranked by hand.

My mother said Grandfather was none too happy about his daughter marrying a "grease monkey"! Eventually, though, he reconciled himself to Daddy's occupation and all was forgiven.

—*Audrey Thibodeau, Mesa, Arizona*

Packard Had Timeless Appeal

By Nathalie Meadors, Oceanside, California

NEITHER OF MY parents ever learned to drive. We lived in Chicago, so we traveled by streetcar, elevated train and taxicab.

In July 1924, shortly after my 16th birthday, my father bought a big new Packard Eight. Free driving lessons came with it, and I became the family chauffeur.

My instructor was the neighborhood milkman, who covered his route with a horse-drawn wagon. He warned me that if he ever saw me driving incorrectly, he'd holler at me from his wagon.

The Packard became my pride and joy. It had a 143-inch wheelbase, making it one of the longest cars on the road. Everyone seemed to give me clearance and stay out of my way!

The car had red hubcaps and extra tires mounted on either side, with a rearview mirror attached to each. Inside were two "jump seats" that folded down between the front and back seats.

The only trouble we ever had with the car was that the dashboard clock refused to work and remained permanently fixed at 9:30.

I loved chauffeuring family and friends, and I was permitted to drive

"Father bought a Packard—driving lessons included..."

the Packard to Northwestern University in Evanston, where I was a student in the School of Speech.

After 7 years, Dad sold the car to the Checker Cab Co. A few months later, he returned from an out-of-town trip and told me, "I rode in our old Packard today."

"Oh, Dad," I said. "All the Checker cabs are painted green. How could you tell?"

He laughed and replied, "The clock said 9:30!"

HOMEMADE TRANSPORTATION. Merritt Scoville pieced together this "sports car" in 1924, at age 18. His father and uncle were Nebraska mail carriers whose cars wore out quickly, so he used parts from their old vehicles to build a unique machine of his own. In 1925, he sold the car to a friend for $75.

He Built "Sports Car" With Salvaged Parts

MY FATHER and an uncle were mail carriers in Nebraska, and the dirt roads and unimproved trails they drove were very hard on their cars. Engines had to be replaced yearly, and the cars themselves were replaced every 2 years. That left me with lots of worn-out cars and parts to experiment with, and in 1924, at age 18, I built my own sports car.

The back of the seat was formed from a sheet of corrugated steel, but there were no cushions. After a 20-mile trip over rough dirt roads, I ended up with a blistered back! And it was impractical to drive through mud, as there were no fenders over the wheels.

I even had to rebuild the car once, after hitting a tree and losing the front axle. I sold the car to a friend the following year for $75.

—Merritt Scoville, Queensbury, New York

Teen Embarrassed by Battered Essex

By Berniece Vaughan
Lodi, California

FOR YEARS, we traveled to town and church in a farm wagon or buggy. Only rich people owned cars, and there weren't many rich people around.

Then one day our friends Orville and Annis Yerrington came driving up to our farmhouse in a shiny black Reo. Orville opened up the hood to show Dad all the latest innovations in modern gas engines. I'm sure Dad didn't understand half of what Orville told him, but when the Yerringtons left, he had a burning desire to own a car.

Before long, a beautiful green Essex with the top rolled back was parked in front of our white picket fence. The dealer came to teach Dad to drive, but he wasn't very successful. (My father lived to age 86 and never did learn to drive well. Once, when crossing the railroad tracks that ran through our farm, he killed his pickup truck's engine on the tracks and had to jump out before the train hit it!)

After a couple of years, Mother decided she should learn to

drive the Essex. That, too, was a disaster. She'd been at it only a few days when she drove right through the garage in a shower of broken glass and lumber. She never drove again.

Still, as we moved from farm to farm, the Essex went with us. By the time the Depression began, the poor old car had lost its top, the metal was show-

FAVORITE WHEELS. Wearing his "plus fours", George Biringer sat on the fender of his 1929 Pontiac convertible for this treasured family photo. "Our first family car was a 1921 Studebaker touring car that could easily do 200 miles a day," recalls George's wife, Edna, of Bella Vista, Arkansas. "But this convertible was his favorite."

ing through the green paint, and Mother had covered the holes in the seats with old quilts.

I was in high school then and didn't want any of the town kids to know about our "primitive" life—the backyard privy, the wash basin on the porch, the worn linoleum floors. But the greatest embarrassment of all was that old Essex!

Dad persisted in herding the poor old thing to the grocery store, and everyone in town knew when he was leaving. The car would sputter, choke, bang and clatter before it finally started with a wild high shriek. Sometimes, as I walked home from school, I'd hear it approaching and would hide or scurry down side streets rather than risk being offered a ride in that terrible contraption!

I hated the car at the time, but it was a part of our lives for so long that it almost seemed like one of the family.

I'm sorry now that I was so shallow and prideful and ashamed of my father and his car. I'd give anything to have that old Essex back...it certainly would be the talk of the town!

'Elizabeth' Was No Tin Lizzie

By Howard Campbell, Santa Barbara, California

I'LL ALWAYS remember 1927 as a sensational year. I was 13 then, and I got my first automobile, a gorgeous shining black '23 Model T. I named her "Elizabeth". Other people called their cars "Tin Lizzies", but my car was far too fine for that. She deserved respect.

I wasn't old enough for a driver's license (the required age then was 14) so Mother handled the details, paying with $35 I had earned selling newspapers.

The seller, an elderly man, delivered the car to our house. He stood for a moment, patted the hood gently, wiped a tear from his eye and walked away. (If he'd known what was about to happen to his beloved car, he would have *really* cried.)

As soon as he was out of sight, my chum Tommy and I were all over the fascinating machine, lifting its hood from both sides, poking everything and looking under the front seat to see how much gasoline was in the tank. It barely wet the end of the wooden dipstick, but who cared! Gasoline was only 12¢ a gallon.

This was a first-class automobile—it had a *starter*. It also had three pedals—forward, reverse and brake—so it would be a cinch to drive. The emergency hand brake on the left was pulled back, holding the gears in neutral and braking the rear wheels somewhat, so we were per-fectly safe. That's what we told my mother, but she fled into the house.

Tommy went in front to pull the "gooser" at the radiator. I pushed up the spark lever and pulled down the gas lever, like I'd seen Grandpa do on his Model T truck. The starter groaned and the motor sounded with a roar.

I downed the spark lever, upped the gas lever and the motor chugged contentedly. This was just great! Tommy climbed in beside me and we reveled in wiggling the steering wheel and banging on the Klaxon horn. What a glorious moment!

Take 'Er for a Spin!

With the emergency brake still set, I pushed down on the "go" pedal. The car crept forward, in low gear, toward the garage. I pushed the reverse pedal and Elizabeth crept backward. After creeping forward and back a few more times, we figured we'd mastered it and backed into the street.

"You hafta give it lots of gas and push the brake handle forward," Tommy advised. (That would put the car in *high* gear, but we didn't know that.) I pulled down the gas lever and, with engine roaring, pushed up the brake.

Elizabeth lunged forward, bounced over the curb and went straight for our front porch! I swerved left and we went charging across our wide front lawn, through the hedge, across our neighbor's lawn and through *their* hedge.

Nowadays you'd just take your foot off the gas pedal, but Elizabeth had only the hand gas lever, and I was busy steering. The thing to do was aim her back to the street.

I made another sharp left, plowed through a rose bed and we were back on the street. We roared straight across it and bounced over the curb. Then I remembered the gas lever, banged it closed and pulled back on the emergency brake. We came to rest astride another neighbor's hedge as Elizabeth chugged contentedly.

What Would Neighbors Say?

The neighbors came out and laughed their heads off. It was the grandest excitement they'd had in a long time. Tommy and I still had to mow their lawns for the rest of the summer, though.

In no time, Tommy and I were veteran drivers. On lonely country roads, we'd race Elizabeth at her top speed of 42 mph. This was pretty scary, so we often stopped and checked under the hood

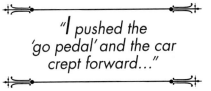

"I pushed the 'go pedal' and the car crept forward..."

on the pretext of making sure everything was all right.

The day before my 14th birthday, we were going along at a pretty good clip when a man backed fast out of his driveway. I skillfully slammed down all three pedals and *almost* didn't hit him. His fender crunched and he exploded, shouting words our mothers had told us never to use. We were scared silly.

The man stormed up to us and shouted, "Are you old enough to have a driver's license?"

"Yes, sir," I said, "tomorrow I will be. I've studied all the driving rules, and you shouldn't back out of your driveway so fast."

The man stopped short and grinned. "You're a smart little feller, aren't you? You know who I am?"

"No, sir."

"I'm manager of the Motor Vehicle Department in this town."

"Oh, golly!" I blurted.

Luckily, he was a nice man. Grinning, he patted me on the head and said, "You drive careful now. I'll see you tomorrow." ⚊

TIME TO RE-TIRE. It was a long way from Milwaukee to Madison, Wisconsin in '25, as Earl Ziegler learned patching a flat on his Model T Runabout. Thanks to Mary Ann Koebernik, Franklin, Wis., for photo.

Steamer Gave Boy Ride of a Lifetime

FILL 'ER UP...with water, that is. This is a Stanley steam car! Steamers enjoyed *some* popularity in the early part of the century and lived on into the '20s. When the self-starter was introduced, however, the "no-crank" steamers started to lose their appeal, and although steamers were fast, gasoline was here to stay.

By George Baker
El Dorado Springs, Missouri

IN 1921, we lived in Cedar Falls, Iowa, where city traffic was driven by both gasoline and horsepower. Flivvers and trucks chugged along impatiently behind horse-drawn delivery vans. I was 8 and fascinated by the cars. I longed for the day I'd get to drive one.

Across the street from our house lived a friendly plumber who owned two steam cars. He tinkered with them incessantly, and I loved to stand by and watch him work, jumping at the chance to hand him a wrench or hammer.

One of the steamers, a Stanley, resembled a conventional automobile. The other—I believe it was a White—had wooden spoke wheels taller than me, and skinny rubber tires.

There was no body on this car, just a wide seat fastened to the frame. In front, just behind the wheels, was a big round washtub of a boiler, which was connected to the rest of the machinery with an amazing array of pipes, valves and gauges.

The plumber told me this was a "flash boiler", which could deliver steam pressure much faster than the half hour other boilers required. He assured me the "gas car" was just a passing fancy and would be obsolete when people saw how efficient steam vehicles could be.

One summer day, I watched bug-eyed as the genius of steam fired up his contraption, and oh, what sights and sounds!

Car Was a Marvel

Steam hissed from numerous leaks, hot oil dripped on the brick pavement and the burners roared. The whistle made a gorgeous sound—deep, loud and mellow. That horn alone would make driving a steam car worthwhile!

I stood watching, awestruck, as my friend tightened the fittings, adjusted the valves and read the dials. Finally, having conquered most of the leaks, he shut the burners down.

"Tomorrow, we'll take a ride," he said with a grin. "Ask your ma."

At first light the next morning, I was at our living room window, checking for any sign of life from the plumbing shop. After hours of gut-wrenching anxiety for fear the ride had been scratched, I saw the big door open. My idol appeared and busied himself with the steamer, and I was at his side in seconds.

After considerable preparation, he "lit off" the burners, manipulated the valves and thumped the gauges. When he told me to climb in, I practically floated to the seat.

Ready to Roll!

He settled his bulk behind the wheel on the right side, made one or two final valve adjustments, pulled a couple of mammoth levers protruding from the gorgeous machinery under the frame and eased us majestically from the curb.

Only the skipper of the *Queen Mary* on her maiden voyage could have understood my ecstasy!

Within half a block, we'd collected a gallery of spectators. Kids ran along the curb, pointing and shouting and, I knew, envying me. Teamsters leapt from their delivery carts to hold their frightened horses' heads as we huffed and puffed along.

My friend eased the car to a stop against a high curb. After a few seconds, he slowly advanced the throttle and the

> *"He eased us majestically from the curb..."*

car climbed the curb—not with a bump, but slowly and deliberately, with a tremendous show of power. A crowd of college kids cheered.

With the wind in our happy faces, puffs of steam and the smell of hot oil all around, we returned to the plumbing shop. I raced home to tell Mother about my exciting ride. I was in such a hurry, I don't think I even thanked my host for the wonderful experience!

The "gas car", of course, was more than a passing fancy, but there's still much to be said for a steamer. Few of my childhood experiences offered a thrill to compare with that memorable ride. ⊱

Chapter Seven

Lasting Memories of Life in the '20s

NEW YORK, NEW YORK was a grand adventure for some, like Stanley Field of San Diego, California, who sent the photo on the opposite page. Stanley's fond memories of his first job in the hustle and bustle of the big city during the '20s can be found on page 146.

Lasting Memories of Life in the '20s

Maybe the '20s really were "the good old days" that the old folks like to talk about. You can probably make a case for it, if only because it was a decade in which we weren't at war—or about to go to war—with someone. Americans knew they had just finished winning "the war to end all wars", and the future looked rosy indeed.

Immigrants poured through Ellis Island as people from all over the world came to the land of boundless opportunities. The son of an Italian immigrant family told me about his 16th birthday present—a pair of long trousers and a dime.

"Louie, you're a man now," his dad declared. "Use the dime to take the bus downtown, and don't come home until you find a job." And Louie did, as office boy for a dollar a week. Fifty years later, he retired from that same company as a highly paid vice president.

Yes, the good old days. The corner grocery would deliver your order and let you pay the bill once a month. The early-morning hours brought the clop-clop-clop of the milkman's horse and the clank of bottles as they were put on your doorstep.

On summer afternoons, the air was filled with the whirr of hand-pushed Eclipse lawn mowers and the quarreling of blue jays overhead.

Old Doc made house calls when the home remedies of castor oil and mustard poultices failed. Mom had her sewing machine, which she used to turn out dresses, blouses and aprons. The leftover scraps of material went into the "scrap bag" and eventually became heirloom quilts.

The backyard garden yielded a bounty of vegetables and fruit, and the excess was canned for winter enjoyment. The butcher obligingly threw in a soup bone with your order and a scrap or two for the dog. The mailman made two deliveries a day.

Respect Was Still the Order of the Day

Men wore suits with vests and neckties, and doffed their hats upon meeting a lady on the street.

Women wore hats and gloves when they appeared in public. Personal dignity was important no matter what your station in life. My grandmother always referred to Grampa as "Mr. Stevens" except inside the home.

Children were respectful of elders and in awe of their teachers. My tiny mother earned her 2-year teaching certificate and was in charge of her own one-room school class when she was 20. Some of the boys were bigger than she was, but discipline was never a problem. Their parents saw to that.

Life was full of simple and inexpensive pleasures, if nothing more than an evening walk around the neighborhood, pausing to chat with folks sitting on their front porches. You could be sure someone would ask you to "come and sit a spell" for a glass of lemonade (hand-squeezed from *real* lemons) and some baked-that-day cookies.

Holidays were celebrated with gaudy parades, band concerts and family picnics with hand-churned homemade ice cream. They were grand occasions, made all the more special because days off from work were rare and to be savored to the hilt.

Just read the memories that appear on the following pages and see if you don't find yourself nodding your head, agreeing, "Yes, those *were* the good old days!"

—*Clancy Strock*

Library of Congress

Florida Nightlife Dazzled Newlyweds

By Percelle Paddock
Lexington, North Carolina

ALABAMY BOUND. Even "Prince" the pooch came along for the ride when Perc and Ada Leidy took a trip to Birmingham, Alabama in 1928. The couple spent the '20s in Florida, enjoying the good life.

AFTER MY PARENTS married in '23, they headed south from Toronto for their honeymoon. Their adventure-filled road trip ended in Florida, where they saw their first palm trees and decided to stay. *(See "Couple Honeymooned to Florida Home", page 55.)*

After renting a two-room flat in Jacksonville, the young newlyweds set out to explore this exciting city. Nightclubs were hopping with jazz bands, bootleg booze, and flappers dancing the Black Bottom and Charleston.

The new styles proved infectious to Mom, who soon got her hair bobbed and bought a new wardrobe of short dresses and cloche hats trimmed with beads, feathers and fur. She even bought the brown Turkish cigarettes that were the rage for liberated women—although she never really learned to smoke them.

One night, my parents went to a club with their next-door neighbors. The husband was the club's orchestra leader and introduced Mom and Dad to a lot of people, including an imposing man with shiny black hair and a cream-colored suit.

To Dad's amazement, the man later offered him a job establishing new offices in the South for a large New York finance company. There was lots of money to be made in Florida now that the great land boom was on, and with the pay being more than he *ever* could have made as a fledgling lawyer back home, Dad accepted.

Stars Came Out at Night

Settling into life as Jacksonville residents, Dad went out and bought several white suits and Panama hats. He quickly found that most business was conducted on the golf course and in country clubs rather than behind a desk. Everybody wanted to have fun, and people seemed to race through their days—eager to make money—then have a good time.

Mom played a lot of tennis and mah-jongg with the wives, then she and Dad would go out almost every night.

During this time, movie stars and European royalty were flocking to the land of palm trees and

PAIR OF POSES. "Flapper" the cat makes a cuddly hood ornament for the Reo while Ada stands in front of plentiful palm fronds in '25.

REAL REO. The Vinoy Park Hotel in St. Petersburg provided a background for Ada and Reo.

orange blossoms, and many of my parents' dinner companions wore jackets full of jewel-encrusted medals and spoke of the deteriorating political condition of Europe.

Mom got to dance with Sydney Blackmer and Douglas Fairbanks Jr., and she even chatted with Mary Pickford, who enjoyed meeting a fellow Canadian.

The exotic movie-star styles were being emulated by many. Mom was surprised to often see a well-dressed woman wearing a live chameleon on her lapel, secured by a tiny gold chain and ring around its neck!

Many ladies took their daily walk accompanied by a majestic Afghan or Irish wolfhound…breeds almost unheard-of in this country before the '20s. Mom got a kitten named "Flapper" and a German shepherd, "Prince", who went everywhere with them.

After Dad opened his company's Jacksonville office, they moved on to do the same in Orlando, St. Petersburg and Tampa. There weren't banks on every street corner like today, so it was his practice on Friday nights to take the weekly receipts from St. Petersburg to a safe in Tampa, driving his low-slung Reo roadster with red leather upholstery.

"The Mob" Struck Fear

That car was the source of adventure on another night. Mom and Dad were driving across a long bridge when Dad noticed another car bearing down on them. He pulled over as far as possible, but the driver wouldn't pass and raced closer and closer. When the car was almost on the Reo's bumper, it suddenly switched on its floodlights, blinding Mom and nearly causing Dad to plunge through the guardrail!

Suddenly, several men in dark suits rushed forward and surrounded the Reo, aiming submachine guns at my terrified parents! The men were Revenue agents who'd gotten a tip that a Reo with a similar "desert-sand" paint job was being used for bootlegging in the area.

Once the agents had crawled through the roadster and apologized for their mistake, they got quite a tongue-lashing from Mom, who'd thought the agents were mob members. Dad was amazed that his ladylike wife even *knew* such words.

Weekend activities usually included a movie Friday night, and everyone took in at least one dance. Mom and Dad did the Lindy and Quick Step to the music of Rudy Vallee and other stars.

Hotels with grand ballrooms were springing up everywhere, and many believed they were funded by mob money. Mom and Dad attended a dinner-dance at the posh Don CeSar hotel. A large party of dark-suited men and bespangled women arrived, and as the group was led to the room's best table, one man glanced admiringly at Mom and paused long enough to give her a gentlemanly bow.

Mom smiled at him, but Dad looked horrified. "Don't you know who that is?" he hissed. "It's Al Capone! I've seen his picture in the papers." Nothing more was said, but Mom always insisted that was the night Dad's hair started turning gray.

As the decade drew to a close, Mom and Dad decided to head back to Canada and raise a family near grandparents, aunts and uncles. The move surely gave them a welcome sense of security, but I know it was mixed with regret at the passing of the razzle-dazzle '20s. ⇒⊹

FASHIONABLE MOM. When Perc's mother, May Leidy, visited the couple in Jacksonville in '25, she was right in style.

IN THE RUMBLE SEAT. Perc was proud to "chauffeur" Ada and a friend in the roadster.

FRONT-SEAT DRIVERS. Ada and Perc smiled in their Reo roadster in 1926, but their grins would disappear when agents mistook their car for a bootlegger's!

Archive Photos

Views Along Boardwalk Couldn't Be Beat

MY MEMORIES of summers at Coney Island in New York City go way back to the '20s.

Tuesdays were set aside for elaborate displays of fireworks, and residents flocked to the Boardwalk for the best views.

A holiday atmosphere prevailed, and Mama would give me a dime to spend. I usually bought an ice cream pop that was dipped in chocolate right before my eyes.

The Boardwalk was several miles long, but it wasn't unusual for me to walk its entire length and back. I always paused to look through the entrance to Steeplechase amusement park, and one of my favorite stops was an open-air room with a small platform where stood "Mighty Atom, the Man of Steel".

Mighty Atom wore a leopard skin, had *long* hair and lectured the crowds in his German accent on the merits of psyllium seed as a digestive aid.

Ven you get up in de morning, he commanded, *take vun tablespoon mit a full glass of vater. It's good for the digestion and helps eliminate gas.*

At this point, the audience roared, but he kept a serious face. *Only in dis coun-try, ven we talk about eliminating gas, people respond by saying "disgusting." In Europe, vere I come from, ve say "gesundheit" (to your good health).*

Following a humorous lecture, he'd perform feats of strength and was world-famous for being able to move a car that was tied to his hair.

Many years later, I spied a newspaper article that said at age 90, Mighty Atom was still performing feats of strength. What a man!

—*Barnet Chernick*
Brooklyn, New York

Trip to Bathhouse Left Us "Clean as Newborns"

IN THE LATE '20s, Mama took my sister and me to the public bathhouse in Brooklyn every Saturday morning when the weather permitted. Although we had running water in our railroad flat, as apartments were called then, there were no showers or tubs; toilets were in the hallways and shared with other tenants.

Mama would load up the shopping bag with soap, talc, dry clothing, stockings, combs and shawls to cover our wet heads, plus some oranges and dark Russian rye bread.

She believed being in or near water stimulated the appetite. "Look how hun-gry you get at Coney Island," she'd say. (Of *course,* we did—Coney Island had Nathan's, with its delicious hot dogs, pastrami sandwiches and root beer!)

The bathhouse was an imposing gray stone building on Wilson Avenue. The humidity and constant mopping made the marble floors shimmer like the surface of a lake.

Towels rented for a nickel, and a shower stall with dressing room cost a dime per person. We always took a tub for 25¢, which was a flat rate—no matter how many people tumbled into it.

For my sister and me, the tub seemed as vast as a swimming pool, or even the ocean. "Mama," we'd cry, "watch me hold my breath…watch me float…watch me swim underwater!"

Sometimes the steam made Mama feel faint, but we'd throw cupfuls of cold water on each other so no one swooned.

After a long soaking, we were sprinkled with talc, like deep-fried doughnuts getting a dusting of sugar, then we squirmed into fresh clothing. We felt almost sterilized—clean as newborns— and ready to start a new week. The only hard part was trying to *stay* that way until Sunday morning. —*Anita Wilson*
Highland, California

CONEY ISLAND has long been a popular summer spot for New Yorkers.

Chicago Was Her Kind of Town!

By Vivienne Lindsay, Lancaster, California

CHICAGO WAS a magical place in the '20s for a little girl.

I loved riding the elevated train, as it seemed like we were racing along the rooftops. I also loved the double-decker buses, and always insisted on riding up top in the front row!

My mother and grandmother often took me on the "El" to Marshall Field's—their favorite store. The toy department there had a nursery where children were entertained while their parents shopped, and on my birthday, we always had lunch at the store's Narcissus Room, where I'd feed the goldfish in the fountain.

Our next stop was the public library, where the children's room was guarded by a sign reading: "No adult admitted unless accompanied by a child".

There was a lot of traffic downtown even then, and I remember dashing across busy Michigan Avenue. We sometimes had to stop at safety islands before we got completely across. Grandmother referred to these as "Thank the Lords".

My grandfather's medical practice was in the Atlantic Hotel, which was frequented by theater people and housed many permanent residents who were retired show people.

Marie Dressler and Al Jolson were among Grandpa's patients, along with Madame Berzac, who had an animal act featuring two ponies, two dogs and a mule. (The ponies were so old that Madame had to chew up their carrots for them!) We often stood backstage at her shows and watched the act from the wings, then later went to her dressing room.

"The City" Had Countless Attractions

I loved the Lincoln Park Zoo, the Field Museum, the colored lights on Buckingham Fountain, and the landmark Water Tower that had survived Chicago's great fire. We enjoyed picnics in the Forest Preserve, attended concerts at Ravinia Park and children's theater performances at the Art Institute, and went swimming in Lake Michigan.

It was in the 1920s that I attended my first circus, where I saw the famous Lillian Leitzel in one of her last performances.

One Fourth of July, my mother made me a costume from red, white and blue crepe paper so I could march with my dad, a World War I veteran, in the big parade down Michigan Avenue.

In summer, we drove our gray Chevrolet to the country to buy fresh corn and other produce, but I really loved my grandfather's long Cadillac. It had two jump seats that folded into the floor, a wool lap robe for cold weather and two crystal vases for flowers. Grandfather had a standing order with the florist for fresh blooms to put in them every day.

Chicago may have been known as the home of speakeasies and gangsters, but I was never exposed to any violence or corruption. *My* Chicago was a city of beauty and delight.

GRANDPOP THE DOC. One of the high-lights of Chicago jaunts was going to Grandpa's office. His patients included Al Jolson and Marie Dressler.

ANIMAL ACT. Another famous patient was Madame Berzac, whose animal act included dogs, ponies and a mule!

ENCHANTED OUTINGS. Enjoying Chicago in the '20s, Vivienne Lindsay is flanked above by her mother and grandmother, while her father is at left.

"Delicate Condition" Was a Delicate Subject Around Kids

IN THE '20S, ladies who were expecting children were said to be "in a delicate condition", "in the family way" or "eating for two". The subject was never discussed around children, and I don't believe I ever even heard the word "pregnant" while I was growing up.

One afternoon, I came home and found my mother and a neighbor chatting on the porch swing.

"Mama," I interrupted, "I just saw Louella downtown pushing her baby carriage, and her stomach was *real big*! What's wrong with her?"

My mother and the neighbor exchanged horrified glances, and ignoring me, the neighbor exclaimed, "What are things coming to? The *idea* of showing herself on the street like that! Someone should speak to her about it."

"Will she be all right?" I prodded.

"Of course, she will," my mother answered. "I'm sure the doctor can help her." I was quite puzzled, but said no more. —*Helen Riser, Ocala, Florida*

A Quarter Brought The Lights Back

WHEN the lights dimmed in our flat in Newark, New Jersey, someone had to run down to the basement and put a quarter in the gas meter. This would bring up the lights almost immediately.

I also recall the mantle, the white sock-like object that covered the gas flame on our lamp. When it ran its course, one had to use great care in removing it. Just a slight touch would turn it into a fine white ash. —*Art Kimberley Petaluma, California*

Prize Was $25,000 For "Bunion Derby" Winner

IN 1928, a promoter named C.C. Pyle announced he would award $25,000 to the winner of a transcontinental footrace from Los Angeles to New York. The event became known as "The Bunion Derby", and contestants from all parts of the world entered.

The runners traveled 30 to 40 miles a day, accompanied by timekeepers, foot doctors, health officials, shoe repairmen and a company of others selling souvenirs, hot dogs and program booklets.

The race followed Route 66 from the West Coast as far as St. Louis. Our town of Conway, Missouri was one of the overnight stops where the runners spent the night in the high school gymnasium.

It was a carnival-like atmosphere the afternoon the runners began arriving and had their lapsed time recorded, and I remember how dark brown they had gotten from their run through Arizona and New Mexico.

This was one of the most exciting days of my young life, and it was the first time we'd seen people from other countries. The race was finally won by a man from Claremore, Oklahoma.

We were so proud to be part of a grand national event! —*Ralph Miller Cordova, Tennessee*

Ethnic Neighborhood Was My "Paradise"

YORKVILLE, NEW YORK was a child's paradise in the '20s…and a place where I always felt safe. It was like a microcosm of the League of Nations, with people of different nationalities and ethnic backgrounds. I grew up understanding words in Polish, Hungarian, German, Greek and Yiddish.

There was no racism or animosity then, and the whole neighborhood was family-oriented. Doors and windows were left open so neighbors could come and go freely. We all struggled together and were very protective of each other.

On summer mornings, we kids often went to the hilltop playground at Rockefeller Center. There we felt as though we were in the country among the green grass, yellow dandelions, shade trees, swings and slides. We were given free milk as a snack, and I still remember the refreshing taste of that cold milk in a paper cup.

A mere five pennies provided food for the entire day. I lunched on hot sweet potatoes called *mickies*, hot corn sold by the push-cart vendors, and a charlotte russe or crushed ice with fruit juice poured over it for dessert.

In the afternoons, I sometimes accompanied my mother to the kosher poultry market, where she'd pick the fattest, most belligerent chicken for me to catch.

Once the chicken was slaughtered, Mom would carry it home, ignoring the old women who plucked the feathers for only a penny. (Why pay them when *I* could do it?)

My reward came later—eating the rendered fat, called *schmaltz,* with fried onions on thick bread. What a treat!

Our kitchen had a large washtub that substituted as a bathtub—except on Thursday nights when the live carp Mom bought for the Friday night gefilte fish were left swimming in the water. (A symphony of chopping was always heard throughout the building on Friday afternoons as the tenement women prepared supper.)

Our family may have been poor, but I never felt deprived. I lived life to the hilt, enjoying the simple pleasures and colorful people around me.

—*Grace Flitt, Teaneck, New Jersey*

SKATE KEY KIDS found their own fun in neighborhoods during the '20s. All it took was a few friends, some clamp-on skates and a stretch of sidewalk.

Children Reveled In Wonders of 'The Street'

By Alice Thompson, Pepin, Wisconsin

MY FAMILY lived along a bustling street in Minneapolis, but despite a few parental warnings, "the street" was a pretty safe place for children in those days. We saw it as a mecca of excitement.

Across the street was a playground for playing pussy wants a corner, run sheep run or fox and geese.

The big church on the corner was off limits for exploring, but we watched from a distance as parishioners arrived and were awed by the ladies with their big feathered hats, beaded bags, fox furs and high buttoned shoes. And their escorts were *so* handsome in hard-brimmed straw hats, green wool suits and orange square-toed oxfords.

One day, big poles called "traffic lights" were installed at our corner. Now we could cross the street several times a day and visit with the people at the streetcar stop! Another favorite pastime was identifying the different cars like Maxwells, Overlands and Pages.

WHERE'S THE FIRE? The horse-drawn fire wagon was just one of the many wonders that could be seen on city streets back in the 1920s.

Evenings found us perched along the curb, exchanging eerie ghost stories and trying to spot the first star of the night so we could make a secret wish.

We declared we could see the features of "the man in the moon" and decided that was God's night-light, enabling Him to watch over people everywhere. The 9 o'clock siren was our signal to disband and scramble home.

One of my most vivid memories is of running breathlessly down the street in ankle-high button shoes. The heavy hand-crocheted lace of my petticoat slapped against my knees as I tried to keep up with the older kids racing…but no matter. We were on our way to the fire barn!

In summer, the barn's huge sliding door stood ajar, allowing us to peer in-

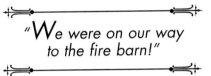

"We were on our way to the fire barn!"

side the dark building. On this lucky visit, fireman Mike invited us in, and we marveled at the sleek red fire wagon with polished brass fixtures and folded hoses and ladders flanking the sides.

At the rear of the building, four handsome white horses stood in wooden stalls, contentedly swishing away flies with their silky tails.

Should We Cry or Run?

Suddenly Mike reached up and touched a button, and a great clanging reverberated through the building. The horses snorted, reared and pawed at the heavy timbers. Their eyes grew wild and nostrils flared as the tendons bulged in their powerful thighs. We didn't know whether to cry or run!

Just then the clanging stopped. With a chuckle, Mike stepped over to one of the horses, gently pulled its face even with his own and gave her a loving pat. "Calm down, girl," he told her. "There's no fire."

Kids no longer imagine about the man in the moon like we once did. Rather, they speak with authority about men *on* the moon. Still, whenever I see my old lunar friend, I'm filled with nostalgia as I recall the loving memories and values I learned growing up in the '20s.

Tree Sprayers, "Rivet Man" Thrilled Urban Youngsters

SUMMERS IN DETROIT, Michigan were filled with thrilling events— like the annual arrival of the tree sprayers.

The procedure was announced by a man walking down the street, shouting, "Close your windows!" through his megaphone.

Then a huge noisy truck with an attached tank followed as men wearing yellow slickers and wide-brimmed hats sprayed the elms and poplars with high-pressure hoses.

As the trees swayed back and forth, we kids scampered to find a safe place to watch from. (Rumor had it that your skin would be "eaten off" if any spray got on it.)

The arrival of the street flusher was no less exciting, as the big water truck lumbered down the street, flushing the pavement with sprayer nozzles from each side. We'd strip off our shoes and socks and stand near the curb to get a cooling foot wash.

One summer, there was a steel-framed building under construction nearby…and the rivet man was a show unto himself!

He'd heat rivets in a charcoal fire while turning a crank to keep the fire hot. Then he'd take out a red-hot rivet with a large pair of tongs and toss it up high to the "catcher", who deftly caught it in a funnel-shaped container and placed it in a rivet hole. Two men with air hammers then pounded the heat-softened rivet into a tight fit.

You sure don't see things like *that* anymore.

—*Robert Meyer*
Clinton Township, Michigan

Quarantine Kept Loved Ones Apart

By Barbara Gray, Loveland, Colorado

"QUARANTINE" warned the blazing-red sign on our front porch in spring of 1922. My 3-year-old brother had scarlet fever, a dreaded and contagious disease at that time.

Mother insisted on doing the nursing, so she sealed herself and Bobby in the living room while Granny moved in to take care of the baby and me. This arrangement allowed Dad to go to work every day.

Most children avoided going near houses under quarantine, or would walk on the other side of the street. Some daring boys took a deep breath, held their nose and dashed through the danger zone, prompting horrified

TOGETHER AGAIN. Once Bobby (right, with author) was cured of scarlet fever, family life got back to normal.

shrieks from the girls on the other side of the street. Now *our* home was the focus of this after-school drama.

A porch window was low enough for me to peek in for assurance that Mother and Bobby were near. Granny or Daddy would hold Mary Ellen to the glass to wave or blow a kiss. There were tears on both sides until the baby got used to Mother being out of reach.

At mealtimes, Granny moved a table under the window and put food, dishes and water on it. Mother wouldn't open the window until Granny left the porch.

Kids Longed for Mother

After she and Bobby ate, Mother washed and boiled the dishes on the living room's coal heater and put them back on the table. I remember how flushed her face was from the overheated room and worried that it meant she had scarlet fever, too.

The days crept by. At first Bobby was very sick, and all we could see of him was a red splotched face on a white pillow. Later he began sitting up a bit and gave us a wan smile.

One evening, I pressed my face against the window, hoping a germ would squeeze through and make me sick. Then *I'd* be the one on Mother's lap, being rocked while she sang lullabies.

I strained to hear the familiar words, but Mother's pretty voice sounded like a faraway bird's. Tears spilled down my cheeks, and I fled to my favorite "crying place".

The next day, my sad feelings were eased by the sight of Mother at her treadle sewing machine, making an Easter outfit for each of us. She held up a piece of sunshine-yellow dotted Swiss, indicating it was for me.

When the quarantine was finally lifted, all the sheets, towels and bedding had to be washed and boiled by Mother, and the books and toys Bobby used had to be burned.

New Clothes Were Fumigated

The lovely clothes Mother had made were the subject of a heated discussion between her and a Health Department representative. He finally agreed she could keep them, unboiled, if she'd hang them where they could be fumigated. I watched from the porch as Mother stretched a clothesline across the room and hung up the clothes. The room looked like a store full of pretty things, and there were even petticoats to match the dresses.

Soon after that, Mother and Bobby emerged, scrubbed and purified, for a joyous family reunion. The only damper on our joy was the baby's refusal to go to Mother's arms, and it was several days before she forgave Mother for staying out of reach in that room!

The house was left for the fumigators while we went to Granny's for the night. Here my memory fades, but I'm sure that on Easter Sunday, we felt splendid walking off the porch in our fumigated finery. ⚊

CATTLE CURE. Still too weak to walk, little Russell Sproul took the "bovine bus", thanks to brother Frank.

His Spirits Soared At Signs of Spring

IN 1925, at age 5, I became ill with typhoid fever, which developed into double pneumonia. Our doctor didn't expect me to survive, and I remember neighbors and relatives came for a "final" visit.

I was in bed for 6 months, and on my worst nights, my mother and sisters made up hot onion poultices for my chest all night long.

By spring, I had improved greatly but was still too weak to walk. One warm day, my mother and my brother Frank put me on the back of our gentle, faithful family cow and took me on a riding tour of our yard and barn lot.

After all these years, I've never forgotten the kindness and concern of my nine older brothers and sisters, or the pleasure of seeing the renewing signs of green grass and blooming flowers once again.
—*Russell Sproul, Waynesfield, Ohio*

Dollar Went a Long Way For Food, Entertainment

A DOLLAR went a lot further in 1929. Rent on our spacious Seattle apartment was $12 a month, and haircuts cost 15¢ —although the fancier shops charged a whole quarter.

A hearty lunch of beef stew with a beverage was 15¢, and generous-size burgers at a chain called "Filling Stations" cost a nickel. Other eateries featured hotcakes and coffee for a dime, with extra butter for a penny, and one of our restaurants had family-style chicken dinners for a quarter.

I was a delicatessen clerk in the Seattle Public Market and earned about $10 a week. One day, the boss had just mailed some checks and needed to make a bank deposit to cover them, so I sprinted out the door trying to get to the bank before it closed at 3.

About a half block from the bank, I saw the guard pulling the curtains as he prepared to close up. He saw me running and waved me on in. I returned to the deli and proudly announced, "Mission accomplished."

We soon came to regret my speed, because the next day, the bank didn't open! In a few weeks, our store joined the growing list of businesses that failed after the crash of '29. —*Chet Noland*
Federal Way, Washington

Payday Candy Had to Last

DURING THE WEEK, Mother would send me to the neighborhood grocery. Along one wall was a rack filled with account books with everyone's name on the end. The grocer tallied the prices in our book and gave me the top copy to take home to Mother.

Saturday was payday, so when Dad came home from work, he'd wash up, then we'd all go to the grocery to settle the week's bill. Sometimes it was a whole dollar—which is what Dad earned in one 12-hour day as a mechanic.

Once the bill was paid, the grocer gave my sister and me a small sack each and let us go behind the counter to select as much penny candy as we could stuff into our bags. This is the only candy we ever got, so we savored it all week until payday came again.
—*Bruce Thompson*
San Bernardino, California

DANCE DUO. In the spirit of the '20s, Bruce Thompson and sister Thelma try their feet at the Black Bottom. Perhaps they're celebrating payday and penny candy! (See memory above.)

Mother's Ingenuity Saw Family Through Lean Years

By John Van Der Sande, Helena, Montana

OUR FATHER was killed in a car accident in 1928, leaving Mother, at the age of 27, with five children to raise. Her only assets were her Yankee ingenuity and fierce independence.

The State of Wisconsin offered a monthly widow's pension of $15 for the first child, $10 for each succeeding child and $7.18 for the widow. Work was scarce, but Mother was able to clean houses and scrub floors for $1 a day.

At least food prices were lower then. Sugar was 6¢ a pound, flour 90¢ for 50 pounds, eggs 8¢ a dozen, unpasteurized milk in glass bottles 6¢ a quart, coffee 16¢ a pound and peanut butter 27¢ a quart jar. Mother baked up to 14 loaves of bread a week and canned up to 500 quarts of fruit and vegetables each year.

Spring meant fresh watercress and dandelion greens, and a summer garden provided lettuce, tomatoes and young beet greens. We boys scoured the streams and fields for fish and game.

In fall, we scavenged for fruits and berries. We had no refrigerator or icebox, so everything had to be eaten at once or canned. Nothing was wasted —we didn't even own a garbage can for years!

During the school year, we had bread or hot cereal for breakfast, then walked home for lunch to share a quart of home-canned fruit and a loaf of bread.

For supper, Mother sometimes splurged and bought two pork chops to dice for gravy, served with about 5 pounds of mashed potatoes.

Other nights, we'd have mashed potatoes with catsup, boiled rice sprinkled with sugar and cinnamon, or baking powder biscuits with white gravy. We also ate a lot of soup, since stew bones could be obtained for little or nothing. On Saturdays, we looked forward to a great delicacy—Boston baked beans with salt pork.

Mother did all her cooking on an old wood and coal range, which was also our only source of heat. On cold winter nights, we'd gather around it while she sang to us or told stories of her childhood in New England. Sometimes, rather than wait until the bread was baked, she'd slice some dough and fry it on top of that old stove.

Until Mother remarried in 1938, we lived in an uninsulated two-bedroom house for $25 a month…but I think those years were the best of our lives. We were denied material things, but our mother taught us to make do, respect the rights of others and appreciate that the best things in life were free. ⚬

ALL IN A ROW. John, Aiden, Joyce, Audrey and Robert Van Der Sande made it through hard times in the '20s, thanks to their mother's spunk.

'Cheap Dates' Were Full of Fun

By June Chatterton, Milan, Illinois

I WAS born in 1912, so I was there in the Roaring '20s when fun was cheap—especially for a young woman and her date.

For instance, a lady could don her $1.98 hat, a $12.98 dress and an $8.50 pearl necklace, dust on some fine Armand powder, which cost $1, and be ready for a date.

Her fellow would arrive on time, thanks to his $1.50 Ingersoll pocket watch, carrying a 1-pound box of fine chocolates purchased for $1.

Away they went to play Tom Thumb miniature golf, then perhaps catch Will Rogers in *So This Is London* at the Capital Theater matinee for 25¢, which included a vaudeville show.

For a snack, the couple might go to Kresges for a 15¢ afternoon special at the fountain (only 10¢ with coupon), and to finish off the date, a lovely moonlight excursion on the steamer "Capitol" could be had for 75¢.

Yes, those were the days…and whenever I look at these old ads from my scrapbook of the late '20s, I'm reminded of the good times we enjoyed…for the right price.

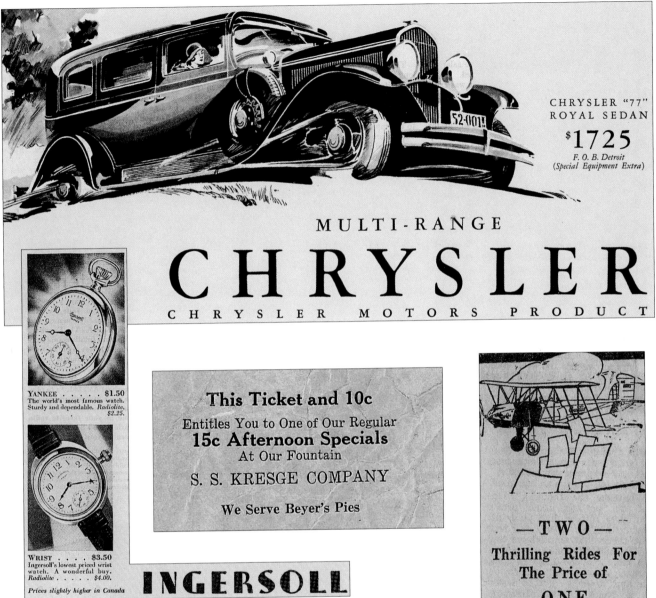

CHRYSLER "77"
ROYAL SEDAN

$1725

F. O. B. Detroit
(Special Equipment Extra)

MULTI-RANGE

CHRYSLER

CHRYSLER MOTORS PRODUCT

YANKEE $1.50
The world's most famous watch.
Sturdy and dependable. *Radiolite,*
$2.25.

WRIST $3.50
Ingersoll's lowest priced wrist
watch. A wonderful buy.
Radiolite . . . . . $4.00.

Prices slightly higher in Canada

INGERSOLL

This Ticket and 10c
Entitles You to One of Our Regular
15c Afternoon Specials
At Our Fountain
S. S. KRESGE COMPANY

We Serve Beyer's Pies

—TWO—
Thrilling Rides For
The Price of
—ONE—

Moline Airport
SUNDAY

"Penny-a-Pound"
Rates

—

Glider Activities
Music
Night Flying

—

CURTISS-WRIGHT
(Flying Service)

Moonlight Excursion
VETERANS OF FOREIGN WARS
F. W. Galbraith Post 828
Wednesday, July 16
Lv. Davenport 8:15 P. M.—Rock Island 8:30
TICKETS 75 CENTS
Steamer CAPITOL

Dad's Chip Biz Catered to Stores And Speakeasies

By Nana Becker
Petersburg, Michigan

MY DAD established the first potato chip company in Detroit, Michigan around the early part of '26.

He rented a building and bought two round stainless steel kettles about 12 feet in diameter. The chips were made with peeled raw potatoes sliced wafer thin, then fried in hot peanut oil and sprinkled with salt.

The chips, sold in bulk to grocery stores, were put into 3-1/2-pound cans and delivered in a panel delivery truck. Dad also sold caramel corn, which was popped in brass kettles and mixed with brown sugar and butter.

The products were taken by truck to candy stores, groceries and speakeasies, which in those days were called "blind

CHARTER CHIPSTER. Looking chipper in his new truck, Nana Becker's father delivers homemade potato chips. It was the first business of its kind in Detroit.

pigs" since they operated outside of the law. My mother used to help Dad with the deliveries there and told me that when she knocked on the door, she had to wait to be recognized before entering with the potato chips.

Dad always reminded her to avoid certain areas of Detroit then where the mafia men known as "the Purple Gang" ruled.

Mom is now 90 years old, and I can't tell you how many times I've asked to hear her stories of those exciting days again and again. ➤

Kind Boss Took Stock of Young Worker's Plight

By Stanley Field, San Diego, California

WHEN I GRADUATED from high school at 15 in 1926, I dreamed of attending college, but my dear parents were struggling. My older brother had quit high school so he could work and help out, and it seemed only fair that I do likewise. I enrolled in night school and started working for Tishman Realty as an office boy.

David Tishman was a real estate magnate and construction pioneer. He built the first fully air-conditioned building in Manhattan, and the Tishman apartments on Park Avenue were considered the height of elegance.

Despite his power and influence, Mr. Tishman was kind and thoughtful. He offered to pay my tuition so I could become an architectural draftsman, but I couldn't draw a straight line, even with a ruler. He assigned me to assist the rental director, and later the comptroller.

One evening as I was leaving, Mr. Tishman's secretary called me in. After Mr. Tishman finished checking some plans, he wanted me to rush them to the architects. She informed me I might have to wait half an hour or more.

"I have a class tonight," I told her. "I'll be late."

"I'm sorry," she said. "Your job comes first." Mr. Tishman happened to hear this and came striding out of his office. "Oh, no," he told her, "his education comes first."

He turned to me and motioned, "You go ahead, and don't be late to class," he said. "We'll get a messenger."

On another occasion, Mr. Tishman called me in and said he was about to have an important conference. "Afterward, I'll have a check that must get to the bank before 2 o'clock," he said. "Please wait."

It was then 11 a.m. I waited and waited. Noon. Twelve-thirty. At 1 p.m., Mr. Tishman came out of his office. "I'm terribly sorry," he told me. "I know you've missed your lunch hour, but we're almost ready. Thank you." (In the midst of a crucial meeting, he had taken the time to worry about an inconsequential office boy.)

At 1:20, he hurried out with the check, told me to take the subway and handed me a $5 bill. "Have a good lunch," he said.

When the Great Depression began, our office staff was pared to the bone. In 3 years with the company, I'd saved a few hundred dollars and invested it in Tishman stock. I'd bought it at $57; now it was up to $80. If I sold, I could make a $200 profit—quite a windfall for a teenager with no business acumen.

When I asked our comptroller for his advice, he smiled benignly. "Don't be foolish," he said. "The stock's going up to $100. Hold on." So I did.

That was October 25, 1929. Four days later, the stock market collapsed.

Many of us lost our jobs after that. On my last day, the comptroller followed me to the elevator and handed me a sealed envelope. "Mr. Tishman wants you to have this," he said. "Open it when you get home."

I couldn't wait. As soon as I was out of the building, I peeked inside and found a check for $600—every cent of my lost stock investment, including the broker's commission.

Is it any wonder I still remember David Tishman after all these years?

Girl Saw Bright Future as a Nurse

By Kathleen Selsam
Mount Vernon, Ohio

I SAW A NURSE for the first time at age 6, the evening before my mother died during surgery. My future was years away, but I knew immediately that nursing would be *my* vocation.

Getting there wasn't easy. During my last 2 years of high school, I did all the housekeeping for Dad and me, including cooking and laundry.

Every Monday, I was up at 4 a.m. to wash our clothes before going to school. We had a water-power washer, but I still had to cope with Dad's heavily starched overalls and jackets. He was a railroad engineer, and his clothes were black and greasy after working with those coal-fired steam engines.

I taught myself to sew, and my grandmother encouraged my interest in handcrafts. I knit a sweater for the Red Cross to send to soldiers during World War I, and later when I was in high school, I taught Dad to knit. He was good at it, too.

After high school, I became a student nurse. With no air-conditioning and never enough fans, summers were hot. We soon replaced our petticoats with starched blue and white gingham uniforms topped with white aprons and bibs. We rolled our stockings below the knee and learned to anchor our caps on short hair.

I never learned the Charleston or Black Bottom. Our 9-hour shifts, which included up to 4 hours of classes, were followed by study time and a 10 p.m. curfew, which didn't leave the time or energy for dancing.

My father deserves a great deal of credit for guiding me through those years. How could a man, alone, with no role model or instructions, cope so deftly with a teenage daughter in that time of change? But he did.

Dad never broke a promise and he taught me to be responsible for my own life. He made sure I knew he'd love me no matter what happened.

My aims were clear. I worked hard and did what I had to do. At 89 years old, I am still a registered nurse and have most of the credits for my license renewal in 1995, which will probably make me the oldest R.N. in the state!

HARD-WON GOAL. Thanks to Dad's guidance, Kathleen Selsam (right, with fellow student nurse Margaret Tilghman in '26) became a registered nurse and worked at Bethesda Hospital in Zanesville, Ohio. This year, Kathleen will renew her license—at age 89!

AFTER GRADUATING from high school in 1922, Edith Tollefsrud found a job at the Parker Pen Company in Janesville, Wisconsin. "My first earnings were spent on flapper garb, as seen in these pictures of me and my uke and wearing the popular galoshes," recalls Edith, who now lives in Rockford, Illinois. "At work, I played piano in the office lounge during lunch while others danced to *Yes, Sir, That's My Baby*, and *Has Anybody Seen My Gal?* One day, a bashful boy in the mailroom invited me to a vaudeville show. We double-dated with my cousin Hazel and her boyfriend, and she and I splurged on marcels. It was a warm evening, but my date kept the top closed on his fire-red Reo to protect our hairdos. On the return trip at 1 o'clock in the morning, however, we turned the top back and zoomed along at 70 mph on a dark, deserted road. Our hair was in strings by the time we got home, but that wild ride was worth it! At the end of this crazy decade, I met a man who liked plays, family dinners, Sunday trips in his Star coupe and smoking a pipe—a welcome change from the popular cigarettes. We soon married, and my favorite song became *My Blue Heaven*. My 'roaring' days were over."

Patient Found Castor Oil Hard Medicine to Swallow

I'M 89 years old now, but I clearly remember a funny thing that happened when I was working as a nurse in a hospital surgical ward in 1925.

Doctors then often prescribed castor oil before many operations, and one of our patients bragged that no one could get *him* to take castor oil.

When his doctor ordered it, I took the patient a tray that contained a teaspoon of bicarbonate of soda and two glasses of orange juice—one with castor oil on top.

I told him the doctor wanted him to take the powder to settle his stomach, and that I'd mix it with orange juice, which would foam like a Bromo-seltzer. He was to drink it quickly, then drink the second glass of juice (the one without the castor oil).

The patient followed instructions and all was fine—until I told him he'd just had his castor oil. He was in shock for a second, then he blew up and called me, and everyone around him, some pretty vile names.

Needless to say, the other men were convulsed with laughter because of his previous bragging. The patient never spoke to me again.

—*Ethel Walker, Shelton, Connecticut*

Newsboy's Throwing Arm Threw Some for a Loop!

By Merlin Norris
Mountlake Terrace, Washington

FROM 1923 to '26, I was a carrier for the *Bozeman Daily Chronicle* in Montana. Six days a week, I reported to the newspaper building at 4 a.m. to pick up a stack of papers and fold and stuff them in a bag for delivery by 7 a.m.

When the weather was decent, I rode my bicycle. On cold days, I always looked forward to deliveries at the apartment buildings on my route, where I could get out of the snow and wind for a few minutes.

Those pre-dawn hours were cold during winter, so carriers had to dress warmly. We often were out before city workmen had cleared the sidewalks with their horse-drawn, wedge-shaped snow-plows. I wore knee-high leather boots, well-greased to make them waterproof, plus heavy wool socks and a stocking cap.

One of my customers lived in a one-story brick house fairly close to the sidewalk. The porch window was usually open about a foot, and one morning I threw the paper and it sailed right through it. To my horror, I heard a grunt, so I raced up the street as fast as I could pedal.

The next morning, the customer was waiting for me, sitting on the porch steps in his night-shirt. "Sonny," he said, "if you throw that paper through the window every morning, I'll give you a quarter each month. Yesterday the paper landed right on my stomach, so I turned on the light and read it before I got out of bed!"

After that, I was especially careful with my aim, and always tossed the paper through the window so it would land on the bed.

PAPER PEDALER. Read all about how Merlin Norris nearly made headlines tossing papers from his bike.

Another customer had a beautiful copper screen door. One morning, I was a bit careless and threw his paper so it struck the door. This customer, too, waited for me the next morning.

"Please don't hit the screen door anymore," he said. "That door cost me a lot of money. I don't want it damaged." From then on, I was careful to throw his paper to another part of the porch.

Near the end of my route was a square house with a recessed porch in one corner. I always threw the paper so that it landed at the door at the rear of the porch.

One morning, I was about 10 minutes behind schedule and riding as fast as I could, then tossed the paper without looking first. Meanwhile, the lady of the house, who was rather stout, had just stepped out the door (expecting her paper to already be there) in a long white nightgown.

When the paper hit her square amidship, she threw both hands in the air and let out a scream that I'm sure was heard for miles. Believe me, I pedaled out of there in a big hurry!

I lost a lot of sleep in those years and occasionally dozed off during class, but I do have fond memories of that early-morning job. I suppose it could be called a family tradition, since all four of our children had paper routes during their growing-up years.

Satisfied Boarders Made Aunt Mag "Miss Popular"

AUNT MAG never had any children, but she mothered everyone she knew—including me, her namesake. She was about 5 feet tall and weighed 100 pounds, and always pulled her white hair into a neat bun.

When Aunt Mag's husband died, she was left with many debts and decided to take in boarders. Her business became so successful that she built a large boardinghouse and employed a staff of six.

Many of her boarders were young men who worked in the business district nearby. Aunt Mag fondly called them her "boys". She often said she'd rather have men than women there, as they were "not near as much trouble".

In 1924, when the local theater sponsored a contest to name the most popular girl in town, Aunt Mag's "boys" nominated her and got busy selling tickets in her name. Although she was nearly 60, she won the title—and the grand prize of a brand-new car. This picture of her, sitting proudly in the car in front of the boardinghouse, is one of my favorites.

—*Margaret Nigh, Terrell, Texas*

Boys Saved Their Best Scowls for Picture Man

WHEN MY FUTURE mother-in-law learned that "Walter the picture man" would be coming to town, she was thrilled. Her boys were getting so big, and they hadn't had their picture taken in 4 years.

Mama spent the next few days washing and starching shirts and polishing shoes. When the picture man came, she'd be ready.

The boys weren't happy with all the fuss. They wanted to play mumblety-peg and catch crawdads and fireflies…but every time they went outside, Mama was there to caution them. "Now boys, don't get too dirty. The picture man may come today."

The boys eventually decided that when the picture man *did* come, they would retaliate by looking just as mean as possible for their portrait.

Days later, the picture man finally arrived while Elmer and Woodrow were drawing water for the cows. Mama got them into their good clothes and washed their faces as gently as if they were babies.

She sat them in two good chairs from the dining room and perched straw Easter hats on their heads. They looked so handsome! Mama was so excited that she didn't even notice their grim expressions.

When the pictures arrived 2 weeks later, Mama looked as if she might cry. Then she laughed and said, "Well, it certainly *looks* like you two." She vowed to keep that picture forever.

Many years later, long after Woodrow and I were married, Mama was going through an old trunk. There, wrapped tenderly in tissue paper, was the picture of her two precious boys…looking just as mean as could be!
—*Marcella Reeves*
Leeds, Alabama

Savvy Salesman Knew How to 'Sew up' a Deal!

By Abbie Thomas, Lubbock, Texas

ONE DAY in 1922, a sewing machine salesman pulled up to our house in a Ford roadster that had been converted to a truck. The bed in back carried a chicken coop and an Elgin sewing machine.

Mother loved to sew and was excited to see what the machine could do. She warned the salesman she couldn't buy it without Daddy's approval, and he'd be plowing the rest of the day. The salesman brought it in anyway.

My sister, brother and I were just as excited as Mother as we gathered around to watch the salesman demonstrate all of its wonderful attachments.

"Oh, wouldn't I love to have that machine," Mother murmured.

"I tell you what let's do," the salesman said. "Let's take the machine to the field for your husband to see."

"Can we do that?" Mother said.

The salesman put the machine back on the truck, then climbed in front with Mother. We kids clambered into the back with the machine and the chicken coop. We bumped up and down across the rows of cotton toward the far side of the field where Daddy was plowing.

Once he spotted us, he tied the mules to the plow and started walking out to meet us. By the time he got to the truck, the salesman had the machine ready for another demonstration.

As the salesman put the machine through its paces, Daddy was watching Mother's excitement. He knew she'd needed a sewing machine for a long time. But the price was $12.75—more than we could afford.

"Lucy," he told Mother, "I want you to have this machine if we can work out a way to pay for it."

The salesman assured him they could work something out.

"All I have to my name is $2," Daddy told him. "Can you take produce?"

"Sure," the salesman said. "What do you think that chicken coop is for?"

We all set about collecting what Daddy figured to be $10.75 worth of produce. The salesman went on his way with Daddy's $2 plus 15 fryer-sized chickens, 8 quarts of peach preserves, four watermelons, eight cantaloupes, a bushel of black-eyed peas, a gallon each of cane syrup and honey, six bars of lye soap and a cured ham!

Mother used the machine day and night. She made all the dresses my sister and I wore, sometimes using printed feed sacks. Later, during the Depression, the money she made sewing for ladies in town helped save our farm.

I learned to sew on the Elgin by making gauze sacks to stuff the sausage in at hog killing time.

Mother used the machine until 1962, when she bought an electric Singer she didn't have to pedal. She gave the Elgin to a lady who had no sewing machine at all—and was just as happy to receive it as Mother had been 40 years earlier in the cotton patch.

My Old School Still Stands—on 'Memory Lane'

By Carl Gregory
Higgins Lake, Michigan

THE ONE-ROOM country school is long gone, but not forgotten for those of us with rural roots and a good memory.

Both my parents graduated from the same school I went to in central Michi-

> *"The boy next to me lifted the cover of his dinner pail and grinned..."*

gan, and as the '20s came in, it was now my turn to walk down a dusty country road on a crisp September morning.

My first day began with the teacher writing my name on the top of my desk and giving me a handful of shelled corn to trace the chalked letters with.

There was a wall in the cloakroom for our "dinner pails", those shiny containers with a copper bail and removable tray at the top for dessert.

Youngsters from poorer, large families often carried their dinners in syrup pails designed by the manufacturer for just that secondary purpose.

ROOMFUL. A teacher of a one-room school had her hands full. Carl Gregory (right, front row) has great memories of classmates in this 1923 shot.

I remember one time in early fall, we were sitting alongside the schoolhouse enjoying the sun while we ate, when the boy next to me lifted the cover of his dinner pail and grinned. Looking into the pail, I saw two hard-boiled eggs floating around in sweet cider.

My best friend's dinner frequently consisted of two huge sandwiches made with thick cream slathered between two slices of homemade bread...*not* my idea of a gourmet meal.

Once on my way to school, I got into a fight that soon developed into a dinner pail-swinging fray. When I took the cover off my pail at noon, my mother's butterscotch pie looked as if it had just lost a bout with an egg beater.

Surprise at the One-Room Schoolhouse

AS CHILDREN in the Montana mountains, we rode to school on milk trucks and got to watch as the men loaded cans of milk from farms and ranches along the way.

At the end of the day, we walked home. It was only 2 or 3 miles, but it felt like a thousand. School was in session from early spring to late fall, because winter travel was too difficult on our dirt mountain roads.

We never had more than six children in school at one time, and all were in different grades. There was no sloughing off when you were the only one in your class!

Since we had no plumbing, I carried our drinking water from a nearby farm and was paid $3 per term—the first money I ever earned. I had to walk over to the next valley to collect my check from a school board member.

One day in July, we ran out of water and I had to go for more. It was hot, and I was feeling sorry for myself. When I returned, I was greeted with my first surprise birthday party! That long walk in the hot sun was quickly forgotten.

Early each term, we'd have a lesson on dental hygiene. It became routine to brush our teeth after lunch in the meandering willow-lined creek outside the school yard.

What a life for kids. We had specialized training, learned our lessons well and never heard of—nor dreamed of—the perks students get today.

—*Joseph Martina*
Oceanside, California

SUMMER SCHOOL. When Joseph Martina went to Brown's Gulch School in Montana, it was mostly in the summertime because the roads were too bad in the winter. This recent photo shows the little school in the mountains...still standing after all these years.

Sudden Gift Still Flowers in Her Thoughts

By Jennie Roberts
Pasadena, California

IT WAS JUNE 1925 in Boston, and we were lined up by twos in the school auditorium for eighth-grade graduation.

Except for me, everyone had a red rose. The girls, all wearing white organdy dresses, carried theirs, and the boys' were tucked into their lapels.

At that time of year, roses had to be bought from a florist, so I hadn't even mentioned it to Mother. She was having a hard enough time making ends meet on the little money she made cleaning houses. Besides, it hadn't seemed that important.

But now, as I was the only one standing in line without a rose, it *was* important. Every glance in my direction made me feel out of place. Where would I get the courage to walk up to the stage to receive my diploma?

By the time we began marching into the hall, I was close to tears. Suddenly I felt a rush of air at my back and a gentle touch on my shoulder. Standing at my elbow, trying to catch her breath, was Florence Dunbar, my English teacher, who held out a red rose for me to take. With a heartfelt "thank you", I clutched the flower close and marched proudly down the aisle, putting all my heart into our graduation song.

And then I caught sight of Miss Dunbar, standing on stage with the principal and the other teachers. Everyone was sporting a rose—except her. Bless her! It remains one of my most cherished memories. ⇒+

Young Trappers' Odor Was Trapped in School

ON A CHILLY fall morning in 1927, I was just about to ring the bell at a one-room school in Colorado when one of my students ran up to me.

"Teacher," he pleaded, "send Bob and Pete home!" When asked why, he just said, "You'll see!"

Puzzled, I rang the bell and stood aside as the children filed in. Bob and Pete came in last, and as they walked past, I understood their schoolmate's request. What a *horrible* odor.

It turned out the two brothers had been trapping small animals to sell the pelts for spending money, and early this particular morning they'd skinned a skunk!

When they finished, they knew they had to do something about the smell, so they slipped into their house and found a bottle of their mother's perfume, then liberally splashed it on each other.

Now, skunk odor is bad enough, but with perfume, it's simply awful!

Well, I opened all the windows in the schoolhouse and told the kids to put on their coats. We all "toughed it out", but it was a very long day...and still a vivid memory at the age of 91. (By the way—I married Bob and Pete's older brother the next year.)
—*Dorothy McCormick*
Newport, Washington

Miss Culpepper Gave Us Music and More

By Estelle White, Severna Park, Maryland

ON MY FIRST DAY of school, Mama coaxed me out of my overall cutoffs and into a pretty cotton dress, slippers and socks. I knew all my classmates; they'd been partners in my tomboy escapades. The only person I felt shy about was the teacher.

Miss Culpepper was wearing a pale pongee dress, a long rope of pearls and a crown of golden finger-waved hair. Her voice was soft as she called me by name and showed me to my desk. The moment I saw her, I knew that I, too, would be a teacher.

I began to wear dresses without a fight, and copied Miss Culpepper's speech and mannerisms. My resolve never wavered. I wanted to be just like her.

I can still see her surrounded by students, her long fingers flicking the beads of a large wooden bead board. As we counted, I watched Miss Culpepper's fingernails, shining with clear nail polish. I started licking my own nails so they'd be shiny, too.

As the months passed, I grew to love Miss Culpepper for more than her beauty. "Whole child development" isn't a new concept; she practiced it naturally. She instructed us to keep our hands washed, and to hang our clothes on a chair by an open window at night. "You are really *my* children," she would gently tease us. "I just let you go home to sleep."

Our little town was poor—so poor, some said, that later when the Great Depression came and went, no one even noticed. Few of us had seen a phonograph, so Miss Culpepper decided to expose us to a little culture. She brought in a Victrola, and every day she cranked it up and played one of the three records she owned.

The one I remember had a Kellogg's cornflakes commercial, which the cereal company sent to the schools for free. To the tune of *Here We Go 'Round the Mulberry Bush*, a mother sang: "You lazy Mary, will you get up, will you get up, will you get up? You lazy Mary, will you get up, will you get up today?"

Mary refused, so her mother suggested several different things for breakfast. Mary rejected them all—until her mother offered Kellogg's cornflakes. Then Mary sang, "Yes, Mother, I *will* get up, I will get up today".

These days, kids are bombarded with commercials on TV. I wonder if it was "lazy Mary" who started it all! ⇒+

FIRST COMMERCIALS? Even the old records had ads, says Estelle White.

Trip to America Was a Wonderful Adventure

By Magda Hartwig, Wyoming, Iowa

WHAT A THRILL it was the summer of 1923, when Dad came home and gathered us around the kitchen table to tell us we were going to America!

The endless preparations to leave Germany began, and Mom had a lady come to our house to sew dresses, all alike, for us girls. Then we had a family picture taken for a passport photo. I was so proud to stand next to Dad and hold his arm.

We soon had a sale of our household goods, and Dad made several trunks to pack our belongings in to take with us.

After teary good-byes in our town of Husum, we rode the train to stay with

---

*"Grandmother knew
she would never
see any of us again..."*

---

my grandparents, and there was a big party for us the night before we left for America.

The next day when we went to the train depot, Oma didn't go, but I remember her at an open window waving a handkerchief to us. While I didn't realize it at the time, my grandmother knew she'd never see any of us again.

We spent several unpleasant days in Hamburg undergoing physicals and delousing, and our clothing was fumigated. This was especially demeaning for my mother, who took pride in the cleanliness of her family. All of our new white underclothing came out yellow!

Finally on the Way

We finally boarded our ocean liner on November 1. The first few days were wonderful with so much good food, and there were band concerts, dancing and a snack shop where you could buy things we'd never seen before, like bananas. Our favorites were pickled herring and oranges.

Ellis Island was *not* so thrilling. All immigrants had a fear of "the Island of Tears" because many unhealthy or undesirable people were sent back.

We girls and Mom were separated from Dad and Pete and placed in "holding pens" for more physicals. Then we were informed we'd have to stay for another day because my sister's health was questionable. How frightening to think we may have to turn around and go back after all we'd been through!

We were finally allowed to proceed with our plans, and Dad was so relieved that he went to a fruit stand and bought us the biggest "oranges" he could find. (They turned out to be grapefruit.)

After a long train ride to Oxford Junction, Iowa, we were greeted by many relatives and we had to curtsy for each one. Next came our first automobile ride to the home of Mom's aunt, where we stayed for the next 2 weeks.

The first winter in America, Dad worked cutting wood and as a hired man on farms. He was finally able to rent a farm on his own and we became independent. Life wasn't easy, but from our parents, we learned a strong work ethic, which we have tried to pass on to our children and grandchildren.

We all became citizens, and have done our best serving church and community for this great United States.

First Sight of "The Lady" Left Lifelong Thrill

IT WAS a bitterly cold day in January of 1925 when our ship *Andania* arrived in New York. My parents and I were new arrivals from Berlin, Germany and had just endured a rough 13-day trip on the Atlantic.

I recall standing on deck in the freezing weather, eager to get our first glimpse of "the Lady". We were thrilled when we finally caught sight of her!

While on board, we had undergone numerous inspections for lice and were checked for vaccinations. When we finally disembarked, we were taken to Ellis Island, where we stood in long lines to be inspected again.

When the lady inspector looked at our passport, she pronounced my name "Lizzie Brittensteen". I was as indignant as a 10-year-old could be and replied, *Nein, ich heisse Luzie Breitenstein!*

She smiled and said, "In this country, you'll be known as Lizzie Brittenstein." Right then and there, I decided I wasn't going to like this country…but as you can see, I later changed my mind, as it has been 70 years since I've settled in my adopted country!

—*Luzie Darner, Dayton, Ohio*

PASSPORT PHOTO. Before coming to America in 1923, the Petersen family had this photo taken in Husum, Germany. Magda Hartwig is proudly holding her father's arm.

PROPER PAPERS. Everyone looked happy for these passport photos taken in 1922. George Murdock, then 8, was coming to America with his grandparents to join his family in Seattle.

Kind Strangers Comforted Our Sad Arrival

I REMEMBER sitting on the long benches in the Ellis Island registry room in September 1928. We came from Greece on an old American ship called the *Thomas Edison*. The trip had become a sad one when my older brother was kept back due to an illness.

A kind man finally brought my mother and me a basket of fruit, pinned notes on our jackets stating our destination and led us to the train.

We arrived in Detroit and had to wait for a transfer to another train to Kalamazoo. Since we couldn't speak English, we had no way to ask for food during the long trip to meet my father. A kind stranger realized our situation and took me to the dining car for a meal. My mother and I could only smile our thanks.

My brother joined us from Greece 3 months later. How excited I was telling him of the schools that had toys, playgrounds and helpful teachers…and that there were diamonds in the sidewalks! As we walked home from the train station, I pointed out a stretch of sidewalk where the cement sparkled as if sprinkled with diamond dust.

My arrival to this wonderful country is still vivid. My husband and I now have four children and three beautiful grandchildren. My first return visit to Greece was in 1987 with my children.

—*Eva Fleckenstein*
Kalamazoo, Michigan

Scottish Family Sailed to Land of Opportunity

By George Murdock
Toledo, Washington

I WAS BORN in a cotter's house on a beef farm in Scotland. Work as a farmhand was hard for my father, and the promise of a better life in the United States eventually led to the emigration of our entire family.

I stayed in Scotland with my grandparents until 1922, then we sailed on the *SS Columbia* from Glasgow to New York in June, spending 7 days at sea. Since we were used to very plain and mostly boiled food, the rich foods and seasickness were a problem.

I'll never forget passing through Ellis Island. At first, there was a hassle since my name was Murdock and I was being brought by the Leslies. Fortunately, my father had served the USA in World War I, so I automatically became a citizen.

The passageways out of Ellis Island were lined with thick, tall solid cement walls and were stopped with very heavy metal gates. It was a scary sight.

We finally made it out and took the train to Portland, Oregon. The scenery on the way was wonderful! We were met by an aunt and uncle and worked in their prune and walnut orchards. At the end of the summer, I went to Seattle to live with my parents.

I graduated from the University of Washington in 1936, taught school, served 5-1/2 years in WWII, then served as a high school principal. I retired after 15 years as school superintendent.

For us, the United States really did turn out to be "the land of opportunity".

Country Kids Found Big City a Fright

MY FAMILY came to Boston from rural Nova Scotia in 1928, then boarded a ferry to cross the harbor to our new home in East Boston.

Dad had planned to take a streetcar the rest of the way, since our new flat was clear across town, but we country kids had never seen such a thing and refused to get on one! Dad was mad as a wet hen. Still, no matter how much he pleaded, we wouldn't budge. We ended up walking all the way across town, toting our luggage!

The bustle of city life was frightening to a bunch of country bumpkins. We shrunk from the traffic in the street, staying as close to the buildings as possible. Scared? You bet. Our folks couldn't get us out of the house for a week!

—*Cecil Nickerson, Somerville, Massachusetts*

LADY OF THE LAMP. The Statue of Liberty was a hopeful symbol of *America, at last,* to immigrants eager for their long journey to be over.

Surefire Tip Made Mama Suspect No. 1

TOTS FOR TEMPERANCE. Ruth Stewart (right) and sister Naomi only knew one temperance song, but they were a big hit when they sang it.

We Were a Regular "One-Hit Wonder"

DURING PROHIBITION, my father and a local preacher often discussed temperance issues and trying to close down the saloons. I was very young, so I didn't really know what they were talking about.

My sister, Naomi, and I had been taught to sing at an early age, so one evening, the preacher asked if we could sing at one of his temperance rallies. I was 5 and Naomi was only 3.

Father took us downtown in the buggy to meet the preacher. His old flatbed truck was parked on Main Street, surrounded by a crowd of people. I still recall a poster on the back of his truck depicting a child whose dad was a drunkard.

Father then lifted us onto the back of the truck, and my sister and I began to sing *The Drunkard's Child*. When we finished, there were a lot of cheers for us to sing again, but that was the only temperance song we knew.

—Ruth Stewart, Granbury, Texas

By Esther Ronshauger
Brookings, South Dakota

MY MOTHER was president of the South Dakota Women's Christian Temperance Union for 24 years and traveled all over the state giving talks.

She always carried a great deal of temperance literature with her, and one time when she was to go on a 3-week trip, she bought an expensive new suitcase with two straps and a wonderful lock on it.

At home, we packed it full of temperance literature, and boy, was it heavy. When Mama left on her trip, she checked the big suitcase.

When she got to her first stop, Mama saw her suitcase sitting on the platform to be picked up and gasped. The straps were torn and the lock was missing!

It was weeks before we learned what had happened: Two government officers had been in the baggage car because they'd had a "hot tip" that someone was sending bootleg liquor in suitcases.

"I'd loved to have seen their faces when they found temperance literature," laughed Mama, "but I wish they had put the lock back on after breaking it so I at least could have had it repaired!"

One of my life's greatest moments took place many years before this incident in the summer when I was 4. We learned we were to have a great guest in town—Carry Nation herself was coming to one of our temperance meetings.

I kept asking Mama if I would be able to hold Mrs. Nation's hatchet, but Mama said no. "If she lets you, be glad," Mama advised, "but don't ask her."

Papa, Mama and I were among those who met her train. She was carrying one large suitcase, a smaller bag and an umbrella. When Papa offered to carry her bags, she told him, "You can carry the large valise. I'll carry the small one."

Everyone went to our house for lunch, then on to City Hall for the meeting. Mrs. Nation opened the small valise, took out her famous hatchet and put it on the table. No wonder she'd wanted to carry that bag herself!

Soon after the meeting began, Pete, the town drunk, tottered in. I knew all about him because Papa had told me in secret. Someone asked if he should be taken outside, but Mama said he'd soon fall asleep—and he did.

Mama had put me in the front row, where I could almost touch the hatchet. (I noted that Papa had one almost like it in his woodshed). After Mrs. Nation finished speaking, she asked me to hold the hatchet for a few minutes. What a great moment!

Then something even more wonderful happened. Mrs. Nation was selling hatchet pins, and Papa bought two— one for Mama, one for me.

Mrs. Nation had me stand up and fastened my pin just above my heart. "Esther Irene," she said to me, "promise that all your life you'll work against alcohol and its evils." I did, and it's a promise I've kept for more than 90 years.

I wore that pin often and I keep it in my jewelry case to this day. ✦

"Hard" Sell Convinced Children to Join WCTU

WHEN MY FATHER was pastor of a church on Chicago's south side, he invited a lady from the Women's Christian Temperance Union to speak to us children about the ill effects of "booze".

I really don't recall her talk, but we were fascinated when she took some bottles out of a small black bag and lined them up on a table. She explained that half the bottles contained water, and the others contained alcohol.

The woman then held up a bottle of the water containing a piece of meat and shook it. We didn't hear anything…but when she shook a bottle that contained *alcohol* and a piece of meat, there was a clinking noise because the meat had hardened. She repeated the demonstration with bottles containing an egg yolk, with the same "shocking" results.

After she went through the row of bottles, we were quite willing to sign the cards she passed around, making us members of the WCTU. We were convinced that if we drank liquor, our insides would end up like that piece of meat and egg yolk!

—Evangeline Spence, Chelmsford, Massachusetts

Bootleggers Did Their Part For a Good Cause

THE ERA of Prohibition was filled with stories of Al Capone and other kingpins of illegal bootlegging in the Chicago area.

My mother was a widow with five children, eking out an existence with a few dollars and a lot of needs. We lived on a small farm in northern Wisconsin—only a couple of miles from a huge moonshine operation.

We could hear the trucks going back and forth down the dirt road at night, and when the wind was right, you could even smell the mash.

Everyone in town knew about the operation, and some of the locals took money to stay quiet. The bootleggers approached my mother, but she refused to take their money—though she could have used it. The fear for her children's safety was incentive enough to keep her quiet.

As Christmas approached, the teacher at our one-room school gave all of us a batch of Christmas Seals to sell. It was for a charitable cause, and the child who sold the most would receive a pencil box loaded with pencils, crayons, rulers and a sharpener.

Oh, how my sister and I longed for that box! Our chances were slim, so we decided to try selling the seals at the still back in the woods.

We started out directly after school, so Mother was unaware of our plans as we trudged down the 2-mile road behind our farm. Stopped by a tall wire gate, we scrambled through and kept going.

Suddenly two men came toward us. "What do you kids want?" they demanded.

When we told them about our seals, they bought them all with no discussion, then barked, "Now, get out of here!"

We were elated, and as we ran home, we decided to get more seals to sell the next day. After all, we had a real good market for them.

After telling Ma about our good fortune, we didn't get the reaction we'd expected. Her face turned pale and her knees shook as she reached for the nearest chair. Dismay, anger, fear and relief flashed across her face as she explained the danger we had been in. Forbidding us to go there ever again, she threatened we wouldn't be able to sit down for weeks if we did.

A few months later, "the feds" raided the still and put it out of business, snaring about 20 men. As for my sister and me—we won the pencil box.
—*Helen Peters, Crete, Illinois*

***MOTHER OF THE MOVEMENT.** Leading the temperance cause was Carry Nation, wearing the ax pin that symbolized her weapon of choice to destroy saloons.*

"Home Brew" Traveled to Party on Ice—Literally!

DURING PROHIBITION, some rural dwellers put in a barrel of cider every fall. By spring, it had often turned to vinegar or hard cider.

The vinegar was used in cooking, and the hard cider was consumed during haying, trading or on some other special social occasions—but always discreetly.

When I became the heir to my Aunt Ethel's small estate, I found a humorous letter she had written. It tells of a time when some of the neighborhood folks planned a social gathering during the "dry" era.

It seems that some friends of my aunt's made "home brew" for the party and cleverly transported it to the host's home in an old-fashioned ice cream freezer packed with ice. Aunt Ethel said they carried the freezer right out in the open, and the neighbors never even suspected!
—*Gerald Kimball*
Gray, Maine

We Stumbled on A Secret Stash!

ON A WARM sunny day in the spring of '28, my sister and I were walking home from school when we saw some bright orange flowers in a pasture.

We decided to pick a bouquet for Mother, and as I crawled under the barbed wire fence along the country road, I saw a length of rusty old stovepipe hidden in the grass. Inside the pipe were four bottles lined up end to end. We'd stumbled on a hidden stash of whiskey!

I was only 8 and didn't really understand much about Prohibition, but I knew my parents didn't approve of drinking, so I didn't, either. (Mama wouldn't even touch the root beer my father sometimes brought home.)

Although we had never heard of Carry Nation, we acted just as zealous as she would have for the cause of temperance. My little sister and I diligently removed the caps, poured the whiskey into the grass, then put the bottles back in the pipe just the way we found them.

We hurried home without picking any flowers, and never told our mother about the incident. But I'm sure Carry would have been proud of us!
—*Janet Van Velzor, Lancaster, Ohio*

"SHE WAS ONLY a moonshiner's daughter, but I loved her still..." as the old song went. In this case, the moonshiners' stills were piled up in the yard of a neighbor who was a genuine "revenuer", says Mary Bussey of Arlington, Texas. That's Mary's sister, Merle Loggins, peeking out between the knees of her friend Ruby Mae Snearley, as the girls posed with the results of numerous raids made by their Texas Ranger neighbor. The moonshiners might've been temporarily out of business, but during Prohibition, it was a full-time job keeping the local men from obtaining what was known as "moonshine", "corn likker" and "white lightnin'". Mary also recalls that the neighborhood ladies saw to it that mason jars filled with John Barleycorn were smashed after this particular raid, and the local chickens became some "happy birds" as they pecked through the fermented refreshments from the jars.

perance League. One of the mothers played piano, so our activities often included the following song. Boy, could we sing!

When we are tempted and offered a drink
Of sparkling cold liquor, we surely must think
Of the danger and damage that first drink can do,
So we'll turn down our glasses and say, "No, thank you!"
Refrain:
We'll turn down our glass,
We'll turn down our glasses,
We'll turn down our glasses and say, "No, thank you!"
We'll turn down our glasses,
We'll turn down our glasses
We'll turn down our glasses and say, "No thank you!"
—Lois Ralston, Arlington, Texas

Parents Really "Rocked" Singing Temperance Songs

IT WAS IRONIC my parents lived in Bourbon County, Kentucky, where its whiskey namesake was first distilled. You see, they used to sing together at temperance rallies, and one of the songs stressed the desire that the whiskey-producing area be put out of business.

I can still see them sitting in rocking chairs on our front porch as they practiced at the top of their lungs: "Bourbon's going dry, Bourbon's going dry...Glory hallelujah, Bourbon's going dry!"
—Frank Florence
Butler, Kentucky

Nerve Medicine *Really* Made Her Nervous

I WAS quite young when this took place, but my father often told of an amusing incident regarding the leader of our local Women's Christian Temperance Union.

Outspoken, unforgiving, intolerant and aggressive...many of the townspeople considered her to be perfect for the role in this movement to cleanse the nation of the evils of alcohol.

One of her favorite targets happened to be her own doctor, and she was always on his back for prescribing medicines that contained alcohol. For years, she'd seen him for a nervous condition that seemed to dominate her life. During this time, he had prescribed certain medications, making sure that all of *her* medications were alcohol-free.

Suddenly, she stopped coming to see him. When she finally returned after a couple of years—to reprimand him again for dispensing alcohol—he inquired about her health. She told him everything was just *perfect*, thanks to a patent medicine she was now taking.

The doctor turned to his bookshelf and found this particular medicine listed in one of his references. As he read through the ingredients, he looked up and said quietly, "I see that this medicine contains alcohol."

With that, the woman ran out the doctor's door and never returned. Dad always laughed that it was no wonder she'd finally gotten some relief from her nervous condition! —William Diven Las Cruces, New Mexico

Church Youth Group Sang Song of "No Thanks!"

AFTER SCHOOL on Wednesdays, my friends and I used to stop at our church for youth meetings of the Loyal Tem-

CHURCH LADIES TOOK THE CHALLENGE. It was often the good women of groups like this who took on the cause of temperance with a vengeance. Esther Neale of Richwood, New Jersey shared this 1926 picture of the local Ladies Bible Class. "It was also called the Joy Class," Esther notes, "but frankly, they don't *look* too happy."

Stranded City Dudes Ended Visit with a Surprise

By James Wodahl
Hill City, South Dakota

GROWING UP on a farm in Minnesota, I remember the last days of the 1920s as a time when money was in severe shortage for us. That was serious…especially with Christmas approaching.

One snowy, blustery night, Mom and I were in the kitchen cranking up the cream separator. Dad had just brought in two big cans of milk from the barn and said there'd be more.

My job was to turn the crank as Mother poured the warm milk into the separator tank. When I had it up to speed, I opened a brass spigot that fed the milk into a spinning mechanism, re-

"Their car had skidded off the road…"

sulting in a stream of cream from one spout and a flow of milk from the other.

Suddenly, there was a loud knock, and when Mom opened the door, two frozen-looking but well-dressed young men said their car had skidded off the road into a ditch.

Mother told them to see Dad out in the barn about pulling them out with the team. As they warmed up in the house for a few minutes, the men became fascinated by the cream separator, and I had to laugh at the questions they asked before venturing to the barn.

"Are the cows mad?" they wanted to

know. "Are they tied up?…Are the horses tied up?"

We knew they must be *real* city dudes. I decided to follow them to the barn and found them *knocking* on the barn door.

After they cautiously entered and Dad said he could pull the car out, they continued questioning: "Are you sure those cows are tied?…How do you heat this big building? Is this a kerosene lantern?"

Dad harnessed up our biggest team, "Fly" and "Charlie", as the strangers watched. "How can you tell where all of those straps go?" they wondered. Dad just chuckled.

The car was a quarter mile down the road, and I carried the lantern. Dad shook his head when he saw the huge Hupmobile buried deep in the snow, but he hooked up a stout chain and said he'd give it a try.

The driver struggled through the snow and got behind the wheel, then rolled down his window. "Don't tip me over!" he called out. I think that angered Dad a little, but the horses soon lurched the car up on the road.

The men were very pleased, and one of them reached for his billfold. When I held up the lantern so he could see, I noticed his billfold was bulging with money.

He pulled out a $100 dollar bill and handed it to dad, who figured the guy made a mistake. "I can't take that," he said. "It's too much."

The young dude took it back, then handed dad a twenty. That was *still* too much, but Dad knew not to protest again, and the strangers were soon on their way.

Heading back to the barn, Dad exclaimed, "That car was loaded with bootleg whiskey!"

Bootleg whiskey or not, we figured it was a miracle, because that $20 bill made our Christmas a happier one. Mother got a new dress that wasn't made of flour sacks. Dad got a new sheepskin jacket. I got a BB gun and a pair of four-buckle overshoes…and Fly and Charlie even got some choice hay and extra oats that joyous season.

Bootleg Brew Saved Baby's Life

THE WINTER after I was born, I became very ill with pneumonia and my heart began to weaken.

We didn't have the medicines that exist today to fight this illness, so the country doctor told my parents to give me a three drops of whiskey every few hours to stimulate my heart. "No more or no less," he warned.

My parents were good Presbyterians and perhaps the most fervent teetotalers in all of Kansas, but my mother appealed to our minister to secure the whiskey. He went to one of our neighbors who was known to patronize bootleggers, and in a short time, he obtained a bottle.

After I recovered, the whiskey sat untouched. When I was about 10, my mother finally took it down from the shelf where it had sat all those years. "I don't believe we'll ever be needing this again," she said and poured it out in the backyard.

Today, I'm a healthy 74 years old and a "non-drinker", but I have to admit, I owe my life to bootleg whiskey!   —*Ruth Teal Safety Harbor, Florida*

CHEERS FOR BEER. Tired of going "dry", protesters wanted what they called the "18th Commandment" repealed. This was 1928…so they'd have 5 more years to wait.

BABY BUGGY BOAT. With the help of an uncle who transformed her buggy into a boat, Evelyn Wallace and baby doll "Bubbles" led the parade in Waukesha, Wisconsin and sailed away with first prize—the suitcase she's holding.

and fluff, these humble containers were transformed into beautiful creations.

In the earliest days, wild violets, sweet William and other flowers, along with apple and plum blossoms, gave the baskets a delightful springtime aroma.

The finished May baskets were filled with popcorn, homemade fudge and penny candies and given to special friends or loved ones. Anyone who was caught delivering a basket was promptly caught and kissed—but no one ever ran very fast!

The giving of May baskets has all but disappeared now, but what a lovely, thoughtful custom it was—and what beautiful memories it brings back.

—*Iris Hanson, Lytton, Iowa*

Girl's Spirits Sailed When She Won Parade

SUMMER VACATION days in Waukesha, Wisconsin were happy ones for me. There were evening band concerts in the park, Italian festivities honoring St. Bartholomew on the banks of the Fox River, and an occasional small circus on the edge of town.

But my favorite were the doll-buggy parades held in various parks. My large doll, "Bubbles", and oversized doll buggy were my pride and joy, and I loved the opportunity to show them off.

Family members were allowed to help entrants decorate the buggies, and I was fortunate to have an uncle who was a designer. For one parade, he removed the hood and used thin slats and crepe paper to transform my buggy into a boat. With white shirt and pants borrowed from a neighbor boy, and sailor caps for Bubbles and me, we were ready to "sail".

I was delighted and honored when I was chosen to lead the parade—and doubly delighted when I won first prize.

—*Evelyn Wallace, Downey, California*

Treat-Filled May Baskets Were Scented with Blooms

AS MAY 1 approached, people spent many evenings collecting butter boxes, oatmeal boxes and other containers to turn into baskets. With some crepe paper, wallpaper samples and bits of ribbon

Whatever Became of May Day?

MAY DAY was a delightful tradition I remember from the '20s.

The winding of the Maypole and making May baskets to leave at the front doorsteps of teachers and older people in the community was a special thrill for us kids.

It was so much fun to create different kinds of baskets with paper or scraps. Mother would bake delicious little cookies to put inside along with candies. I can still smell the lilac blossoms and other little flowers adorning the top of our baskets.

I think it was more of a treat for *us* making these basket treats for others!

—*Page Willis, Bethany, Oklahoma*

Warm Easter Day Was Perfect for an Outing with the Gang

By Marie Freesmeyer, Jerseyville, Illinois

AS DRAB WINTER turned to spring, my life began to change. I could shed my heavy coat, pack away long underwear—and start thinking about a new outfit for Easter.

I began looking for a dress as soon the Sears Roebuck spring catalog arrived. Some years I had to settle for a homemade one, but Mother's creations always looked just like those in the catalog.

With the dress issue settled, Mother would go to town to trade a case full of eggs and a little money she had saved. She usually bought me new black patent-leather shoes, and either a new hat or trimmings to spruce up

last year's Easter bonnet. I was eager to wear all these new "toggins" and looked forward to Easter with great anticipation. For weeks, I wished on the new moon, the first evening star and every wishbone for that special Sunday to be warm and sunny.

On Easter morning, I dashed downstairs for breakfast and raced through my chores. (The only other time I got through chores that fast was on Christmas.) There was no Easter Bunny to bring colored eggs and candy, but there *was* a brand-new outfit waiting to be put on.

At our little country church, the congregation looked colorful and

cheerful. The women and girls wore gay summer hats, and I still recall the squeaking of brand-new shoes as a late arrival tried to slip in quietly.

After dinner, my brother and I made short work of the dishes so we could join our friends. If the weather was nice, a dozen or so of us would meet at a lovely spot in a hollow, where a large creek flowed between flat limestone rocks. It was an ideal place to build a fire and roast eggs, or else boil them in a syrup bucket.

We'd eat eggs, play games and talk until the sun sank behind the cliffs. Then we'd say our farewells and hope to meet there again...on Easter next year.

Despite Traffic, Fourth Was Glorious

MY MOTHER, Florence Burt, still talks about "Cowthumpion" parades that were part of the Fourth of July celebrations held in the early 1920s in Chesterhill, Ohio.

The young ladies in her Sunday school class started weeks ahead of time to prepare picnic baskets that would be bulging with fried chicken, potato salad, homemade buns with fresh butter and raspberry jelly, deviled eggs, cherry and raisin pies, chocolate cake and lemonade.

Ice for the lemonade came from the old icehouse, where the blocks had been stored after being cut from nearby creeks in the winter.

Lots of Laughter

Young men dressed in their finest suits for this event, and the young ladies wore hoop skirts. These were the days of button shoes, corsets, long-sleeved dresses, gloves, large hats with plumes and always a fan. Women *needed* fans in all that garb, especially in July.

One of the young men would borrow his father's team and wagon for the hayride to the picnic grounds. Anyone who could play a guitar or banjo brought it along. The 10-mile ride along dusty roads was filled with songs and laughter.

At the grounds, everyone ate lunch, then gathered to watch the parade. First came the bands, World War I veterans, flag-bearers and horses. There were decorated buggies, carriages, carts and wagons, and ladies bedecked with ribbons, satin, flowers and big hats, competing for first prize.

Don't Forget Cows!

Next came clowns and jugglers, followed by dogs, cats and goats in various costumes. Last but not least were the cows, adorned with flowers, satin ribbons, all types of hats and, most of all, bells. The winning cow was the celebrity of the day.

Baseball games and horseshoe-pitching competitions followed, and before nightfall, the food baskets were opened again and finished off for the day, followed by homemade ice cream.

After dark, everyone enjoyed popcorn while watching the fireworks. Then it was time to return home, do the evening chores by lantern light and climb the stairs to bed, happily exhausted.
—*Helen Davy*
Crystal River, Florida

By Nancy Poltrack
Middletown, Rhode Island

THE FOURTH of July never seemed like much fun for my brother Bob and me, because every year we had to drive to Aunt Lizzie's in Bayonne, New Jersey for the annual family celebration.

Dad dreaded the bumper-to-bumper traffic crawling through the small towns, and Bob felt cheated at leaving our fireworks at home. As the morning progressed, so did the heat and humidity. Tempers flared as Bob and I fought in the backseat.

The only interesting part of the drive was crossing the Hudson River on the ferry. Just watching the cars slip into place was exciting. The deck hands worked with speed and precision, filling every available foot of space.

Once under way, we were allowed to stand at the rail and watch the river traffic. My imagination ran wild. *Who was in that motorboat darting this way and that? Where was the barge headed, and what was its cargo?* Unfortunately, this part of our trip was over too soon.

When we reached Auntie's, tables draped in white cloths were already set on the side porch, complete with place cards, party favors and red and blue streamers.

Auntie always served homemade peach ice cream for dessert, so Bob and I helped spin the crank on the freezer. As the mixture thickened, we worked harder and harder, waiting impatiently for Auntie to declare it frozen.

At last, we took the dasher out and shared the ice cream clinging to the blades, and the freezer was packed in rock salt to await serving time.

Then Uncle Len shooed us out to the front lawn, where he saluted the Fourth by firing his small brass antique cannon. Neighbors cheered and clapped, and all we needed was a marching band.

After lunch, Auntie led us in singing old songs, like *The Owl and the Pussycat Went to Sea in a Beautiful Pea-Green Boat* and *A Frog He Would A-Wooing Go.* It wasn't exactly modern music, but toes tapped and voices joined heartily.

We were exhausted by dusk when we started home for Connecticut. The trip seemed endless and traffic was heavy, but as we drove through the small towns, we passed parks where band concerts were in full swing, and fireworks blazed in the sky, evoking oohs and aahs of pleasure.

In retrospect, it *was* a glorious Fourth. After World War I, people weren't ashamed to demonstrate love for their country. They sincerely believed in democracy and were confident there would be no more wars. ⚞⚟

PATRIOTIC FAMILY. The family of Caesar Pasquesi of Highland Park, Illinois (seen above truck cab, partly hidden by flag) were, like most immigrants, very patriotic. Here they decorated the family business truck for a 1922 Fourth of July parade in Highland Park. Caesar's father and two uncles founded an express company in 1921. His mother, Linda, is standing third from left.

TURKEY CALL. Thanks to the party line on a phone like this, neighbors shared good holiday meal. See story at right.

Rural Thanksgiving Feasts Drew a Crowd

ON THANKSGIVING, we always had a big dinner at our home in the country. We children had plenty of room to run and play hide-and-seek. There were so many kids and places to hide that we had two "seekers". We could've played that game for hours.

When the dinner bell rang, we feasted on turkey or chicken, mashed potatoes, sweet potatoes with marshmallows, gravy, vegetables, salads, all kinds of pickles, fresh-baked bread, assorted pies and cakes and homemade ice cream.

Then there was always the game of "who gets to keep the wishbone", plans to make for coming Christmas parties and time for music.

The highlight of the day was when each person told what they were most thankful for. The grown-ups' answers were interesting, and the children's were hilarious!

—*Mimi Jenkins*
Ventura, California

An Invitation to Dinner The Hard Way

ONE VERY STORMY Thanksgiving during the '20s, my sister and her family, who lived 35 miles away, called to say that because of the weather, they would not be able to come down for dinner.

Mother had prepared a big turkey and all the trimmings, and, of course, we were all disappointed, but the storm *was* bad.

We were on the old party line back then, and shortly after Mother hung up, the phone rang again. It was Harry, a neighbor and dear friend.

"I hear you have some nice pumpkin pie and turkey that perhaps might not be eaten," he said. In the background, we could hear his horrified wife scolding him and yelling…*Harry! Harry Richenberg!*

We all got to laughing, and Mother told him, "Come on over!" They did, and we all had a happy, happy Thanksgiving.

Oh, for the good old days!
—*Marion Johnson, Halma, Minnesota*

Mail Carrier's Kids Helped Him "Play Santa"

MY DAD, C. "Roy" Stryker, was a rural mail carrier in Brady, Nebraska and served as a personal friend to all of his patrons.

He knew firsthand their deep disappointment when some of the Christmas orders from Montgomery Ward or Sears Roebuck hadn't arrived by December 24. Those families would have a sad and dreary day ahead.

Normally, the government forbade Dad from taking passengers on his regular route, but on Christmas Day—a legal holiday—he was free to do as he pleased.

Early that morning, he'd load his car to the roof with all of the late-arriving packages (some said "mama" or jingled a lot). Then my older brother and I would climb on top, and away we went to "play Santa" and make those people happy.

Thinking back, I don't think Dad could have taught us a better lesson. On those crisp, exciting mornings, we had the true spirit of Christmas in our hearts.
—*Jocelyn Schmidt*
Arroyo Grande, California

We Spent Christmas on a Banana Boat!

MY PARENTS made every holiday a special event, so we never knew what the next adventure would be. In 1924, it was celebrating Christmas aboard a United Fruit Lines banana boat!

The captain was a friend of the family and had invited us to join him on board since the ship was in port for a winter layover.

On Christmas Eve, we all climbed into our old touring car for the trip from Brooklyn to the Hudson River pier. The city looked and felt like a giant icicle. I was just 8, but I recall the tire chains clanking as we drove through deep snowdrifts. When we arrived, a mixture of snow and freezing rain was swirling around the pier.

On board the ship, we children settled into a tiny stateroom for our overnight stay. We were excited, but a little fearful that Santa Claus might pass us by. After all, how would he know to look for us on a banana boat?

It was a relief to find a decorated Christmas tree in the ship's lounge. As we added our gifts to the ones already there, I wondered where Santa might make his entrance. There was no fireplace like the one at home. We were assured that Santa *would* find us and would have no trouble landing his sleigh on the deck.

The next morning, we quickly donned robes and slippers and ran to the lounge, where our parents and the captain were already having coffee. Just as promised, Santa had indeed found the boat, and aside from the usual dolls and games, he had left us a beautiful multicolored parrot in a huge wrought-iron cage. It took quite a bit of encouragement from Father before Mother agreed to let us keep him on the sun porch at home.

The gift-sharing ended all too soon. After breakfast, we went off to dress for the holiday meal of turkey and all the trimmings. That night, we youngsters were so exhausted from the excitement that we slept the whole way home.

Miraculously by morning, all of our goodies had arrived in Brooklyn, including "Pirate Pete, our Polly Pal".

—*Sara Riola, Lakewood, New Jersey*

Old-Fashioned Christmas Programs Played to a Packed House

By Gladyce Carlson, Webster City, Iowa

WHEN I was a young girl back in 1922, the churches in our little Iowa town of Boxholm were always packed for the children's Christmas programs.

Our pieces were handed out the week after Thanksgiving at Sunday school. Mom would pin mine to the kitchen curtain and help me learn it as we did the supper dishes.

When the day finally arrived, we'd eat an early supper and quickly finish our chores before getting dressed in our best clothes.

As we began to bundle up in our warmest wraps, Dad headed for the garage with an 8-quart kettle of boiling water. There was no antifreeze for radiators in those days, so people waited until the last minute to fill them.

Huddled in Car

When Dad came back to the house with an empty teakettle, it was time to wrap my little sister, Ruthie, in a warm comforter, blow out the lamp and head for the car.

Brother Benny and I huddled in the backseat with a heavy robe on our laps as we made our way down the frozen ruts of a dirt lane. At 35 miles an hour, the frosty 3-mile trip to town seemed endless in those days before heaters!

When Dad finally turned down the street to our church, our chattering teeth were forgotten as we glimpsed the welcoming glow through the stained glass windows of our Swedish Methodist Church.

Church Was Warm

We entered the bright warmth of the church, made cozy by the coal-burning furnace. The pulpit furniture had been removed and replaced with a stage for us to stand on while we recited our parts, and in the corner stood a 10-foot Christmas tree decorated with ornaments and tinsel.

There were no lights on it, though, as electric bulbs were unheard-of and candles were too dangerous.

Benny went to sit with his fourth-grade class and I sat with the third graders. We children grew restless as the church filled, then at 7 o'clock, the program began. The Sunday school superintendent announced each recitation

and dialogue and named each child. The program was all about the Christ Child, Mary and Joseph, the shepherds, angels, wise men, Bethlehem and joy.

Carols were sung by different groups of children throughout the program, and after the offering was taken and the benediction pronounced, everyone was asked to remain seated.

A Sweet Conclusion

Soon the ushers came forward carrying bushel baskets filled with sacks of candy, which were handed out to every child in the church.

It was now time to get our wraps back on and head for home. Once there, Dad let us off at the front gate, then drove into the garage to drain the radiator.

The rest of us headed for the dark cold house, where Mom lit the lamp. Then she shook the grate on the kitchen range, put some cobs in the firebox and poured kerosene over the top before putting a match to them.

We could soon feel the heat as wood was added and another fire was built in

YULETIDE YOUNGSTERS. The 1922 church Christmas program is a cherished memory for Gladyce Carlson (center), pictured with her brother, Benny, and her sister, Ruthie.

the dining room. By that time, Benny and I were into our candy sacks, which had been filled with assorted hard candies and peanuts in the shell.

It was late when the house was finally warm and we three sleepy children headed up the stairs for bed. The long-anticipated Christmas program of 1922 was now just another happy memory.

Young Church Musicians Took Duties Seriously

CHRISTMAS WAS always a beautiful time of year, especially when we walked to church under a cold, clear, star-filled sky.

We children took part in the church Christmas program as soon as we were old enough, and we considered it a privilege.

When I was 6, my 8-year-old brother and I were to play a duet of *Silent Night*. I had begun taking piano lessons from Mrs. Gaynor (she used a ruler to reprimand students who played a wrong note), and my brother Richard took violin lessons with an instructor at the teacher's college.

We practiced our number at home many times and had it down pat, but this would be my first time playing it on the church's old pump organ.

We were both so excited looking out that night on so many people in the pews. I sat down at the organ, and my feet just barely reached the pedals. My brother tucked his violin under his chin and began to play.

Things were going quite well—until I missed a note. Without missing a beat himself, my brother lowered his bow and whacked me over the shoulder. Needles to say, my composure was now completely shattered!

Still, we felt good afterward when everyone told us they thought we did well.

In later years, I've often played that favorite old carol in other churches, but the memory of that first time always makes me chuckle.

—Ruth Marie Jorgenson, Eugene, Oregon

Mom's Love Turned a Gray Christmas to Gold

By John Doll, Fillmore, California

IN CHICAGO, the weather alone could dampen anyone's holiday spirit, but in 1925, things were especially grim for my brother and me. Our father had died 3 years before, leaving Mom with only her pride and a strong back.

While my older brother, Ned, was in school, I went along with Mom to the only job she could find—that of a cleaning lady. I watched her hour after hour, scrubbing floors on her hands and knees, or sitting on the outside of a windowsill in freezing weather, washing windows four stories up—for 25¢ an hour.

That Christmas Eve when Mom finished working, we headed for the streetcar. She'd been paid $2.25 for 9 hours' work, plus a jar of tomato jam as a Christmas present. She lifted me onto the rear platform of the noisy red car, searching through her precious coins for our 10¢ fare. We held hands as we sat on the cold cane seats, and the roughness of her skin almost scratched mine.

I knew it was Christmas Eve, but I didn't expect anything more than snow, some extra food and a visit to Marshall Field's window display of toys. Still, the "Big Brothers" had delivered a basket of food the night before, and that gave me a warm sense of security. These baskets came at Christmas, Thanksgiving and Easter, and always had vegetables, a canned ham, walnuts, and an apple or two on top. On rare occasions, there would be a soft but sweet orange.

We passed a large department store

GRATEFUL SON. John Doll (with older brother prior to their father's death) still remembers his mother's gifts.

just about to close and could hear the happy cries of shoppers. Tears streamed down Mom's weathered face.

The bitter cold struck us as we stepped down from the streetcar onto the icy street. As we walked toward our flat, I peered into the front-room windows that framed brightly lit Christmas trees. Mom walked straight ahead, without a side glance, and as we passed

an empty lot where Christmas trees had been sold, she picked up a bundle of discarded branches.

The inside of our flat felt like a refrigerator. The only heat came from a potbellied stove in the kitchen. We fed it with coal that dropped off railroad cars, or wooden fruit boxes Ned and I found in the alleys.

Mom prepared our Christmas feast, and we ate our canned ham, vegetables and bread facing the stove. At bedtime, there was no anticipation about what I'd receive for Christmas, and I quickly fell asleep.

Around 5 a.m., I woke realizing Mom had not come to bed. *What if something happened to her?* I lay in the icy stillness, afraid to get up but unable to sleep. Then I heard a grinding sound from the kitchen.

I slid out of bed and inched toward the light glowing from the kitchen door. I could see Mom's breath, as the fire had been out for hours. Her back was toward me, a blanket draped over her to ward off the cold. She was working at

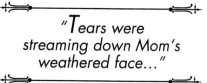

"Tears were streaming down Mom's weathered face..."

the old table, and on the floor was her favorite broom with its handle whittled off.

In front of her stood what appeared to be a strange, disfigured tree. Mom was using her broken-handled kitchen knife to gouge holes in the broom handle, and inserting the branches from the tree lot into the holes. Some were held in place with butcher's string. It was the most beautiful Christmas tree I had ever seen.

At Mom's feet was a small can of red paint and a wet brush. Two towels had been spread on the floor and were almost covered with red toys—a fire engine with two wheels missing, an old steel train with the caboose roof bent in half, and a jack-in-the-box with no head.

I felt no cold or sadness anymore, but rather the greatest flow of love I have ever experienced. Tears poured from my eyes, and she never heard me as backed out of the room and returned to bed. I shall never forget my mother or the Christmas of 1925.

Fragile Paper Tree Made Durable Memories

I WAS BORN in 1922, one of seven children. Dad's paychecks were slim, but our parents always saved enough for Christmas every year so we could look forward to the Italian tradition of a good hearty soup, candy and gifts.

One memorable Christmas, we woke to find a 3-foot tissue-paper tree in the center of the kitchen table. It was the honeycomb type that could be folded flat. We'd never had a Christmas tree before.

The room was lit by oil lamp, since we didn't have electricity, and that beautiful tree was surrounded by roasted chestnuts, dishes of hardtack, pastel candy almonds, assorted nuts and a large bowl of apples, oranges and bananas.

Red and green crepe paper had been strung from the four corners of the ceiling, with a red tissue-paper bell hanging in the center.

And Santa had been there, too, bringing the youngest of us each small glass containers shaped like a car, lantern or telephone and filled with candies. There was also a new wooden "kiddie car". What fun we had taking turns riding around the potbellied stove, warmed by a crackling fire!

—*Lucy Karnek, Burgettstown, Pennsylvania*